W9-COJ-320

Dames of the Theatre

Dames of the Theatre

Eric Johns

ARLINGTON HOUSE·PUBLISHERS
NEW ROCHELLE, N. Y.

Printed and bound in Great Britain by Butler & Tanner Ltd

Library of Congress Catalog Card Number 75-1486

ISBN-0-87000-310-0

To Sybil Thorndike

First star I ever saw on a London stage.

First actress I ever met backstage.

First to encourage me to persevere in my desire

to earn a living writing about the stage.

Contents

Acknowledgments

In paying tribute to those actresses who have been honoured with the title of Dame, I am deeply indebted to:

Peggy Ashcroft, Cicely Courtneidge, Edith Evans, Anna Neagle, Flora Robson and Sybil Thorndike for inviting me to their homes, where they reminisced about their careers under ideal conditions.

John Gielgud, Basil Dean, Joyce Carey, Stanley Hall, Andrew Cruickshank, Marie Ney, Glen Byam Shaw, George Howe, John Fernald, John Goodwin, Tom Courtenay, Peter Graves, Freddie Carpenter, Ronald Waters, Malcolm Farquhar, Peter Saunders, Herbert de Leon, John Casson, Herbert Wilcox and Ronald Millar, who all devoted valuable time and threw light upon those Dames with whom they had been closely associated.

John Casson, Raymond Mander and Joe Mitchenson, Eileen Robinson, Assistant Librarian of the Shakespeare Centre at Stratford-upon-Avon, Vivienne Byerley of H. M. Tennent Ltd, and the Hon Mrs Celia Mitchell Anderson, daughter of Isabel Jay, who put rare pictures at my disposal from their unique collections.

Major-General P. B. Gillett of the Central Chancery of the Orders of Knighthood, Mary Harrison, Branch Librarian, East Sussex County Library at Portslade, and Peter Taylor of the Administration Department of Dulwich District Library.

Douglas Blake for revising the manuscript and offering so many constructive suggestions.

Eric Johns

Dames of the Theatre

Date created a Dame	Actress	Age at time of being honoured
1918	May Whitty	53
1921	Geneviève Ward	83
1925	Ellen Terry	78
1926	Madge Kendal	77
1931	Sybil Thorndike	49
1937	Marie Tempest	71
1941	Irene Vanbrugh	69
1943	Lilian Braithwaite	70
1946	Edith Evans	58
1956	Peggy Ashcroft	49
1960	Flora Robson	58
1960	Judith Anderson	62
1967	Margaret Rutherford	75
1967	Gladys Cooper	79
1970	Anna Neagle	66
1972	Cicely Courtneidge	79

The Title of Dame

Dame is a pretty dreary four-letter word. It evokes equally dreary associations and mental images. It seems to apply to essentially matronly ladies. When I was a young lad in the North, all girls, even those in the same class at school, were known as tarts, and likewise any lady approaching her fifties was automatically labelled an old dame. One expected the old dame who lived across the street to favour a cottage-loaf coiffure, to wear dowdy, neutral-coloured clothes and possibly mittens and elastic-sided boots. A gamp, as umbrellas were then called, would be an indispensable accessory to the ensemble.

Yet when it was decided to honour distinguished women with a rank equivalent to the men's knighthood, the title chosen to bestow upon ladies who had rendered valuable service to the state was that of Dame. When the Order of the British Empire was established in 1917, it contained Statutes authorising the appointment of ladies into two categories of the Order in which their male counterparts would be Knights. An appropriate term of address for such ladies was required and it was decided to use the previously accepted form of address of Dame, because in the Middle Ages the wife of a Knight was always described as a Dame. To indicate a lady had 'earned' her appointment in the Order of the British Empire she was entitled to add the post nominal letters of GBE (First Class) or DBE (Second Class).

The considerable number of actresses – almost a score – who have been created Dame during the past fifty years are naturally immensely proud of having been singled out for such distinction, but without exception they have all disliked the specific title of Dame. In the theatre a Dame usually suggests a pantomime comedian, often the bizarre mother of the principal boy hero – an eccentric red-nosed creature with George Robey eyebrows, a Nellie Wallace hat and red flannel bloomers.

When people enquired what I was doing during the period I was working on this book, I would reply, 'Writing a book on Dames.' Immediately it would be necessary to specify that I was not writing about pantomime comics, but compiling a collection of appreciations of actresses who had been honoured in recognition of their significant contributions to the theatre – such active living legends as Sybil Thorndike, Edith Evans, Cicely Courtneidge, Peggy Ashcroft, Flora Robson and Anna Neagle.

Oddly enough, even when popular leaders of the stage are made Dames, their title is not always used even by their adoring admirers. Possibly on account of their advanced age, Dame Sybil and Dame Edith figure in common everyday speech, but one rarely hears people talking about Dame Anna, Dame Peggy, Dame Cicely and Dame Flora. They are all too well known and regarded with too much affection to require a title – and especially one as unattractive as Dame.

On the other hand, because the Knight's form of address of Sir is so much more flattering than that of Dame, one frequently hears the use of Sir Michael, Sir Ralph and Sir Laurence when Michael Redgrave, Ralph Richardson and Laurence Olivier are being discussed. Olivier, incidentally, still prefers to be addressed as Sir Laurence, in spite of having been given a Life Peerage and elected to the House of Lords for his services to the theatre.

Whoever spoke of Dame Ellen Terry instead of Ellen Terry? Mrs Kendal remains Mrs Kendal and very rarely becomes Dame Madge, even though the title would have suited her Victorian Dowager appearance, with a bonnet as famous as Queen Mary's toque. As internationally famous ballerinas are robbed of their christian names by their own public, Markova and Fonteyn are never in danger of being called Dame Alicia and Dame Margot. Dame Margot, by the way, sounded quite ridiculous when in 1956 Fonteyn became the youngest-ever stage Dame at the age of thirty-seven, when on stage she still looked about twenty-five.

American theatregoers get incredibly confused over the use of the title. Dame May Whitty was the first actress-Dame they encountered in Hollywood, where she became an outstanding personality in the film colony at the time she made *Night Must Fall*. She was called Dame Whitty and even Mrs Dame Whitty, but hardly ever Dame May because Americans considered they might be committing a *faux pas* by addressing a distinguished foreign actress by her christian name.

One bewildered American lady, meeting Dame Edith Sitwell on a lecture tour asked, 'Why do you call yourself Dame?' 'I don't,' replied Dame Edith, 'the Queen does!'

Nothing can be gained, more than fifty years after the creation of the first theatre Dame, by complaining about the ugliness and inappropriateness of the title bestowed upon her and upon her illustrious successors. Rather let us rejoice in the knowledge that the artistic achievement of so many famous actresses has been publicly recognised.

Way back in the reign of George V, the title of Dame seemed to be reserved for a great actress in the twilight of her life, with her career no more than a glorious memory as she lingered neglected in retirement. Geneviève Ward – first as well as the most elderly actress to be made a Dame – was eighty-three and lived barely a year to enjoy the honour. Next came Ellen Terry at seventy-eight, with only three years to live, followed a year later by Mrs Kendal at seventy-seven.

Sybil Thorndike created something of a sensation in 1931 by becoming a Dame at the height of her career at the youthful age of forty-nine. She was, at that time, the youngest actress ever to be so honoured. Peggy Ashcroft, a quarter of a century later, was also only forty-nine when made a Dame.

Gladys Cooper and Cicely Courtneidge were both within sight of their eightieth birthdays. Edith Evans was fifty-eight when she was honoured, as was Flora Robson. The remaining Dames are Judith Anderson, honoured at the age of sixty-two, Anna Neagle at sixty-six, Marie Tempest at seventy-one, Irene Vanbrugh at sixty-nine, Lilian Braithwaite at seventy and Margaret Rutherford at seventy-five.

Strangely enough, the very first actress to be made a Dame was May Whitty in 1918, three years before Geneviève Ward, but she was honoured for her remarkable services to charity during the First World War and not for her contribution to the theatre. Yet this was no embarrassment to her or to the profession because it so happened that late in her career her performances reached an eminence worthy of the highest official recognition. As the terrified, elderly victim of murder in *Night Must Fall*, her spine-chilling acting still haunts the memory of all who were lucky enough to have seen it, either on stage or screen.

George Howe, the most famous Polonius of our time, who has acted with a number of Dames since his early days with Marie Tempest, considers the title should apply essentially to distinguished actresses remarkable for their discipline, dedication and domination; three qualities which must also be illuminated by the individual magic of the star's own personality. Such players would never be guilty of walking through a performance. If the audience consisted of no more than a handful of people on a blazingly hot summer afternoon, Dames worthy of their title would continue to give the finest performance of which they were capable.

May Whitty 1865–1948

May Whitty is the unique actress-Dame. In 1918 she had the distinction of being the first actress to be created a Dame, three years before Geneviève Ward was honoured, but she was appointed DBE for her beneficent charity work during the First World War and, not as Miss Ward was, for her services to the theatre. She was a public-spirited woman and during the 1914 war she pioneered such causes as shows for army camps and workrooms for out-of-work actresses and she also helped to establish the Star and Garter Home for Disabled Servicemen at Richmond. Her honour reminds us of Melba's. The idolised *prima donna* celebrated her twenty-fifth season at Covent Garden with a memorable fanfare in 1913, and then spent the war years in her native Australia and America where she raised a record amount for British war charities. In recognition of her generosity George V honoured her with the title of Dame. The fact that she happened to be one of the greatest operatic singers of her time had no bearing on the case.

Yet it so happens that Dame May also rendered valuable service to the theatre as an actress and as an organiser. She did much towards getting the British Actors' Equity Association firmly established as a powerful trade union, capable of bargaining with managements and preventing actors from getting stranded by bogus managers who ran off with the box-office takings and left artists to fend for themselves in far-away places.

As Flora Robson remarked, 'May Whitty was a wonderful committee woman. In the chair she knew how to use her gavel to keep order and to keep vital discussions from branching off at a tangent.'

As an actress May Whitty first appeared on the stage at the age of sixteen at the Liverpool Court Theatre in the chorus of *The Mountain Sylph* in 1881. The following year she was first seen in London in the Offenbach comic opera, *Boccaccio* at the Comedy Theatre, playing the part of Fillippa. Strange to relate, three years later at the same theatre, in a revival of the same comic opera, Marie Tempest made her first

1

appearance on the stage playing the part of Fiametta at the age of nineteen.

After playing in *Boccaccio*, May Whitty moved to the St James's Theatre to work for the Hare and Kendal management. She understudied and appeared in *The Ironmaster* and in *A Scrap of Paper*. Throughout her career her work bore the impression of Mrs Kendal's excellent training.

May Whitty's name is always affectionately linked with that of Ben Webster, the actor she married in 1892. Their devoted companionship lasted until 1947, when Ben died in America only a year before May. In St Paul's Church, Covent Garden, known as the Actors' Church, a simple memorial plaque, not far from the silver urn which contains Ellen Terry's ashes, records the fact *They were lovely and pleasant in their lives and in their death they were not divided.*

Ben was a grandson of Benjamin Webster (1797–1882), a famous Drury Lane Harlequin, who appeared with Mme Vestris at the Olympic and later took over the Haymarket which he managed for sixteen years, engaging the finest actors of the day in a series of notable plays. Grandson Ben, who had three sisters on the stage, was intended for the law, his father's profession, and was called to the Bar in 1885. But he deserted it for the theatre, appearing for a few performances with Hare and Kendal in *A Scrap of Paper* and *As You Like It*. He was so successful the management offered him an engagement with them in 1887 in *Clancarty* and also in *The Ironmaster*.

Later he joined Irving at the Lyceum and was also in the companies of Alexander, Ellen Terry and Boucicault, appearing in plays by Shakespeare, Shaw, Pinero and Barrie. In later life he appeared in *Richard of Bordeaux* and on the outbreak of war in 1939 went to America where his reputation stood as high as it did in England. He remained there until his death, his last appearance being as Montague in the Broadway production of *Romeo and Juliet* which starred Laurence Olivier and Vivien Leigh.

May Whitty joined Irving's company at the Lyceum to play a number of fairly colourless parts from 1895 to 1898. They included Marie in *Louis XI*, Julie in *The Lyons Mail*, Emilie in *The Corsican Brothers* and the Gentlewoman in *Macbeth*. Together with her husband, she went to America with the Irving company in 1895. Recalling Irving, or the Guv'nor as he was always called, May said he was a stern, rather forbidding taskmaster. If she met him backstage at the Lyceum, as the company was assembling in readiness for the evening performance, she would never dream of speaking to him unless he first addressed her. Ellen Terry, on the other hand, was a fairy princess, with a word for everyone.

After the Irving engagement May made a favourable impression as Susan Throssell in Barrie's *Quality Street* at the Vaudeville Theatre and she was in constant demand in the West End, appearing in such successes as *Trelawny of the Wells* and *The Madras House*.

After the First World War, when May divided her time between the stage and patriotic war work, her style as an actress seemed to acquire more assurance and domination. Her face and figure in maturity expressed a downright common-sense motherliness. She improved as an actress and gave her finest performances in the latter part of her career. She was the old nanny in John Van Druten's *There's Always Juliet* and at the age of seventy, in 1935, she gave the crowning performance of her career in the Emlyn Williams thriller *Night Must Fall* in which she appeared as the victim, Mrs Bramson – a frighteningly realistic performance of a terrified woman which she later repeated in a Hollywood film. *The Lady Vanishes* and *Mrs Miniver* are two other classic films in which May made an indelible impression.

With Ben she lived the remainder of her life in Hollywood and she played the Nurse in the Oliviers' Broadway production of *Romeo and Juliet* in which Ben played his last part. Lewis Casson recalled that Ben, almost to the time of his death in 1947 at the age of eighty-two, continued the loving nightly custom of brushing May's hair. She died just a year later in Hollywood.

In London they lived for years in a flat in Bedford Street, Covent Garden, overlooking St Paul's, the Inigo Jones Church where that plaque now serves to remind us of the fifty-five happy years they enjoyed together. Their London home was a meeting place for English and American actors. The Barrymores might just as easily be there as some totally unknown player being given a helping hand on his bewildering first visit to London. Their home was always a refuge and a comfort for those in trouble.

Their daughter, Margaret Webster, was a great joy to them, making her own significant mark in the theatre without leaning upon either of her parents. She appeared with Sybil Thorndike in *The Trojan Women* and was the Gentlewoman in *Hamlet* when John Barrymore played the Prince of Denmark at the Haymarket in 1925. Her greatest success was scored in America, where she directed a number of distinguished Shakespeare productions. Her 1943 production of *Othello* in New York, in which she played Emilia, broke all records for a Shakespeare play there, with 295 consecutive performances. Later she turned to opera and directed *Don Carlos, Aïda* and *Simon Boccanegra* at the Metropolitan Opera House in New York. She also devised and toured a one-woman show based on the life and works of the Brontë sisters. She died in London in 1972 at the age of sixty-seven.

Geneviève Ward 1838–1922

George V made 1921 a milestone in the history of Honours and Awards for in March of that year he chose to create the first actress Dame. Nowadays the creation of a Dame is usually announced at the time of the New Year Honours on New Year's Day or on the occasion of the Queen's Birthday Honours in June. But because Geneviève Ward's honour was unique and the first of its kind it took the form of a personal greeting – a letter from Windsor Castle on the morning of her eighty-third birthday.

The King's decision meant as much to the acting profession as Irving's knighthood of 1895, which resulted in actors and actresses being accepted socially and no longer despised as rogues and vagabonds. The delicate matter of choosing the first actress to receive this supreme distinction called for considerable diplomatic discussion, but those who advised George V were strangely out of touch with popular feeling when they suggested he singled out Geneviève Ward as the first actress to receive the highest British honour in respect of her services to the stage.

Apart from being the first actress to be created a Dame, Geneviève Ward still remains the oldest ever to be thus honoured. She was eighty-three and had but one more year to live. The public appreciated her distinguished career and the fact she had appeared with Irving and Benson, but she was, after all, an American and not one of the great names born and bred in our own illustrious theatre. What about Ellen Terry, ten years her junior?

At that time – as throughout her long career – Ellen Terry was the most idolised actress in Britain and no one could understand what had prompted the King to choose an American, whose contribution to our theatre was far less significant than Ellen Terry's. The embarrassing situation was adjusted four years later, when Geneviève Ward was already three years dead. But the damage had been done and the adored

4

and adorable Ellen Terry had to be content with the doubtful honour of becoming the second actress to be made a Dame. By that time she was a frail and absent-minded seventy-eight.

Geneviève Ward had a remarkable career, both as actress and opera singer. Hers is a story which reads more like a fictional saga than a real-life biography. She was born in New York in 1838 and decided to make her name as an internationally famous soprano. She studied for the grand opera stage under Fanny Persiani, the diva for whom Donizetti composed *Lucia Di Lammermoor*. Geneviève Ward sang under the name of Ginevra Guerrabella. She came to Europe and appeared as Lucrezia Borgia in the Donizetti opera of that name at La Scala, Milan, and went on to the Paris Opera to appear as Donna Elvira in *Don Giovanni*.

She sang at Covent Garden for one season only in the autumn of 1861. During the summer of that same year Patti had made her sensational Covent Garden début in *La Sonnambula*, following this blazing triumph with sold-out performances as Lucia, Violetta, Zerlina and Martha. Patti had departed by the time Mme Guerrabella arrived in London to sing in one performance of *Maritana* and eight of *Robin Hood*, with the popular Louisa Pyne and Charles Santley in support. She could not be expected to compete with the fabulous Patti, but it was nevertheless quite an achievement to have sung leading soprano roles at Covent Garden.

The following year she sang Violetta in a New York production of *La Traviata*. Soon afterwards she sustained a crippling blow of fate in Cuba, where she contracted diphtheria. She recovered only to discover she had lost her singing voice for ever and her operatic career which had shown such promise in Milan, Paris and London had to be abandoned.

But Geneviève Ward was a woman of iron determination. She had no intention of feeling sorry for herself for the rest of her life. Her illness had left her with a good, sound speaking voice, so she decided to scrap her glamorous *prima donna* name and start life as an actress under her own name of Ward. It took ten years to complete the transformation.

By the time she was thirty-five in 1873 she returned to England and tried herself out at Manchester as Lady Macbeth. She felt convinced she had not made a mistake by going on to the legitimate stage and made plans to try her luck in London the following year. She subsequently made a favourable impression as Antigone, Belvidera in *Venice Preserved*, Portia in *The Merchant of Venice*, and Emilia in *Othello*. At Drury Lane she played in *Ivanhoe* and was seen as Lady Macbeth, playing opposite Hermann Vezin. She appeared 162 times in *The*

Prayer and the Storm in London, which was quite an achievement for those days.

She went into London management in 1879 and presented *Forget-Me-Not* by Herman Merivale and F. C. Grove at the Lyceum, with Johnston Forbes-Robertson as her leading man. It was a cast-iron success and became the most popular drama in her repertoire. She played the leading part of Stephanie de Mohrivart more than 2,000 times in various parts of the world. She was an accomplished linguist and played Lady Macbeth in French at the Porte-Saint-Martin in Paris.

Irving invited her to join his Lyceum company in 1893 while Ellen Terry was still his leading lady. She played Queen Eleanor in *Becket*, Queen Katharine in *Henry VIII* and Queen Margaret in *Richard III*. Together with Ellen Terry she appeared with Irving in the Lyceum productions of *King Arthur* and *Cymbeline*.

Her appearances became somewhat spasmodic after 1900, but she was drawn towards Frank Benson's company, making a dynamic impression as Volumnia in *Coriolanus*, which served as a memorable finale to her long and enterprising career. Her very last appearance was with the Benson company as Queen Margaret in *Richard III*.

Geneviève Ward was a tall, commanding woman with fine features and striking good looks. In her youth she bore some resemblance to the great Italian actress, Adelaide Ristori, to whom the critics often compared her. A striking 1906 painting by Hugh Rivière now in the Royal Shakespeare Theatre Picture Gallery at Stratford-upon-Avon endows the actress with a serenity which possesses a curious magnetic quality.

She happened to be a friend of C. B. Fernald, whose son John Fernald met her at tea under the roof of his family home on several occasions. John, a very little boy at the time, was only admitted to the drawing-room, when the great lady paid a visit, as long as he sat very still and did not utter a word. He still retains a vivid recollection of a very regal, dominating old lady, quite awe-inspiring in her manner. She must have been the most powerful of those actresses then labelled tragediennes, who spent their lives playing tragic victims of great misfortune.

Ellen Terry 1847–1928

When George V decided in 1925 to confer the title of Dame upon a second actress there was only one possible choice – Ellen Terry – the darling of the British public who had been so surprisingly overlooked four years earlier in favour of Geneviève Ward. Ellen Terry's admirers considered she had been slighted and treated disgracefully. She had been on the stage since 1856, the year of the Crimean War, and after gaining invaluable experience on the road and in London productions she had reigned at the Lyceum with Irving for a quarter of a century and continued to be idolised even in her late seventies as the most famous actress of the English-speaking world.

The investiture proved quite an amusing incident for George V. The ceremony was held in private at Buckingham Palace because at the age of seventy-eight Ellen Terry had become a rather absent-minded, frail old lady. Her daughter Edith Craig was in attendance at her reception by the King and described her mother's graceful curtsy as slow, stately and very expressive. The ageing actress sought Edy's guiding hand as she groped her way out of the audience chamber. Suddenly she laughed and exclaimed, 'I quite forgot to walk backwards!' She did not realise the King was only a step behind her and was both surprised and relieved to hear him laughing with her. He escorted her to another room where Queen Mary awaited them, eager to reminisce with Ellen Terry about memorable nights when she had seen her playing at the Lyceum.

The occasion was a tremendous event in Ellen Terry's life. The monarch had done for her and her profession what Queen Victoria had done for Irving when she had knighted him thirty years earlier. But she loathed and dreaded the idea of being addressed as Dame. Despite her advanced age and her failing faculties, she was, to use John Gielgud's felicitous phrase, a Fairy Godmother in spectacles, and the title of Dame did not fit the lovable image cherished by legions of admirers and well-wishers. Time was to prove that few could bring themselves to call her Dame Ellen, which sounded so incongruous and totally out of character.

Ellen Terry's Tudor farmhouse at Smallhythe in Kent, where she spent so much time during the last thirty years of her life, is now a fascinating museum, housing personal treasures and preserving her bedroom just as it had been in her lifetime. Mrs Molly Thomas, the dedicated curator who has lived there with Ellen Terry's ghost for quite a number of years, always refers to the actress as Miss Terry, which speaks for itself.

Bernard Shaw once said, 'Ellen Terry is the most beautiful name in the world; it rings like a chime through the last quarter of the nineteenth century.'

Without ever being stagestruck, as Irving was, Ellen Terry, daughter of strolling players, was on the boards at the age of nine, when she played Mamillius in Charles Kean's production of *The Winter's Tale*, with Queen Victoria and Prince Albert in the Royal Box at the Princess's Theatre. In due course she became the First Lady of the English-speaking theatre. Never, in any walk of life, has there been a more suitable and popular candidate to qualify for the highest honour a woman can receive in her own right.

When the Keans retired Ellen Terry went to Bristol to join the excellent stock company at the Theatre Royal. She was only fourteen and one of her colleagues was the year-younger Madge Robertson, who was to become famous as Mrs Kendal. While working with her own sister Kate in Bristol, Ellen Terry decided the height of her ambition would be to become a useful actress and that desire remained her guiding principle right throughout her long career. 'Usefulness . . .' she wrote, 'on the stage it is the first thing to aim at. Not until we have learned to be useful can we afford to do what we like.' She never had any grand ideas about stardom and during her long years at the Lyceum she was quite content to play second fiddle to Irving.

Shaw accused her of trifling with her career. At sixteen she married the painter G. F. Watts, but the vast difference in their ages meant their life together was doomed to failure from the start and later she left the stage for six years to live with the eminent Victorian architect Edward Godwin at Harpenden. By him she had two illegitimate children, eventually to make their own significant mark upon the theatre as Gordon Craig and Edith Craig.

Charles Reade, the popular playwright, was out hunting near Harpenden one day in 1874 when purely by chance he ran across Ellen Terry. He wondered where she had been hiding for so long and insisted upon her returning to the stage. Ellen Terry and Godwin were deeply in debt at the time, so by way of a joke she said she would consider nothing less than £40 a week. To her astonishment Reade agreed to her demand on the spot and Ellen Terry returned to the

London stage at the age of twenty-seven, with two illegitimate children to bring up.

Charles Reade was fascinated by Ellen Terry, whom he described as an enigma. 'Her eyes are pale, her nose rather long, her mouth nothing particular. Complexion a delicate brickdust, her hair rather like tow. Yet somehow she is beautiful. Her expression kills any pretty fancy you see beside her. Her figure is lean and boney; her hand masculine in size and form. Yet she is a pattern of faun-like grace. Whether in movement or repose, grace pervades the hussy.'

The next great milestone in Ellen Terry's career was her Portia of 1875, with the Bancrofts at the Prince of Wales Theatre, which occupied the site of the now demolished Scala Theatre off Tottenham Court Road. She accepted the invitation of the Bancrofts to join them with a note which read, 'My work will I feel certain, be joyful work and joyful work should turn out good work.'

Alice Comyns Carr, costume designer and wife of one of Irving's playwrights, saw this remarkable Portia and described the impact Ellen Terry made upon the audience on the first night.

'As the curtain rose upon Nell's tall and slender figure in a china-blue and white brocade dress, with one crimson rose at her breast, the whole house burst forth in rapturous applause. But her greatest effect was when she walked into the court in her black robes of justice, and I remember my young husband, who had rushed out between the acts to buy the last bouquet in Covent Garden, throwing his floral tribute to her feet amidst the enthusiasm of the audience.

'What Ellen established as the characteristic of her performance in an age when pompous, rhetorical, windy, and monotonous acting was still the rule, was an utter naturalness of manner which came directly from her own essential nature. As soon as she put her foot on the stage she did not assume artificial limbs and an artificial voice – she intensified by careful study and the thoughtful invention of 'business' her own natural reaction to whatever part she was playing. Her high spirits led her to find her fullest realisation in comedy; her own suffering led her to understand the human aspect of pathos and compassion.'

Ellen Terry began to seek out the human aspects of all the various characters she played after the creation of that Portia. Sybil Thorndike saw a much later Portia in Ellen Terry's career and recalls the wondrous inner light which shone from her. She had a never-failing sense of humour, as well as perfect enunciation, and succeeded in taking the audience completely into her confidence.

Henry James drew attention to Ellen Terry's remarkable charm, which beguiled people into thinking her an accomplished actress. Pinero said the moment she came on the stage there was something about her that made every man in the audience want to take her in his arms and carry her home. Her own son, Gordon Craig, maintained Ellen Terry was never genuinely criticised, because the moment she walked on to the stage the critics fell under her spell and that was that. He also declared she played but one part – herself. Instead of an actress playing Ophelia, Nance Oldfield or Beatrice, playgoers saw Ellen Ophelia, Nelly Oldfield or Nell Beatrice. She had the rare gift of identifying herself with the personages she presented, and when a part was not herself she could not play it.

Sybil Thorndike deplores the fact that Ellen Terry was not more closely identified with the characters she played. 'She could have done such exciting things had she got away from her own personality; but this never happened because the public would not have accepted her'. So she was always Ellen Terry and thus always the object of their hero worship.

Ellen Terry devoted a great deal of attention to details of her stage appearance, to her make-up, her costume and her movement. When *The Times* critic, A. B. Walkley, saw her as Imogen he wrote, 'Hers is a figure that dwells in the memory as one of absolute beauty.' When Graham Robertson saw her playing the same part at the age of forty-nine he recalled, 'Such a radiant embodiment of youth that when she first appeared the audience gasped – there was silence, then thunders of applause.' Johnston Forbes-Robertson, as fine a painter as he was an actor, described her as a vision of loveliness.

Godwin was the only love of her life, though she was to marry three times – first Watts, then the pedestrian actor Charles Kelly and later the American actor James Carew in 1907. She was with Godwin for eight years and then he tired of her; there were constant money problems and the presence of the two children did nothing to ease their domestic worries. They parted in 1875 and two and a half years later Irving called on Ellen Terry at her house in Earl's Court to invite her to join his company at the Lyceum. She was offered a salary of forty guineas a week and never looked poverty in the face again.

Irving was already forty; she was thirty-one and during the spectacular years they starred at the Lyceum from 1878 until 1902, the most famous roles she played were Ophelia, Henrietta Maria in *Charles I*, Jeanette in *The Lyons Mail*, Portia, Desdemona, Juliet, Beatrice, Marguerite in *Faust*, Lady Macbeth, Queen Katharine in *Henry VIII*, Cordelia in *Lear*, Rosamund in *Becket*, Guinevere in *King Arthur*, Imogen in *Cymbeline* and Volumnia in *Coriolanus*.

Perhaps her most glorious achievement was Beatrice. It was near-perfection because she was at her best when her sense of fun and her high spirits could join forces with her strength, her intensity and her grace. With every sign of complete spontaneity, her performance was a work of precisely calculated art. Sybil Thorndike is convinced Shakespeare wrote Beatrice just as Ellen Terry played her.

Irving lost the Lyceum as his London home in 1902 and that meant the end of their legendary partnership and really the end of her own histrionic splendour. She was to live another twenty-five years, but it was an anticlimax as far as her stage career was concerned. Apart from playing Lady Cecily Waynflete in Shaw's *Captain Brassbound's Conversion* in 1906, she did very little of real significance after leaving Irving at the age of fifty-nine.

By the end of the 'nineties, considering their advancing years, there were only three productions in which Irving and Ellen Terry could appear to real advantage – *Charles I*, *Madame Sans Gêne* and *The Merchant of Venice*. His Shylock and her Portia had been a never-failing box-office draw for some twenty years and they played these parts right to the end. They played *The Merchant of Venice* together for the last time at the Lyceum in July 1902 and just a year later they acted together for the very last time on July 14 in a Drury Lane charity performance of the same play in aid of the Actors' Association.

The last time they ever met was at Wolverhampton in the Spring of 1905. Irving had been taken ill on tour and she rushed to see him. They sat in silence for most of the time, both very moved. Afterwards she said, 'He looked like some beautiful grey tree that I have seen in Savannah. His old dressing-gown hung about his frail yet majestic figure like some mysterious grey drapery.' He died in Bradford, after a performance of *Becket* on Friday, October 13, 1905.

Their professional parting had been neither at her suggestion nor by her desire. There were no bitter feelings, but what pained her most of all was the realisation that Irving no longer considered her a 'useful' actress. She had to face the future alone and failure of memory made her regard new parts with some degree of apprehension. Her face, her dress and her movement still retained beauty and her voice remained thrilling and youthful to the end. But the prospect was bleak. The full blaze of her glory was over.

She put on *The Vikings* by Ibsen and *Much Ado About Nothing* at the Imperial Theatre in Westminster so that her son Gordon Craig could exploit his genius as a stage designer, and the next and last event of any consequence was *Captain Brassbound's Conversion* at the Court Theatre in Sloane Square in 1906, the year of her stage jubilee. Shaw drew the character of Lady Cecily entirely from the scores of letters Ellen Terry had written to him. He did not meet her until the play was finished. He hardly ever saw her, except across the footlights, until the inevitable moment came when they were in daily contact at *Captain Brassbound* rehearsals. After the run of the play, which had been specially written for her, their meetings were few and in every case purely accidental.

In 1902 Oscar Asche half jokingly suggested Tree should play Falstaff in a season of *The Merry Wives of Windsor*, with Ellen Terry and Mrs Kendal as the wives. Tree leapt at the idea, but knowing Mrs Kendal was decidedly jealous of Ellen Terry's eminent position in the theatre at the turn of the century, he gave her first choice of part. She preferred Mistress Ford, so Ellen Terry was given Mistress Page with no alternative.

Ellen Terry's very last appearance on any stage was in a charity performance of *Crossings* by Walter de la Mare at the Lyric Theatre, Hammersmith, in 1925. Ten-year-old Phyllis Calvert made her stage début on the same occasion, playing a child haunted by the ghost of an old lady. To maintain the illusion of the supernatural, Ellen Terry dusted her face with French chalk and was instructed on no account to touch the child. But when she glided on to the stage with outstretched arms she could not resist hugging the little mite, who frantically whispered, 'You're not supposed to touch me!'

Much consternation was caused in the interval when Princess Helena Victoria and Princess Marie Louise left their box and drove off in a car. Later it transpired they had received news that the aged Queen Alexandra was dying.

Even in her late seventies Ellen Terry remained gracious, kindly and interested in young people. George Howe recalls playing Puck in *A Midsummer Night's Dream* at the Kingsway Theatre in 1923. Ellen Terry saw the production and at a reception afterwards insisted upon meeting the young Puck because she had played the part at the age of twelve in Charles Kean's company and thus had a special interest in it.

When Sybil Thorndike was starting her career Ellen Terry was to her synonymous with Theatre. The great actress had long passed the peak of her career by that time, but when Sybil Thorndike played every part imaginable during the First World War at the Old Vic for 'ten bob a show', Ellen Terry used to appear at the Old Vic Shakespeare Birthday Festivals and it was on one of these occasions that Sybil was able to marvel at the glorious indignation of Ellen Terry's Queen Katharine in *Henry VIII*.

Ellen Terry's costumes were so much a part of her they acquired a sort of magic, which was why Edith Craig never liked to have them cleaned. She created an unforgettable series of stage portraits – as Ophelia, Juliet, Imogen and Portia. She was everyone's idea of Portia, maintained Sybil, in her dynamic impression of Ellen Terry, which was recorded when Sybil paid tribute to her at a National Portrait Gallery lunchtime recital, using as a backcloth Sargent's majestic portrait of Ellen Terry as Lady Macbeth in her green beetle-wing dress – a full-length masterpiece lent by the Tate Gallery for the occasion.

Her barbaric Lady Macbeth, explained Sybil, was not in the Siddons tradition because Ellen Terry was incapable of whispering certain lines which Siddons insisted should only just be heard by the audience. Rosamund in Tennyson's *Becket* was one of her astonishing creations because the part hardly existed. She had to make bricks without straw for the simple reason that Tennyson did not know enough about women to write a really convincing part for an actress.

Sybil never ceased to be amazed that so great a stage personality should be totally devoid of personal ambition. She was content to be a prop for Irving during the best years of her professional life and was always ready to play any part requested of her. As an actress she was never interested in herself or her career. She conquered the world with her charm and a voice which never ceased to sound young. She was always gay and would talk about anything under the sun except herself.

Shaw told her anyone could play Shakespeare and indicated she was wanted for other things, but she was not attracted by the idea of appearing in *John Gabriel Borkman* or as any of Ibsen's dark ladies. She considered the theatre existed to gladden tired working people. Sybil reminds us that Ellen Terry was ready to go out into the provinces to play in grim, colourless towns for nothing as long as she could make life more joyfu to those who lived there. Such was her gospel. Even so, the theatre was never her first love; she was too occupied in giving happiness and love to others and worrying about her children and her grandchildren to devote undivided attention to her career.

Although I was already twenty when Ellen Terry died I never had the good fortune to catch a glimpse of her, either on the stage or in the street. Yet I feel I have met her because I have been a frequent visitor to the Tudor farmhouse at Smallhythe which she loved so passionately. Happily, this picturesque dwelling near Tenterden is now a National Trust property for all to visit.

She first saw it back in the 'nineties when she lived at near-by Winchelsea. One summer evening she was driving through Small-hythe with Irving, going to see a puppet show at Tenterden. She fell in love with the mellowed old house at first sight. She stopped the brougham and made some enquiries from an old shepherd, who said the house belonged to a Miss Hope. It had been in her family for 200 years, but she was the last of the line. Ellen Terry gave him an addressed postcard and asked him to send it to her if the house ever came up for sale. He kept his word, at a time when she was on her penultimate American tour, but she cabled home to Edy – BUY IT AT ANY

PRICE. It was purchased in 1900 and she was to die there on a lovely summer day twenty-eight years later.

Today it is easy to go to Smallhythe and imagine the relaxed existence Ellen Terry enjoyed in this peaceful spot. Inside the house one can read letters from Oscar Wilde and others, examine her primitive wicker make-up basket and admire many stage costumes already familiar to us through paintings and photographs dating back to her Lyceum days. One can also gaze upon her death mask swathed in the chiffon drapery she favoured in later years.

One can visualise her writing letters to Shaw in her austere bedroom, seated at the old twin schoolroom desk used by Edith and Gordon Craig in their nursery days. Dominating one wall of the bedroom is a large photograph of Eleonora Duse, whose untheatrical, realistic acting so impressed Ellen Terry. Across this arresting portrait Ellen Terry has written in her bold hand: THERE IS NONE LIKE HER – NONE. This admiration was mutual and on the occasion of Ellen Terry's stage jubilee at Drury Lane in 1906, the frail Italian actress travelled all the way from Florence just to stand in homage beside Ellen Terry.

For many years Edith Craig lived in the picturesque Tudor Priest's House, a few yards along the road from her mother's more spacious fifteenth-century house at Smallhythe. Edy shared the Priest's House with her woman-writer friend, Christopher St John, who apart from worshipping Edy and Ellen Terry, had edited the Ellen Terry and Bernard Shaw correspondence as well as Ellen Terry's own memoirs.

Edy had died and Chris was living in the house with their mutual friend the painter Clare (Tony) Atwood, when I was invited to drink coffee they had obtained in vacuum-sealed tins from the Savoy. I was staying in Rye at the time, reading a rough proof copy of Laurence Irving's masterly biography of his grandfather, Henry Irving, so it was only natural conversation should touch on this forthcoming publication.

They admired much about the book, but thought it did not go far enough. Chris maintained that Irving and Ellen Terry had been lovers briefly at the time they first played together at the Lyceum, although Laurence Irving had gone to great lengths in his book attempting to prove they could not possibly have indulged in a physical relationship.

Charles Howson, a trusted and long-standing member of Irving's business management staff, had suspicions about Irving and his leading lady, as I learned in later years from his daughter Clelia. At one time while on holiday in Germany, Ellen Terry had been confined to her room with a severe cold. Irving instructed Mr Howson to go to the post office to send a telegram of good wishes for a speedy recovery. As Mr Howson counted the number of words he was surprised by the warmth and affectionate terms in which Irving had expressed his sentiments. He was convinced he and Ellen Terry were sharing a deeply emotional relationship at that time.

To perpetuate Ellen Terry's memory her daughter Edith Craig converted a large, thatched barn at the bottom of the Smallhythe garden into a theatre and there each year on or about the anniversary of Ellen Terry's death in July a performance used to be given on a Sunday afternoon by leading members of the theatrical profession before an invited audience.

Edith Craig bought a consignment of chairs at 4/6 each, in order to provide seating in the auditorium. Then she cleverly suggested an equivalent number of famous people should each pay her 5/- to cover the cost of chair and delivery. In return each donor had his name inscribed in poker work on the back of a chair.

These anniversary performances usually concluded with an oration delivered by someone who had known Ellen Terry. W. Macqueen-Pope, the theatre historian, once recalled her rare gift for happiness. 'Whenever her name is mentioned in the presence of anyone who saw her, either on the stage or in private life, they invariably smile.'

Audrey Cameron took the stage on another occasion. At the age of ten she had been engaged to play Robin in the Basket Scene from *The Merry Wives of Windsor*, when Ellen Terry toured the variety theatres as Mistress Page, with Edith Evans as Mistress Ford and Roy Byford as Falstaff. When they played the Coliseum Ellen Terry feared the child would not be heard at the back of that vast house. So she instructed her how to speak the lines without giving the impression of shouting. Then, despite her seventy-one years, she climbed up many flights of stone steps to the back of the gallery during a rehearsal, just to confirm that the beginner was audible. Later in her life, when she was seventy-five, Ellen Terry sighed to Miss Cameron, in all humility, 'I've got so much to learn about acting and so little time.'

John Gielgud provided me with a treasured memory in the last oration he gave in the Barn Theatre. He was intensely proud of being her kinsman and reminded us she was so many other things apart from being a great actress. She was a lover of life, with a gift for being interested in other people and putting them at their ease. As a boy he regarded her as an enchanted being.

Though she was so old she had to be wheeled along Brighton Pier to the theatre in a bathchair, she could still dance on to the stage as Mistress Page like a young girl, giving the impression of youth without aping it. On that account she never looked ridiculous because she created an effect of youth that remained unforgettable. After the performance she settled back into her chair to be pushed back to the hotel, swathed in shawls and clutching the enormous reticule from which she was never separated.

Gielgud's final comment: 'She spoke immortal lines as if she had just thought of them herself for the first time.'

Madge Kendal 1848–1935

I saw Mrs Kendal only once, not on the stage, but at Claridges when she walked through a lounge where I was waiting to be joined by Anna May Wong to taste fresh lychees for the first time in my life. Dressed in funereal black from head to foot, she might have been a despotic dowager Empress in exile. With a forbidding and hostile expression on her face she looked, as Queen Victoria so often did, as if she had never laughed in her life.

Suddenly I recalled what the actress Mary Jerrold had once told me about Mrs Kendal's glorious gift for comedy. She had acted supporting parts with Mr and Mrs Kendal for three and a half years from 1902 and said, 'I defy any other actress, living or dead, to get a laugh out of some of the poor lines with which Mrs Kendal simply rocked the house. And what control she had! One moment she would have her audience roaring with laughter and in a flash she could have them quiet as mice.'

Gaiety seemed a far cry from the ageing matron I saw at Claridges. She was by that time Dame Madge Kendal and about eighty-five years old. She looked every inch a Dame, in the most unflattering sense of the word. I suppose she had been known as Mrs Kendal ever since her marriage to W. H. Kendal in 1869 and no one seemed to think of her as Dame Madge.

Madge Robertson, to use her maiden name, was born into a family which had served the theatre for 200 years. Her father William Robertson acted with Edmund Kean and her mother Margaretta Marinus, of Scandinavian extraction, was an actress, though there must have been long periods when she was away from the stage considering she had twenty-two children, Madge being the last of them. The only other to attain fame was the first-born, T. W. Robertson, the dramatist who wrote *Society*, *Ours*, *Caste*, *Play* and *School*, which founded the cup-and-saucer drama because of their realistic domestic settings. At the time they were written, his plays had recognisable rooms, his dialogue was credible and his plots were an immense advance on anything that had gone before. These realistic works established the reputation of the newly-formed Bancroft management at the Prince of Wales Theatre, which stood on the site later occupied by the Scala Theatre off Tottenham Court Road. As he directed his own plays, he has come to be regarded by many as the first of the modern producers.

William Robertson, father of the clan, in partnership with J. W. Wallack, leased the old Marylebone Theatre in London and it was there that Madge made her first appearance on the stage as Marie in *The Struggle for God* in 1854, just before she was six. By the time she was fifteen she had become a seasoned actress, having played in London, Bristol and Bath. At Bath's Theatre Royal in 1863 she played the second singing fairy in *A Midsummer Night's Dream* to the Titania of Ellen Terry, a year her senior. Ellen was wearing an exquisitely pretty dress designed specially for her by Edward William Godwin, who was to become the father of her two children.

Madge Robertson regarded her real London début as having been in 1865, when she played Ophelia to Walter Montgomery's Hamlet at the Haymarket. At the age of seventeen she played Desdemona to the Othello of Ira Aldridge, the first great American Negro actor, billed as the African Roscius. In the last act he made her wear 'toed stockings with sandals to suggest being undressed', pulled her out of bed by her hair and dragged her round the stage before he smothered her. The same year she played Lady Macbeth opposite Samuel Phelps in Hull and was also his Lady Teazle in London.

At the age of twenty-one she married W. H. Kendal in Manchester. At that time she had already played over fifty parts, but after their marriage their careers became inseparable until their mutual retirement in 1908. Kendal was dull and pompous as an actor and as a man. To many they became insufferable because they made a cult of respectability, which made them highly disliked in many quarters, on account of the ostentation with which it was displayed. They had four children from whom they were alienated because they treated them abominably and Mrs Kendal used to decry them in public with such vehemence she was likened to an old-time tragedienne ranting in a cheap melodrama. She used to discuss her family with young Joyce Carey, who admits she often felt like laughing during these vitriolic outbursts.

In her memoirs, published when she was eighty-five, only two years before her death, Dame Madge maintains her husband died of a broken heart and wounded pride because they had both given up all hope of any sign of affection from their children. When their youngest child Dorothy Grimston, the actress, married the manager Bertie Meyer at a register office against her father's wish and was later divorced, Mr

Kendal never raised his head again. As Mrs Kendal remarked towards the end of her own life, 'The divorce court becomes more overworked every year than the year before. I am glad I lived in Queen Victoria's time, for Her Majesty disliked divorce.' I knew Bertie Meyer quite well, but never summoned up enough courage to ask his opinion of Mrs Kendal, though he did say on one occasion she was a difficult mother-in-law.

'My husband never was my leading man,' proclaimed Mrs Kendal, 'I was always his leading lady.' Even so, it was she who was the box-office draw. In those days the public liked man-and-wife leading players who toured their own company round the provinces, with regular London seasons. Irving and Ellen Terry were not married, but their twenty-five-year partnership had an air of respectability and permanency about it. Fred Terry and Julia Neilson were inseparable stage partners; so were Marie Wilton and Squire Bancroft, Johnston Forbes-Robertson and Gertrude Elliott, Seymour Hicks and Ellaline Terriss, Marie Tempest and Graham Browne, all husband-and-wife teams who were stage partners of long standing. It often happened that one half was much finer, from an artistic point of view, than the other. In recent years Alfred Lunt and Lynn Fontanne were equally fine players and remarkably unselfish partners.

Mrs Kendal had a high opinion of her husband's talent as an actor and would often recall the scene in *The Queen's Shilling* in which he displayed his remarkable gift of turning pale whenever he wished, just as Duse had been able to blush at will on stage. Mr Kendal played a wounded soldier and at one point in the action the colonel gripped his arm where he had been wounded and the soldier visibly blanched with pain, often causing women in the audience to faint. The Kendals led a severely disciplined life and disapproved of actors going out to parties two or three times a week. Such artists, in their estimation, could not be considered conscientious. 'The actor must give his best performance and the public value for their money,' insisted Mrs Kendal. She had no time for actors who were out all day at the races or playing golf, arriving at the theatre only just in time to change before the show. 'Artists who walk through a part are not acting; they are just on stage.'

Mrs Kendal held decidedly strong opinions which seem rather out-moded today. As a widow in retirement she became more and more censorious and her outbursts – which always made good headlines in the press – became increasingly bitter and denunciatory. She dressed in an old-fashioned style, often wearing a bonnet rather like Queen Victoria at the end of her reign, but as the Matron of the British Drama, as she liked to style herself, it suited her and she seemed entirely in character when criticising the young for having neither morals nor manners.

The increasing use of make-up off-stage displeased her. She admired Mrs Langtry's beauty as something quite remarkable, but one wonders what she thought of the Jersey Lily's morals. 'She had a complexion like a peach,' recalled Mrs Kendal, 'soft and with a tinge of pink in it – real, real! I wonder where in God's great universe she is and what she thinks of the red cheeks, red backs, red legs, red arms, red nails and red lips of the modern woman.'

Dismissing short skirts as kilts, Mrs Kendal was of the opinion no actress could speak sentiment in what she called curtailed clothing. 'It requires the majestic sweeping of a train or, at any rate, something down to the ankles to suggest romance.' She considered people went to the theatre to hear words and arguments and conversation of all kinds – not to see a lady undress herself.

The ingratitude of young actors came under fire. 'I have taught many actors and actresses the early part of their business – what is called the ground work – but I have never been thanked by anybody except Seymour Hicks.' I am convinced this charge is highly exaggerated, as both Mary Jerrold and Marie Löhr talked to me at length about their early days in the Kendal company and how deeply grateful they were for all they learned from her.

Mrs Kendal thought the acting of her heyday travelled from the brain to the heart and from the heart to the brain. 'Today much of it does not reach as high as the heart, but seems, rather, to be below the belt.' Two of her own children went on the stage. She had no objection as long as they had talent to begin with, supported by industry, perseverance, good health, strength of mind and last, though not least, a little modesty of their own merits. When mothers consulted her about the prospects of putting their daughters on the stage she would indicate the qualifications a young woman should have for a successful career on the stage as being the face of Venus, the figure of Juno, the brains of Minerva, the memory of Macaulay, the chastity of Diana, the grace of Terpsichore and, above all, the hide of a rhinoceros. One wonders how she could ever have encouraged a stage-struck girl to try her luck on the boards. Yet, in the next breath she declares, 'As Matron of the British Drama, I have given my maternal blessing to 30,000 aspirants to the stage. It is a large number. They cannot all play Macbeth and Lady Macbeth. Some of them must only be friends invited to the banquet.'

Drama critics came under fire, too. 'My point of view is that they criticise what they have never done themselves. I maintain that a man must have some practical and not merely a theoretical knowledge of

an art before he can write understandingly of it and its technique.'
She also considered critics mixed too freely with actors and it was
difficult to write adversely about an actor's performance when he
happened to be a friend.

She learned her job the hard way. On Saturday nights in her young
days she would often play leading parts in both *The Hunchback* and *The
Lady of Lyons*, which meant ten acts in two exacting works. She considered an actor must have three successes before he could hope to
stamp his reputation on the public and make his name known. During
the first part of her career Mrs Kendal played most of the great classical
roles, but by the time they reached the 1880s the Kendals were content
to appear in plays which have not survived – plays such as *The Falcon*,
Still Waters Run Deep, *William and Susan*, *The Ironmaster*, *A Scrap of
Paper*, *The Elder Miss Blossom*, *The Wife's Sacrifice*, *The Wife's Secret*,
The Weaker Sex, *A White Lie*, *The Fall of the Leaf*, *Lord and Lady
Guilderoy*, *A Flash in the Pan*, *The Secret Orchard*, *The Likeness of the
Night*, *Mrs Hamilton's Silence*, *A Tight Corner* and *The House of Clay*. It
must be admitted that the Kendals toured in *The Second Mrs Tanqueray*
in the 'nineties and in 1902 she went to His Majesty's Theatre to appear
as Mistress Ford in the star production of *The Merry Wives of Windsor*,
with Ellen Terry as Mistress Page and Tree as Falstaff. The plays which
have now fallen into oblivion must have been good vehicles for her,
capable of filling theatres in London and on the touring circuit, year
after year. When Dame Madge died in 1935 she left only £4,743,
though her husband was able to leave £66,251 in 1917.

There was no great fanfare when they decided to retire from the
stage in 1908. She was sixty, he sixty-five. To quote Mrs Kendal, 'Like
the Arab, we folded our tents and stole away.' They last appeared in
The House of Clay at the Coronet Theatre in Notting Hill Gate. It has
long been used as a cinema; but both Bernhardt and Duse played there
and the Dare sisters made their first appearance on the stage there in
Babes in the Wood at Christmas 1899, when Phyllis appeared as one of
the two children and Zena understudied the Boy Babe and had a
minor part in the cast.

This modest fading-out seems extraordinary as Mrs Kendal was a
first rate snob and in her memoirs takes every opportunity to drop
titled names and refer to the Queen as Her Majesty and to a prince as
His Royal Highness. I would have expected them to have arranged a
gala farewell in the 'gracious presence' of King Edward and Queen
Alexandra at one of the more famous West End theatres.

When I had the good fortune to hear Mary Jerrold talking about the
phenomenal Mrs Kendal she stressed the fact that the great actress was
never a specialist, never cast to type. She was a superlative artist able

to play any part that came her way as well as it ever could be played. She knew her job and triumphed at a time when audiences were far more interested in genuine acting than in magnetic personalities. She frequently played parts that did not suit her personality, but she never failed to fill the house because she knew how to act.

Mrs Kendal returned to the London stage in 1896 after a long provincial tour and Shaw wrote, 'Mrs Kendal, forgetting that London playgoers have been starved for years in the matter of acting, inconsiderately gave them more in the first ten minutes than they have had in the last five years, with the result that the poor wretches became hysterical and vented their applause in sobs and shrieks.'

'She was a rigid disciplinarian,' continued Mary Jerrold. 'To her, acting was a serious job of work and not a lazy way of earning money. She laid down the law and ruled her company with a rod of iron. Young girls who were taken on were told, as I was, to part their hair in the middle and to wash every day without fail. She never permitted flirtation in the theatre; there was a time and place for everything and the theatre was certainly no place for amorous tomfoolery.'

There were certain unwritten laws in the company concerning stage behaviour. It was always considered indelicate for an actor to touch an actress above the elbow. 'Never let an actor take you by the upper arm,' she advised Joyce Carey. 'It looks so ugly.' She had a special technique of playing stage love scenes with Mr Kendal. She would cross her arms and he would lean against her, which gave the effect of intimacy without offending their canons of respectability. Even in an age when it was considered something of a sin to go to the theatre, it was permissible for respectable people to go to see the Kendals without losing caste and getting talked about. Hundreds of people who went to see them would not have dreamt of going to see any other actors. They must had had a severe shock when she toured in *The Second Mrs Tanqueray*, after they had been accustomed to seeing her play heroines of a considerably higher moral standing.

Mary Jerrold admitted Mrs Kendal had no dress sense, yet she insisted upon designing the costumes for all their productions. She specially liked plays that called for crinolines and bustles, covered in frills, bows and flowers. Some of the creations were ghastly to look at, but she meant well and wanted the company to look well dressed.

Marie Löhr, daughter of the actress Kate Bishop and her husband Lewis J. Löhr, treasurer of the Melbourne Opera House, was born in Sydney but by the time she was thirteen and a half she joined the Kendal company in this country for two and a half years, succeeding Mary Jerrold. Marie Löhr hero-worshipped Mrs Kendal, who was playing six different parts a week at that time, so the young girl saw her as every conceivable type of character.

In Marie Löhr's estimation, 'Mrs Kendal was the greatest of them all. No other artist, not even Duse, could so firmly hold an audience in the hollow of her hand. She could break your heart in her tragic roles, not with a display of flamboyant histrionics, but by the sheer depth and sincerity of her acting.' Marie Löhr played maids, *ingénues* and small character parts, so she had a good deal of spare time on her hands. Even so, she was never out of the theatre. On nights when she was not playing she would be in the wings, speechless with admiration for what she saw out on the stage.

Mrs Kendal had the same uncanny power even in parts she had been playing for years, such as the Elder Miss Blossom and Susan Hartley in *A Scrap of Paper*. So vital was her interest in her work, according to Marie Löhr, she did not know what it was to grow stale. 'I do not exaggerate when I say she was always, without exception, on the top of her form.'

Madge Kendal was a perfectionist. Everything she did she did as well as she possibly could. Hilda Trevelyan, who created Wendy in Barrie's *Peter Pan*, relates a story concerning Mrs Kendal being asked to make a charity appeal at Drury Lane long after her retirement. The previous day she went down to the theatre, walked on to the stage and looking out into the vast auditorium where one or two cleaners were at work, she hurled out the question, 'Ladies of the Gallery, can you hear me?' Being answered in the affirmative by the astonished charwomen, she returned home confident her moving appeal would be heard the following day in the furthermost recesses of that enormous theatre.

Had she not been so deeply influenced by her husband's ideas, she might have been one of our most popular comediennes with the immense verve she had at her disposal, but in later years she seemed content to appear in amiable, comparatively unexacting pieces such as *A Scrap of Paper*, *Still Waters Run Deep* and *The Elder Miss Blossom*. She was tall, had a good stage presence and a serene look that suited elderly parts, a quality that Orpen captured to perfection in his portrait now in the Tate Gallery, painted in the actress's eightieth year. Her character was too firm to permit family affection to survive and too robust to make her easy to work with. Even so, she made an indelible mark on the theatre of her time, in which she worked ceaselessly for fifty-four years.

Sybil Thorndike 1882–

The first time I saw Sybil Thorndike on the stage I was afraid I was going to faint from sheer excitement. It was one summer night at the New Theatre in St Martin's Lane during the original London run of *Saint Joan*, which had been hailed as the greatest theatrical experience for many a long day. I was a teenager on holiday, going to my first West End theatre to see this much-discussed star for the first time in my life.

Those were the days of queue stools for gallery patrons. For six-pence you hired a very uncomfortable slatted wooden stool which marked your place in the queue, thus enabling you to wander off until thirty minutes before the doors opened. At that moment I rushed up endless flights of stone stairs at breakneck speed, overtaking the less agile to secure the best vantage point on the hard wooden benches – really no more than glorified wooden tiers, without backs or numbered places – from which you looked down on the stage far below.

I remember taking a fancy to Sybil Thorndike's North Country accent when she made her first entrance. She seemed such a friendly soul and I was on her side from the start. The close of the Cathedral Scene was the big moment for me, after the crowning of the Dauphin, when the solitary Joan declaims:

> Dear Child of God
> Be brave go on
> I am thy help
> God will serve France.

Like a mighty bell Sybil Thorndike's rich voice boomed out and reverberated through the hushed theatre. Each line intensified my excitement and raised me to a state of emotional ecstasy. My head swam, my mouth dried up and my spine turned to ice. For one awful moment I thought I might lose consciousness, but the fall of the curtain saved me just in time. For the first and only time in my life I had been spellbound in a theatre.

Sybil Thorndike was back at the New Theatre six years later in a different play, a Napoleonic fantasy called *Madame Plays Nap*. It was then we first met. I had a problem. I was twenty-two and about to start out in life, hoping I could scrape some sort of livelihood in the theatre, which was my only real interest. I knew no one connected with the stage, so right out of the blue, as a total stranger with no sort of introduction, I wrote to Sybil Thorndike for advice. She replied promptly and invited me to meet her at the stage door of the New one evening before the show.

I was first to arrive and walked slowly up and down the corridor ust inside, tense and very nervous, never having been back-stage before and never having met an actress. The door clanged open and I heard the familiar voice greeting the stage door keeper. As she approached me I was aware of her crooked smile as she exclaimed, 'Ah, Eric Johns! I remember!' Together we went downstairs to her dressing room at stage level. Very hesitantly I told her I thought I could write a bit and I hoped to get some sort of a start in the theatre. What did she think of my chances? I made it clear I did not want to act.

On hearing this, she opened the door and called across the corridor to her husband, Lewis Casson, who was in the opposite room. 'Lewis, come in. There's a young man here who doesn't want to act. I think we can help him!' As I watched her I observed a speck of dust in the corner of her eye and her practical hands looked as if they had scrubbed floors and washed dishes. I felt much less nervous. She seemed genuinely interested in my problem and eager to help. Her suggestions did not lead directly to a job, but this slight connection with the Cassons gave me a new confidence and a curious sense of superiority over people I passed in the street.

Eventually I secured a job as an unpaid office boy at the Everyman Theatre in Hampstead, then enjoying a new prestige, having so recently staged Noël Coward's first sensational success, *The Vortex*, in which he appeared with Lilian Braithwaite playing the part of his sophisticated mother. By a strange coincidence the very first production at the Everyman when I went to work there, starred Sybil Thorndike. It was *Fire in the Opera House* by Georg Kaiser. Sybil played the part of Sylvette, an orphan married to a nobleman who thought her chaste, but in reality she was having an affair with an opera singer and in the Paris of 1763 she was at the Opera Ball with him the night the theatre was burned down. Her husband imagined her cosily tucked in bed. Handsome Vernon Sylvaine, so reminiscent in voice and appearance of Henry Ainley, was the leading man in this play which was so confusingly symbolistic.

Whenever I could sneak a few moments from my endless job of

addressing envelopes for circulars, I used to slip down from the office into the auditorium to watch rehearsals. I soon realised the real life Sybil had the same persuasive quality as the Sybil who played Saint Joan. She was always in a good humour, had a wonderful sense of fun and bubbled over with infectious high spirits. The company obviously adored her and were ready to do anything for her. They were supposed to break for lunch at one o'clock and there were occasions when they would finish a twenty-minute scene at about five-to-one. She would turn to them, while they still had the feel of the situation at their fingertips and say, 'Come on, darlings, let's do it just once more!' Off they would go, without a shadow of resentment, just because it was for Sybil. No one muttered anything about the inconvenience of a short lunch hour.

Late one afternoon Vernon Sylvaine was dropping with exhaustion after a long and trying day. He just wanted to pack up, call a taxi and get to bed in readiness for the next day. Sybil was rather keen to go ahead with the next scene before they broke. 'Come on! Do the next like a cherub!' she urged. Her requests were irresistible and he could only agree. Bursting with energy, she zig-zagged across the stage to take her place, clicking her fingers like a Spanish dancer. 'Let's go slap ahead,' she cried. 'Don't stop for a moment's rest.' Off they rushed through their lines and she kept everyone in a good humour, amusing her colleagues with bright remarks on the stage situations.

I was guilty of outrageously moronic behaviour on one occasion during the run of *Fire in the Opera House*. I still feel ashamed when I recollect the incident. I decided it would be rather smart to smoke Russian cigarettes, so I went across the road from the theatre to a shop where they sold them by weight and I also purchased a cheap red enamel case to put them in. Back-stage that night I was standing alone in the wings, watching Sybil in her hysterical scene on her return from the blazing opera house, and thought it would be a marvellous idea to have one of my Russian cigarettes. To this day I'll never know how such an unprofessional and inconsiderate thought entered my head.

As I smoked the rather strong tobacco, I was fascinated by the cloud of smoke which floated out from the wings until it reached Sybil in the centre of the stage. I should have been taken by the scruff of the neck by the stage manager and pitched down the stairs. As Sybil came off stage she took me gently by the arm and very kindly whispered, 'I want to tell you something. Don't smoke in the wings, there's a darling. It upsets our eyes.' I could have died with shame. What other leading lady would have treated me with such undeserved consideration? I wonder what Marie Tempest would have said to me?

Those were star-studded nights in the London theatre. I would travel back to my room in Bloomsbury from the Hampstead Tube station during the run of *Fire in the Opera House* and while waiting for the train would feast on the great names on the London Theatre Guide poster displayed on the platform. While Sybil was playing at the Everyman, Jack Hulbert and Cicely Courtneidge were in *The House That Jack Built* at the Adelphi; Isabel Jeans and Raymond Massey at the Ambassadors in *The Man in Possession*; Louise Hampton and a very young Kay Hammond in the all-woman cast of *Nine Till Six* at the Apollo; Matheson Lang and twenty-two-year-old Peggy Ashcroft in *Jew Suss* at the Duke of York's; Tallulah Bankhead and Glen Byam Shaw were the lovers in *The Lady of the Camellias* at the Garrick; Marie Tempest was keeping Henry Ainley well disciplined in *The First Mrs Fraser* at the Haymarket; Binnie Hale and Bobby Howes were packing the Hippodrome with *Mr Cinders*; out at Lewisham Hippodrome Ivor Novello and Lilian Braithwaite were to be seen in *Symphony in Two Flats*; Frank Vosper played the lead in his own play *Murder on the Second Floor* at the Lyric; John Gielgud had joined the Old Vic company and was playing Macbeth; Colin Clive and Maurice Evans were in the original production of *Journey's End* at the Prince of Wales; Edith Evans and Cedric Hardwicke were filling the Queen's with *The Apple Cart*; Edna Best, Herbert Marshall, Frank Lawton and Elizabeth Allan were in *Michael and Mary* at the St James's and Madeleine Carroll, with her international film career still before her, was appearing in *Enchantment* at the Vaudeville.

I never lost touch with the Cassons. From time to time I would go and visit them in their cosy book-lined sitting room at Swan Court in Chelsea, where they talked about their plans and their great achievements of earlier years which have now become part of theatre history. Lewis always maintained the most memorable moment of their lives, the very peak of their professional achievement, was when they appeared in Shaw's *Saint Joan*, which Lewis directed.

Shaw had a half-written play about Joan of Arc; he thought Mrs Patrick Campbell might have played the part, but changed his mind after her outrageous behaviour during the stormy rehearsals of *Pygmalion*. So the Joan script, for which Mrs Shaw had done so much research, was left in a drawer unfinished. One afternoon Shaw went to see Sybil as Beatrice Cenci when a few special performances of *The Cenci* by Shelley were staged at the New Theatre. He had seen her in the past, but since that time she had matured and developed beyond all recognition. Her work was a revelation, so Shaw went straight home to tell his wife he had found a Joan and he could therefore complete the play.

This decision caused some embarrassment to the Cassons, flattered though they were to discover Shaw was finishing a Joan of Arc play for Sybil. Joan was a character she had always wanted to play and she and Lewis had already discussed the idea with the poet Laurence Binyon and he agreed to write a play for her. It was only after this arrangement had been made that the Cassons read in the papers that Shaw was writing a play about Joan. Lewis Casson wrote to Shaw about their plans and in reply received one of Shaw's famous postcards: OF COURSE SYBIL PLAYS MY JOAN. He even named another actress who could play Binyon's Joan. Perhaps it was Mrs Patrick Campbell, but we were never told. Binyon gallantly withdrew and his play was never written.

Shaw helped the cast of the original production of *Saint Joan* by taking rehearsals during the morning and handing them over to Lewis Casson in the afternoon. 'He was a better actor than anyone in the company,' recalled Sybil. 'He read the play to us with a rich variety of sound and went through the script with me, indicating the intonations of every single line with such thoroughness that fifty years later I could read it like a musical score. We worked together like one person. Almost instinctively I knew what he wanted me to say and how he wanted me to say it.'

I never thought any of the other Joans were a patch on Sybil's. She was unique because she really made you feel that men would leave their homes and families to follow her. They went because they wanted to go, not because they were forced to go or obliged to do so. No other actress possessed the same remarkable magnetism, which Jeanne d'Arc herself must have possessed. Discussing Joan many years after the première, Sybil said, 'Had she lived today, I should have followed her without question!' Sybil did not make the mistake of presenting Joan as a rough peasant girl. 'She was educated and her family lived in quite an impressive house in the village of Domrémy.'

Discussing actresses who played Joan after her, Sybil was very generous in her estimation of their achievement. 'There was much to admire in those performances, but they were not Shaw's Joan. Joan Plowright came nearest to it, but she did not convey the Belief. The actress playing Joan must be aware that Shaw was a deep and profound Believer. His Joan cannot be played as just a magical theatre part. The Greeks – Hecuba and Medea – are spectacular theatre roles, but Joan goes much deeper.' In the opinion of John Casson, Sybil's first-born, 'Her Joan was pure, untarnished theatrical magic.' Edith Evans said Sybil's Joan had religion, which made it so remarkable and that was the reason why she steadfastly refused to accept an invitation to play the part after Sybil. It was, after all, the crowning achievement of Sybil's career and she admits it was the only time she ever felt nervous on a first night. In appreciation of her superb performance Shaw sent her a copy of the play, inscribed TO SAINT SYBIL THORNDIKE FROM SAINT BERNARD SHAW, and it still remains the most cherished souvenir of Sybil's career.

I wanted to know how young Sybil Thorndike impressed her colleagues right at the beginning of her career, so I went to see Basil Dean who had joined Miss Horniman's company in Manchester at the Midland Hotel Theatre and later at the Gaiety Theatre where she established the first repertory theatre in this country.

Basil Dean had been with Miss Horniman for six months before Sybil Thorndike was recruited to strengthen the ranks of the company which Miss Horniman was to put into the Gaiety Theatre which she rebuilt in the summer of 1908. It was obvious to Basil Dean that Sybil already possessed boundless enthusiasm, deep devotion to the theatre and a sense of mission so rare and surprising in one not yet twenty-five.

Ben Iden Payne, who had persuaded Miss Horniman to take the lease of the Gaiety Theatre, was the first producer of her company. His wife, Mona Limerick, was leading lady and their daughter, Rosalind Iden, was born in Manchester. At first, Sybil was held back, though she could easily have played to advantage most of the leading parts which were naturally given to the producer's wife.

It was not until Mona Limerick left the company that Sybil was given her first big chance. As Basil Dean vividly recalled sixty-six years later, 'It was to play Candida and I still consider her the finest Candida I ever saw. The opportunity meant a great deal to Sybil. She scored an unqualified success and has lived in a state of theatrical ecstasy ever since.'

While in Manchester Basil Dean wrote a curtain-raiser for the Gaiety called *Marriages are Made in Heaven*, and it happened to be the first play in which Sybil Thorndike and Lewis Casson ever appeared together – in 1908 not long before their own wedding. It was a miniature tragedy concerning a Kentish farmhand who is about to marry the girl he loves when he is informed by his rival that she is his half-sister.

Sybil in the Horniman days was spurred on and strengthened by Lewis. Basil Dean was tremendously impressed by her belief in the importance of the theatre in social life – a belief which generations later was responsible for the Cassons touring the Welsh mining towns and villages during the Second World War in Old Vic productions of *Medea*, *Macbeth* and *Candida*.

Sybil never wanted a comfortable career, being cast to type in a succession of parts which amounted to playing the same woman in different guises. She wanted to be playing somebody different and avoid performing the same sort of part twice. She was thirty-two when she went to the Old Vic where she remained throughout the four years of the First World War. For 'ten bob a show' she played, among other parts, Lady Macbeth, Rosalind, Beatrice, Portia, Constance in *King John*, Imogen, Chorus and Princess Katherine in *Henry V*, Mistress Ford, Lady Teazle, Kate Hardcastle, Lydia Languish and Peg Woffington in *Masks and Faces*. Because actors – being at the Front – were in short supply, she also played a number of male roles, including Prince Hal in *Henry IV*, Everyman, Launcelot Gobbo, Puck, Rugby in *The Merry Wives of Windsor*, Ferdinand in *The Tempest* and Lear's Fool. Henry Kendall, who played at the Old Vic for nine months in 1915 before he was called up, played Orlando to her Rosalind. 'She taught me all I know about the theatre,' he once told me. 'During a spell of thirty-two weeks we never played the same part two nights in succession.' Thirty-five years later he said, 'She is still the greatest actress we have and only too ready to move with the times.'

Sybil, once she became established, never played a part unless it attracted her and was never blind to the disadvantages of a long run. 'Long runs are a godsend, but they can also be a curse. They provide an actor with security, but they shackle him to one part for years at a stretch, when he ought to be experimenting and developing.'

I was with Sybil and Lewis in 1958 at the time they celebrated their golden wedding. They talked about the day they became man and wife in the little Kentish town of Aylesford, when she was twenty-five and he was thirty-three. Sybil never looked so plain in her life on her bright and frosty wedding morning, according to her brother Russell, who has recorded that her nose was seasonably scarlet to match the train-bearers' cloaks. After a Christmas honeymoon in the isolated beauty of Derbyshire, the young pair began their married life working side-by-side in Miss Horniman's company at the Gaiety Theatre in Manchester. They turned out to be the only actor and actress in the history of the theatre to be still at the zenith of their box-office popularity at the time they celebrated their golden wedding. During the fifty years of their married life most of their work was done in partnership. Sybil's one spectacular success without Lewis was as Miss Moffat in *The Corn is Green* by Emlyn Williams, which was directed by the author. Apart from that isolated instance, they shared most of their successes; if Lewis did not happen to be in the cast, he was more often than not responsible for the direction.

'Now there's a nice face!' exclaimed Sybil when she first saw a picture of Lewis hanging outside a Belfast theatre. Soon after meeting him she wrote impulsively to her brother Russell, 'I've met a man I could marry! He's raving mad about the theatre and looks as if he ought to be an engineer or a sailor or something to do with real life.' He made a tremendous impression on Sybil, speaking twice as fast as she could think, while criticising her Candida.

He appealed to her because he never talked about himself, he loathed games and was in the thick of all the exciting pioneering work being done at Miss Horniman's theatre. One morning in the Kardomah at Birmingham, Lewis plucked up courage to propose to her over toast and coffee – even before he had called her by her christian name! 'The whole room spun round,' she wrote to Russell, 'and so did the houses outside.'

When the couple finally left Miss Horniman to settle in London, Lewis turned out to be a first rate handyman. He did up furniture which he bought at the Caledonian Market so that they could set up house near Vauxhall Bridge. If we are to believe Russell, Sybil could not cook for toffee and dust never appeared to worry her. She imagined everyone else in life adored housework, so she let them get on with it, while she concentrated on acting which she knew she could do so much better.

From those modest beginnings they eventually reached Chelsea, living in Oakley Street, Carlyle Square and finally Swan Court. I once asked Sybil why she had remained so long in Chelsea and she replied, 'It was good enough for Sir Thomas More, so it is good enough for us. And Ellen Terry used to live just round the corner in the King's Road.'

The Cassons were born troupers – strolling players in the truest sense of the word. Eventually they reached a position when they could have picked plays which would have enabled them to play exclusively in the West End. But there is nothing they would have hated more. They were at their happiest in later years giving poetry and drama recitals in the backwoods of the Australian bush or playing *Macbeth* with a handful of faithful barnstormers in those village halls which they packed to suffocation point in the Welsh mining valleys. With their boundless energy they preferred to go to the other side of the world in search of fresh fields to conquer, rather than lead a cosy existence in Chelsea, with an occasional play, film or television to keep them pleasantly occupied.

When Sybil celebrated her fiftieth year on the stage in 1954 they were both enjoying a lucrative engagement in *A Day by the Sea* at the Haymarket. On the very night of that happy occasion they left the cast in search of new adventures – flying to Australia together to start a gruelling tour of one-night stands with their dramatic recitals. 'That will be *real* acting,' remarked Sybil, 'because we shall have to play parts of all ages.' She had had enough of the West End for the time being and was eager to start pioneering again. Her fifty-first year on the stage started with a typical flourish, letting the world know in no uncertain fashion that they had no intention of resting upon their golden laurels. 'I want to go on, not hark back!' was Sybil's remark as she left the Haymarket stage door that historic night.

At the time they did not realise they were embarking upon a 60,000, mile tour of Australia, New Zealand, South Africa, India and Turkey, which was not a bad achievement for an actor of seventy-nine and his partner of seventy-two. Realising when travelling by air that the take-off and the touch-down were the most dangerous moments of the journey, they always held hands, lest their last moment should be upon them. Sybil always had a mad passion for travel and was delighted on her return four years later to have fulfilled two cherished ambitions; to see the sun rise over Everest and to see it gild the minarets of Istanbul, or Constantinople as she prefers to call it.

Though their wartime tour of Welsh mining towns was a less gigantic undertaking, it was a formidably exhausting engagement. They played *Macbeth*, *Medea* and *Candida* under trying, makeshift conditions and hardly ever in a real theatre. Her Lady Macbeth surpassed any I have ever seen. I saw her at Porthcawl Pavilion when the Banquet Scene had all the suspense of a thriller, even though one saw only Sybil and Lewis seated at the end of a table which stretched away into the wings. They convinced the audience there were scores of guests seated just out of sight, horrified by Macbeth's hysterical outbursts. The next day at tea time I saw them in a modest café in the town. Quite exhausted, Lewis was asleep with his head on the table, while Sybil, cheery and chirpy as ever, was sitting opposite him coping with correspondence. In many towns, too small to boast a hotel, they had to stay with the local big-wigs.

This was a mixed blessing because they would sometimes arrive back after the performance to find their proud hosts had decided to show them off to a gathering of local celebrities invited to meet them. No one seemed to realise they were dropping with fatigue, after performing under the most trying conditions, or that they faced the prospect of a wearying journey the following day. Before getting to bed they were expected to live up to their reputation as idolised players, which meant giving an impromptu performance at the supper table. They always rose to the occasion and never let the profession down, which is one reason why they became the most loved husband and wife team of our theatre.

During both world wars the Cassons were criticised for playing Greek tragedy when so many war-weary people wanted to see *A Little Bit of Fluff* or *Is Your Honeymoon Really Necessary?* Soon after the First World War Sybil played Hecuba in *The Trojan Women* and also Medea at the Holborn Empire and during the Second World War they toured

Medea. She realised light entertainment had its place in wartime, but believed the troops preferred plays which gave them a point of view and lasting food for thought. Just after the Second World War in 1945 she played Jocasta to the Oedipus of Olivier at the New Theatre in St Martin's Lane, while the Old Vic company were waiting for their Waterloo Road theatre to be repaired after bomb damage.

She saw *Oedipus* as a parallel to the troubled times of 1945, even though the original production of the Greek play dated back to 431 BC 'In the play people are troubled because a disease ravaged their country. They do all they can to discover the root cause. They look here, they look there and try one suggestion after another in the hope of stripping off the externals and probing into the core of the evil. Europe blamed Hitler and blamed Mussolini for wishing to exterminate the human race. In other words, history repeated itself in 1945. People then were no wiser than the ancient Greeks.'

'There is a line in *Oedipus* – "The dead can feel no pain" – and I felt that terrible truth when I visited Belsen and saw people in Hamburg just after the war, under rusty, corrugated sheets in a desert of devastation. It seemed to me that those who had died had been fortunate.'

In Sybil's estimation the theatre is not just a means of escapism. It is not simply an opportunity to get away from the physical and mental discomforts of life. It exists to hurt and to heal. *Saint Joan* and *Medea* stab us into awareness of the world about us. Through their tears playgoers see a new world of beauty which might previously have been hidden.

The four Casson children – Ann, Mary, Christopher and John – all went on the stage with a considerable degree of success, though never reaching the heights scaled by their parents. Discussing her relationship with them, Sybil said, 'Strong theatre personalities have a way of making themselves felt in their families. The children either accept the situation or they dodge. Mine dodged!' At one time Ann lived in Canada with her actor-husband, Douglas Campbell, John lived in Australia and Christopher settled in Eire. They have always been a friendly and united family and whenever Sybil and Lewis happened to be near them on their overseas tours they always went out of their way to see them.

Regarding her life-long professional partnership with Lewis, Sybil is convinced happily-mated couples are bound to benefit from their mutual sympathy and understanding when called upon to play together on the stage. So many acrobats and trapeze artists are man and wife in the line of entertainment where it is so essential for one to be able to know what the other is thinking.

'It is an advantage for a man and wife to act together,' continued

Sybil, 'but theatrically speaking it is even more important for them to be artistically in tune than happily married. I have seen brilliant performances from artists who loathe each other off-stage.'

Lewis Casson taught Sybil more about her job than anyone else. *The Thing* mattered most to Lewis, the success of a production as a whole rather than the glorification of individual players. The play's the thing and its essential teamwork was always their guiding motive.

Sybil has tremendous admiration for the achievement of contemporary actors, but she constantly maintains they are less vocally efficient than the youngsters of her day. 'I never remember going to the theatre as a girl and not being able to hear the words. Today actors are too busy being natural – lest they be considered old-fashioned and hammy – and consequently it is often impossible to understand what they are saying. Projection is surely the first essential of an actor, as the author's mouthpiece. Those who make no attempt to project might just as well play their parts in a locked room with the blinds drawn. In the theatre, unlike films and television, there are no technicians at hand to project the actor. On the stage he must project himself and if that is beyond him he must think about another job.'

I was walking along the deserted promenade at Brighton out of season and as I approached one of the glass shelters I heard the unmistakable voice of Sybil Thorndike reading an item of news from the morning paper. As I got closer I discovered Sybil and Lewis together and only then did I realise Lewis's eyesight had deteriorated to such an extent that he was no longer able to read. He had to rely upon a small transistor radio for contact with the outside world, but eventually his hearing also failed and according to their son John Casson, Lewis never came to terms with old age, but Sybil's devotion and constant companionship helped him to learn to live with deafness, semi-blindness and an increasing inability to walk. Even so, three years before his death, which occurred in 1969 when he was ninety-three, Lewis appeared with Sybil and Athene Seyler in a revival of *Arsenic and Old Lace* at the Vaudeville Theatre.

Peter Saunders, who presented the production, praised their supreme courage and refusal to be defeated by advancing years. Sybil was becoming less mobile on account of crippling arthritis. She had Lewis, all but blind and deaf, in her dressing room with her, so that she could keep an eye on him. He had one very brief scene at the end of the play, as the new lodger arriving at the house of the murderess sisters. He used to be led to the wings and given a slight push when the cue came for his entrance. He worked to numbers. By the time he had counted six someone was in front of him ready to shake hands; then he counted three and there was a chair waiting for him to sit down and so the short scene progressed. There was always someone within reach, ready to guide him, but it was so cleverly devised no one in the audience had the faintest idea how seriously incapacitated he really was. His exit was up a flight of stairs on his way to view the room he was about to rent. He counted his own steps to the bottom of the stairs and then the number of wooden steps until he reached a member of the stage staff waiting at the top – out of sight of the audience – in readiness to lead him to safety.

Sybil, in the same production, found it difficult to sit in a low chair without enduring agonising pain, so Peter Saunders had a fake upright chair built. From the front it looked like a conventional armchair and Sybil found it much easier to work with this stage property. Peter Saunders looked into her dressing room just before the show one night and discovered the invariably-cheerful Sybil contorted with pain. He suggested she should not play that night, but she would not hear of it. As long as she could draw breath she insisted upon playing, to keep faith with the public and with herself. She admitted she might have to change a move or two during the action of the play and her colleagues were prepared for any eventuality. And so the performance went on as usual with those two plucky veterans honouring their contract and not letting down the management. It was a most inspiring occasion for the back-stage staff and for the rest of the cast who were in a position to appreciate just what it cost them to go on.

As Sybil and Lewis grew older I often wondered what would happen when one of them died, leaving the other in solitary desolation. I even hoped they might be killed in a flash in an air disaster and perish together – holding hands. But it was not to be. Lewis died leaving Sybil alone at eighty-seven in a state of steadily deteriorating health which became increasingly painful and crippling as time went on. There was no question of giving up the ghost. Once Sybil had adapted herself to the state of being a widow, she accepted the challenge and continued to make future plans and get back into circulation. Mentally she was as sharp as a needle, her memory was remarkable. So she went to the first night of any play that took her fancy and with school-girlish comic groaning she made light of the agony she endured when she had to lower herself into a chair and raise herself out of one or when she had to climb any steps. She never took no for an answer, no matter what the cost in terms of pain.

The new theatre named after her at Leatherhead was almost completed at the time Lewis died. Sybil felt her first obligation when she got back into circulation after the stunning blow of losing her husband was to play on the stage of this splendid Thorndike Theatre. Five months after Lewis died she appeared there as The Woman in *There*

Was an Old Woman, which was a decidedly long and exhausting part, She made up as a rather repulsive down-and-out, such as one might see covered by newspapers, sleeping under the Adelphi Arches and the play proceeded to indicate how she had reached this deplorable state in her existence. There were moments when Sybil enjoyed playing the fool and taking the audience into her confidence with a friendly wink. It was not Sybil at the peak of her greatness, but the mere fact that she was on the stage at all, playing a leading part, was nothing short of a miracle.

I had never looked upon Sybil as old until I went round to see her in her dressing room after that show. On stage she seemed to have remembered all her lines and she had the audience right in the hollow of her hand throughout the evening. Back-stage I discovered a very frail old lady bent with arthritis. She was in constant pain, but admitted it ceased the moment she made her entrance, only to grip her again as soon as she stepped back into the wings. She accepted the engagement because she felt it was something she owed to those who had built a theatre in her name. Once the limited season was over I felt she would go home and die, because having accomplished all she had to do, and without Lewis at her side, there was little more to live for. How wrong I was!

A year later she was in the audience at the opening night of the Young Vic Theatre, just across the road from her beloved Old Vic, sitting upon one of the hard benches among the young people for whom the theatre had been built. No red carpet had been rolled out. She wore a tweed coat and a chiffon head-scarf which made her quite inconspicuous in the crowd. She loved every minute of the free adaptation of *The Cheats of Scapino* by Molière and when I went over to greet her those blue eyes were sparkling and she was bubbling with her schoolgirl enthusiasm as she exclaimed, 'This is my kind of theatre!'

There is no star nonsense about Sybil, which is one reason why she is genuinely loved by everyone who comes into contact with her. She arrived at the Everyman by taxi one morning, and handing the driver a ten-shilling note, she said brightly, 'Give me a bob!' She was then at the height of her glory as the internationally acclaimed Saint Joan, but she was as homely as the woman next door. Quite recently she was telling me about a poetry recital she had shared with Jane Casson, her son John's daughter, for whom she has very high hopes. 'She collared the show,' confided Sybil with intense pride. Her choice of ordinary but warmly expressive words has always been one of her most endearing traits.

The public and her colleagues demonstrated their love of Sybil at two comparatively recent functions. To mark her ninetieth birthday in October 1972, all the great names in the contemporary theatre gathered together to present an entertainment on a Sunday night at the Haymarket Theatre in the presence of Princess Alexandra. It was called *Sybil* and many players recalled dramatic and light-hearted moments in her sixty-eight years on the stage. The entire house rose to acclaim her and from the stage Sybil, deeply moved but enormously flattered by this tribute, spoke her thoughts: 'It is wonderful to be surrounded by people I love and admire. I think you don't find this sort of friendliness in any other profession in the world. All my favourite players are here. I feel so awfully moved and touched. It has been such a real joy tonight, and a tribute to the theatre because I am the oldest working girl around.' Proceeds from ticket sales amounting to £5,000 went, at Sybil's request, towards clearing the debt for rebuilding and enlarging Denville Hall, the home for elderly actors and actresses at Northwood in Middlesex.

The other occasion was at the Royal Opera House, Covent Garden, early in 1973 when the Queen attended a glittering gala to mark our entry into the Common Market. Actors, dancers and singers glowed with pride to be included in the programme, but as far as the public was concerned it was Sybil who gave them the most pleasure. She stepped out of a wheelchair in the wings and was led to the footlights by Laurence Olivier to deliver and act a poem she had learned by heart. Her colleagues had been content to read from scripts! She was recalled again and again by her adoring public who dislocated the split-second timing of the programme schedule in order to give Sybil evidence of their love and devotion. No other living actress could have moved an audience to such affectionate enthusiasm.

When I retired from the editorship of *The Stage* in 1972 I was hijacked one day and taken to the Hyde Park Hotel to be ushered into an anteroom where I was greeted by thirty-odd devoted friends, all waiting to give me a goodwill lunch. It was rather like a *This Is Your Life* surprise. The first person I saw was Sybil, as radiant as ever in one of the favourite floral chiffon dresses I always associated with her. When we were finishing an iced confection which had been named after me, Sybil whispered, 'I'd like to say a few words about you!'

Before I realised what was happening she was on her feet singing my praises in such a manner that my friends were roaring with laughter. She told them I did not know what I was talking about when I maintained we had first met at the New Theatre stage door. 'I'm older than you are, but I remember quite clearly that it was in Cardiff!' She was quite mistaken, of course, but who cared when she had made us all so happy? Cardiff reminded her of that famous wartime tour of *Macbeth* and she amused the guests by telling them a young local boy had to be engaged to play Macduff's son and he was so keen on his job he acted them all off the stage. Lewis used to go mad in the wings every night making frantic gestures in an effort to restrain him. This glorious oration was quite an effort for Sybil and she was trembling a little when she sat down, though no one else was aware of it.

I escorted her back to Swan Court in a chauffeur-driven Rolls, which Ray Jackson so kindly put at our disposal. 'I suppose you'll put your feet up this afternoon?' I suggested. 'Not at all,' protested Sybil. 'I think I'll read *The Trojan Women* in the original Greek.'

The next day I received a letter from her which I shall cherish all my life:

Dear, dear Eric,

Wasn't that a lovely party? It just shows how everyone loves and admires you! I felt so proud to have known you longer than anyone else there. It was all such fun and there was such a feeling of love and affection.

God bless you, dear friend. I was going to say 'dear old friend', but I feel that might be misunderstood.

Yours affectionately always,
Sybil (T.-C.)

The spirit of Lewis still pervades the Swan Court flat in Chelsea, where Sybil lives alone with an Irish housekeeper. Lewis figures in the conversation just as much as if he were still alive, but just happened to be out. Naturally Sybil misses him more than anyone else can really appreciate and there are times when she exclaims, 'Don't let's talk about him any more!' The living room is still unchanged and one corner is occupied by the large atlas globe which their four children gave them as a golden wedding present. It was something Sybil and Lewis had always wanted, to trace the itinerary of their various overseas tours when they slipped into a nostalgic mood.

With tremendous courage and determination Sybil has built a new life for herself, in which there is no place for self-pity or brooding about the past. She wakes about eight o'clock when a tray of tea and bread and butter is brought to her by the housekeeper-companion. With that good lady's assistance she gets up just before ten. She usually has lunch in the restaurant below her flat and tea and supper at home, unless she is going out to a theatre or to dine with the family. Her son John lives just round the corner and so does his daughter Jane, who 'collared the show'. Daughter Mary also lives in London, so between them they arrange for Sybil to have one or two family dinners each week, to keep her in touch with news of the various grandchildren and great-grandchildren. There is no question of Sybil living in grand isolation.

Ann Casson, who succeeded her mother as Saint Joan on the English stage, has spent much of her time working with her actor-husband, Douglas Campbell, at the Crucible Theatre in Sheffield and elsewhere in the North. It reminds one of Sybil and Lewis pioneering at Miss Horniman's theatre in Manchester. They find it difficult to get up to London to see her, but that does not deter Sybil from going all the way to Yorkshire to visit them. It is not so easy for her to travel to Dublin to see her son Christopher, who lives there permanently, but that does not mean that she loses touch with him.

It became apparent that Russell Thorndike was dying soon after Sybil's ninetieth birthday and so that they could spend an hour or two together, Sybil travelled all the way to Norfolk and back in a day to take final leave of her brother.

Sybil's postbag is enormous and she always finds time to keep up to date with her correspondence. A widowed friend comes in to help. Sybil dictates personal replies to all her letters and when she signs them she often scribbles lengthy postscripts on the bottom of the page. Her stream of visitors is endless, so there is no likelihood of her feeling unloved or unwanted. Quite a number of friends – the children are inclined at times to think the number is too large – have *carte blanche* as far as visiting Sybil is concerned. They have been informed they can look in and see her without giving previous notice and the front door is left ajar at stated times when they can walk into the flat without having to disturb either Sybil or her companion. She enjoys holding court and keeping right up to date with all that is going on in her own circle of personal friends.

Originally intending to be a professional pianist until she developed wrist trouble and had to abandon music in favour of acting, Sybil remained devoted to her piano until quite recently. She would play Bach every day; but now her fingers have become so crippled with arthritis she has had to give up any attempt to play the piano. Lewis once said of her that she was musical first and last. It was her imagination and immense powers of application that made her an actress. John Casson recalled that his mother's face would become quite different when she played the piano. It used to take on an ageless look. The time she used to devote to the piano every day is now given to reading the Bible in Greek. On Sundays the vicar's wife calls in her car to collect Sybil for church and she returns her to the flat afterwards.

Like Edith Evans, Sybil has become a mad, avid television addict. Her favourite programmes are sport – racing and rugger – which cause tremendous excitement in the flat from time to time. She sees plays, and watching them from her own armchair saves a good deal of effort and pain which she would have to endure if she went into the West End to attend a public performance. In her more active days

Sybil was of the opinion that television defied the aim of the theatre because in her opinion a play in performance is something which has to be enjoyed by a number of people gathered together. It should be essentially a mass experience.

John sometimes calls for her on warm summer days to sit in his garden, which is his wife's pride and joy, and there Sybil can admire the bronze which is one of Epstein's happiest inspirations and will give future generations as vivid an impression of her as we get of Mrs Siddons from Gainsborough's much-visited portrait in the National Gallery. John's daughter Jane as likely as not will cross the street when she knows her grandmother is sitting in her mother's garden. Jane has inherited Sybil's features and the unmistakable timbre of the Thorndike voice. Sybil is obviously overjoyed in the knowledge that at least one of her grandchildren is going to make a significant impression on the playgoing public. She might become more famous than any of Sybil's own children.

Making the very best of her severely handicapped existence, Sybil is happy to be in close touch with her family, her friends and the world at large. In the ninth decade of her life she has time and interest for everything and everybody. Her memory is good. She can evoke the splendour of her past in a few sentences and she is quite ready to go down in the lift and out into the world for a public appearance whenever the occasion arises – whether to deliver a poem from the Covent Garden stage in the presence of the Queen in all her glittering glory, or to give an unforgettable treat to disabled patients confined to a depressing London hospital.

No actress has been so loved and cherished. As her son John so eloquently said: 'No one has ever been made to feel afraid or insecure by Sybil. Whatever you do, ten minutes with Sybil will make you feel dedicated to it and able to do it better. You will always leave her presence feeling more useful, more capable and more enthusiastic than when you came into it.'

Marie Tempest 1864–1942

It was ten o'clock on a bright winter morning. I was walking down Shaftesbury Avenue near the Lyric Theatre. Coming towards me I saw a tastefully and elegantly dressed woman wearing what in the 'thirties we called Russian boots. With the bearing of an Empress she was kicking out the deep folds of her full-skirted coat generously trimmed with sable. She was Somebody, going Somewhere. Then I realised it was Marie Tempest, probably on her way to rehearsal. She was not in the least actressy, yet she radiated a sort of presence off-stage, even on a London pavement in broad daylight. She wore a jaunty hat, had a twinkle in her eye and she might even have been smiling to herself. People who had no idea of her identity could be forgiven for turning round to wonder who this fascinating creature might be. That was as near as I ever got to meeting Marie Tempest.

As Hector Bolitho was to discover, Marie Tempest was the despair of any writer who hoped to evoke some of the splendour of her stage career, nostalgically coloured with memories stretching from *Carmen* in 1890, through *San Toy* at Daly's and Noël Coward's *Hay Fever* to Dodie Smith's *Dear Octopus*, which turned out to be her Swan Song in the 'thirties. Hector Bolitho hero-worshipped Marie Tempest to such a degree he tried no fewer than fifty times over a period of eight years to nail her down to the task of collaborating with him on her biography. Even though she admired his writing and enjoyed his companionship, she had no time for the past. The present and the immediate future were all that mattered to her, so she was constantly destroying all evidence and memories of her earlier existence, even to the extent of burning letters from Bernhardt, Réjane, Duse, Anthony Hope and Arthur Sullivan, to say nothing of the lines Oscar Wilde wrote to her from Reading Gaol. So Bolitho had to be content with writing a series of contrasting impressions of this rogue in porcelain as Barrie once called her. Thanks to his perseverance and boundless admiration, he produced a lively word-picture of the actress six years before her death.

Music was her first interest and with Julia Neilson for a fellow student, she studied singing at the Royal Academy of Music. Her teacher was Manuel Garcia, whose pupils had included Jenny Lind and Mathilde Marchesi, who in turn taught Melba and Calvé. Her family were horrified when she expressed her intention of going on the stage and they even implored Mr Gladstone to try to get this deplorable idea out of her head. But once she had made up her mind, even Gladstone was powerless to dissuade her. In 1885 at the age of twenty she was engaged to play Fiametta in a revival of Suppé's comic opera *Boccaccio* at the Comedy Theatre. She had a lovely voice and some critics were quick to realise it was good enough for the operatic stage and in addition she was a bewitching comedienne. She became a leading lady right away and stayed one for the remaining fifty-seven years of her life.

The year after *Boccaccio* she was seen at Drury Lane, scoring a personal success with her playing of Rosella in *Frivoli*; the following year she succeeded Marion Hood in the name-part in *Dorothy*, Cellier's comic opera at the Prince of Wales Theatre. She continued to play the part there and at the Lyric Theatre until 1889, by which time the opera had been performed for 931 consecutive performances, then a record for the longest run of a comic opera. After playing the name-part in *Doris*, by the same composer, she was seen at the Lyric in *The Red Hussar*, another comic opera, but this time with music by Edward Solomon. She played the decorative part of Kitty Carrol, wearing a picturesque hat resembling a pyramid of flowers and during the evening she even changed into a dashing Hussar uniform. Then America called.

At the age of twenty-six this captivating creature went to New York to appear in *The Red Hussar* at Palmer's Theatre. Then she joined the J. C. Duff Comic Opera Company and toured the United States and Canada with a most unusual repertoire. Apart from Dorothy, she sang the name-part in the opera *Mignon*, Arline in *The Bohemian Girl*, Mabel in *The Pirates of Penzance* and, what is even more remarkable, Bizet's *Carmen*. She caused quite a stir in Chicago, until she saw Calvé's Carmen, probably the most tempestuous and realistic of all, and then she never wanted to sing it again. Shaw's description of Calvé's astonishing Carmen remains one of the most graphic evocations of a performance long regarded as legendary as Chaliapine's Boris Godunov or Melba's Mimi. One can understand Marie Tempest's decision.

Back in New York at the Casino in 1891 she appeared as Adam in *The Tyrolean*, dressed rather like a pantomime principal boy, she sang a number called 'The Nightingale Song'. The purity of her voice, with its flute-like tones, produced twenty minutes of sheer beauty. Quite a number of ardent admirers used to slip in just to hear this number.

Jean and Edouard de Reszké and Pol Plancon, the famous French bass from the Metropolitan Opera House, probably heard her more often than anyone else. She was a dedicated musician held in high esteem by the leading singers of the day. When she returned to New York many years later she lived at the Knickerbocker Hotel, patronised by Metropolitan Opera stars. She often supped with Caruso and his close friend Antonio Scotti, greatest Scarpia of them all. On other occasions she was the guest of Puccini or Gatti-Casazza, artistic director of the Met and his wife Frances Alda, one of the leading sopranos of the company.

After this glamorous American interlude Marie Tempest returned to London for a five-year reign at Daly's Theatre, as the queen of musical comedy, under the management of George Edwardes. She was Adèle in *An Artist's Model*, O Mimosa San in *The Geisha*, Maia in A *Greek Slave* and San Toy in the show of that name. They provided rather more popular entertainment than the earlier comic operas and all had tuneful scores by Sidney Jones. Today, never a week goes by without a number or two from one of these shows being heard on the radio. As the queen of musical comedy Marie Tempest was treated like royalty. George Edwardes created a unique image for her. She was never allowed to use the stage door with the rest of the cast. Her carriage waited for her after the show at the special entrance reserved for Royalty when they went to Daly's and when she emerged she was always most elegantly dressed. She was what in those days was known as a fashion plate.

Then came the *San Toy* sensation. George Edwardes wanted her to appear in a pair of long trousers in this production. She considered them tasteless and refused to wear them. Before she went on the stage she cut them into shorts. George Edwardes was furious and the incident led to a final break between them. He gave her the choice of either wearing the costumes designed for her or leaving the theatre. She chose to leave the theatre and, what is more, to leave musical comedy for ever. When she left Daly's by the royal entrance for the last time, she left a whole world behind her and decided to become a light comedy actress. A new phase of her career started in 1900 when she appeared as Nell Gwyn in *English Nell*.

When Marie Tempest made the momentous decision to quit musical comedy she was only thirty-six and the top box-office draw of the London stage as far as musicals were concerned. Her exquisite voice was in full bloom, but perhaps she realised it would not last for ever and she preferred to become an incomparable comedienne whose artistry would mature rather than deteriorate with advancing years. Anthony Hope of *The Prisoner of Zenda* fame, offered her *English*

Nell, a comedy he had written with Edward Rose from the novel *Simon Dale* for Ellen Terry. As an added attraction Edward German was invited to write the Nell Gwyn Dances, incidental music now known to everyone.

There was no question of Marie Tempest's unqualified success. She had no regret about having left musical comedy. She further consolidated her new position on the straight stage by playing the title role in *Becky Sharp*, a play written by Robert Hichens and Cosmo Gordon-Lennox from Thackeray's *Vanity Fair*. To round off this enterprising experiment with a flourish, she scored another personal success as Polly Eccles in a revival of *Caste* by T. W. Robertson at the Haymarket, where she was hailed by the critics.

This transformation was not brought about without a great deal of hard work on Marie Tempest's part, but she was a perfectionist and prepared to work like a Trojan to master new aspects of her art. She did not expect the public to worship her blindly in whatever she chose to do. She was determined to be worth the praise they lavished upon her. Straight acting was a closed book to her; she was familiar only with the rather naïve lines which linked one number to another in the ludicrous 'books' of the comic operas and musical comedies in which she had starred at both the Lyric and Daly's.

So when she decided to try her hand at becoming a comedienne, she was quite prepared to admit she had much to learn, but from her singing days she retained superb diction. At rehearsal she was not too grand to invite the producer to come up on the stage and show her what to do. Dion Boucicault taught her all she needed to know as a straight actress and she spent the rest of her life polishing this technique to perfection. She was known to spend an entire morning over a ten-minute scene, working to numbers as she answered the telephone, took off her gloves or poured a cup of tea, which looked so simple and effortless from the front.

Another milestone loomed up in 1902 when Charles Frohman engaged her for his fashionable Duke of York's Theatre to appear as Kitty Silverton in *The Marriage of Kitty*, a comedy by Cosmo Gordon-Lennox, who had become Marie Tempest's second husband. It was an adaptation from the French and remained a cast iron box-office success in the Tempest repertoire for some thirty years. When a new venture failed to come up to expectations she could always fall back on Kitty Silverton.

So thorough was Marie Tempest's study of a role and her preparation for the première performance, it has been recorded that thirty-three years after the original production of *The Marriage of Kitty* she played a scene at her Golden Jubilee Matinee at Drury Lane which was a precise replica of her performance on the first night at the Duke of York's. She never tried to override her producers. She was always ready to appreciate their point of view and to be guided by them, but it was not until they both agreed she was playing the scene in the best possible manner that she was ready to turn the page of the script and move on to the next hurdle. She had an iron sense of perseverance, great courage and enterprise and could never be charged with being a stick-in-the-mud. She was prepared to change her style of acting to suit new fashions in the theatre. After comic opera, musical comedy and *The Marriage of Kitty* she proceeded to appear in works by contemporary writers such as Arnold Bennett, Henry Arthur Jones, J. M. Barrie, A. A. Milne, John Hastings Turner, Somerset Maugham, H. M. Harwood, St John Ervine, Noël Coward and Dodie Smith.

A legendary theatre partnership was formed in 1908 when Marie Tempest and an actor six years her junior, William Graham Browne, first met at the Comedy Theatre in the cast of a play called *Lady Barbarity*. It was the first deep friendship of Marie Tempest's life; it lasted twenty-nine years, until Willie died in 1937, five years before her. From the playgoers' point of view the Marie Tempest–Graham Browne partnership was not like that of Irving and Ellen Terry or Alfred Lunt and Lynn Fontanne. He was not a star actor, but usually appeared in her productions, though not necessarily as her leading man. More often than not he was responsible for directing the plays in which she starred. Their partnership really meant more back-stage than on. So deep was their understanding he knew how to get the best possible results from her; she could relax with him at rehearsal and gave her finest performances under his direction. Willie, who had appeared with Tree, Benson, Forbes-Robertson, Alexander and Olga Nethersole, was a respected member of the profession and adored by the actors in Marie Tempest's company. She was far from easy to work with and part of Willie's mission in life was to pour oil over troubled waters and keep the troupe together and in a reasonably happy frame of mind.

Marie Tempest never took a deep interest in the theatre and Willie was the only member of the theatrical profession she took into her confidence. She married three times. Her first husband, Alfred E. Izard, was a companion from her Royal Academy of Music days and they parted in no time. Then came Cosmo Gordon-Lennox, son of Lord Alexander Gordon-Lennox, whom she married in 1898. He wrote *The Marriage of Kitty*, which must have earned a small fortune. Their own marriage collapsed through incompatibility of temperament, long before she met Willie, but she had to wait until Cosmo Gordon-Lennox died in 1921 before she could legally marry Willie.

As an artist Marie Tempest was under the influence of the American

45

impresario Charles Frohman at the time she met Willie. She was also under contract to him and content to play the parts he chose for her. More often than not they were successful and she was paid a handsome salary for starring at the Duke of York's, Frohman's London theatre. He felt the public liked to see her twinkling smile and to hear her infectious laugh and insisted upon casting her in plays which led the critics to call her the Réjane of the English stage. She had perfected a number of technical tricks that never failed to conjure laughs out of an author's flimsiest lines. People who flocked to see Marie Tempest did not care a jot for the play. All they wanted was to enjoy her sparkling performance. The play was no more than a vehicle and she did not venture to play the great classic parts, as Ellen Terry had done. She was frequently content with a mediocre script offering her an opportunity to perform her celebrated tricks of which the public never seemed to tire. She was a martinet in the theatre. She always had her own way. If anyone displeased her a note was sent to the offender and such was her power she never had cause to protest a second time.

When Willie surveyed the situation he persuaded her to reject some of those favourite tricks, even though they had never failed to get laughs in the past. He helped her to think out new ways of being just as amusing and his methods were better suited to the more fashionable dramatists in whose plays she later appeared. A glorious new chapter began. She knew she had met the man capable of making her life happy; she had complete trust in his taste and his ability to direct the comedies in which she starred. Her playing took on a new warmth on that account and some critics even compared her with Duse.

Life was happy for Willie, too. He directed one money-making success after another and there was never any fear of Marie Tempest having to look for a job. They were set for life, appearing only in the plays that took their fancy and playing just where they chose, whether in Shaftesbury Avenue, Sydney or Bombay. Even so, life was not always easy for Willie, with a temperamental star constantly creating difficulties. Hector Bolitho records that Willie once boasted he and Marie Tempest had never had an unpleasant scene in all the twenty-five years they had worked together. I beg to question that claim. An actress friend of mine, Doris Gilham, played small parts and understudied in the company which Marie Tempest took round the world from 1914 to 1923. She was not with them all the time, but long enough to understand why Marie Tempest was called a Tartar in the slang of the time.

During one performance in Australia Willie dried up and had to be prompted. He was so unnerved by the incident and by the venomous look which Marie Tempest flashed at him, he stumbled over another line within the next minute or two. The action of the play was brought to a standstill for a brief moment, just long enough for Marie Tempest to take the situation ruthlessly in hand. She marched across the stage to the prompt corner, snatched the script from the astonished girl who was holding it and presented it to Willie in full view of the audience. Never can a player have felt so humiliated. Finally, according to Doris Gilham, Marie Tempest made an apologetic curtain speech at the end of the evening, saying she had never been so ashamed at any time during her long stage career. This incident all but caused a mutiny in the ranks. And the star's behaviour can hardly have endeared her to her Australian public.

Willie did however score a minor victory on that same tour, much to the delight of the company. News had come through of the death of Marie Tempest's second husband, which meant she and Willie could marry. The day before the wedding they gave a noon cocktail party to the company. Marie Tempest appeared before Willie arrived. He was late, having been doing a little luxury shopping and celebrating with a couple of 'the boys' in the company. When he appeared, though only a few minutes late, he was given a most embarrassing dressing-down by his wife-to-be in front of all the guests. Beaming good-naturedly, Willie said, 'Let me remind you, my dear. Today you are the Honourable Mrs Cosmo Gordon-Lennox, but this time tomorrow you'll be plain Mary Browne.'

Marie Tempest started this eight-year tour in Toronto in October 1914 and did not return to London until February 1923. Before setting out, she went into management at the Playhouse in Northumberland Avenue, now a BBC studio for sound radio programmes, and appeared in *Mary Goes First*, *Thank Your Ladyship*, *The Wynmartens* and *The Duke of Killicrankie*. She opened in Toronto with *Mary Goes First* and then went on to New York and Chicago and subsequently to Australia, New Zealand, South Africa, India, Straits Settlements, China, Japan and the Philippines. Then she went back to America before returning home. *The Marriage of Kitty* figured prominently in the repertoire as well as *Mr Pim Passes By*. Considering this mammoth tour was undertaken in the days before commercial air travel, it must have been a most exhausting business – having to use boat and train – especially in the blazing heat of the Asiatic countries. It compares with the incredible tours undertaken by Pavlova during the same period when she danced in remote places which many atlases have not mapped.

Marie Tempest continued to rule the company with her iron rod, thousands of miles from London and the sophisticated cities where she had previously been idolised. She would not tolerate slovenliness in any shape or form. They travelled vast distances in their own train and she insisted upon the entire company changing for dinner in the dining car every night, no matter where they were. The men wore black ties and she looked no different than she would have done at supper in the Savoy Grill. It was like a mobile hotel and her maid Annie used to cook the most appetising meals on two spirit stoves balanced on the seat of the water closet.

While on this historic tour in Australia in 1921, Marie Tempest engaged Marie Ney to play in *Mr Pim Passes By* by A. A. Milne. Marie Ney then came to England and made her first appearance on the English stage with Marie Tempest at Brixton Theatre in 1923 as Rosalie in *The Marriage of Kitty*. I was fascinated to discover just how this young actress felt as a junior member of the Tempest company, so I invited her to contribute a few impressions. I was delighted when she agreed to do so and I include them just as she wrote them:

'Marie Tempest played in *The Marriage of Kitty* in Melbourne early in 1917. I had only recently joined the Allan Wilkie Shakespearean Company, my first professional theatre engagement. I went to a matinee of *The Marriage* to see the great English actress of whom I had read so much in the English weeklies, which took five or six weeks to reach us in those days.

'I greatly admired Miss Tempest's precision, the crisp speech, her elegance and especially the charm of her singing. In 1921 I met Miss Tempest. She was again in Melbourne with Graham Browne, her husband, and this visit brought a full company who had toured with her through Africa, India and China. Now an Australasian tour was planned and one new play to be added to the repertoire, A. A. Milne's *Mr Pim Passes By*. There was no one to play Dinah. I was engaged and joined the company.

'I enjoyed the rehearsals enormously and one day suddenly I decided I would try out what I thought a very elegant gesture. I was really copying someone I had acted with.

"And what does that mean?" demanded Miss Tempest stopping the rehearsal.

"Well er – I thought it looked – er nice."

"Don't do anything for which you haven't a reason," crisply admonished Marie Tempest. "This is a school of elimination."

'It was a lesson I remembered throughout my professional career.

'The first night arrived. The drawing room set for *Mr Pim* was suggested with dark drapes rather than a complete built set. Curtains suggested the big French windows in the back wall facing the audience. They were painted hessian, but looked like rich material. Dinah opened the play bouncing on through those French windows, rushing downstage to the piano, then up again looking off to where Miss Tempest sat waiting for her entrance. I accidentally swung one of the curtains

48

in a way which exposed the back of the hessian to the audience. "Put that curtain the right way round," hissed M. T., which I did in the character of Dinah and was not unduly upset. Without actually apologising to me at the end of the act, I was given, metaphorically, a pat on the back as Miss Tempest said I'd done very well and then added to Graham Browne nearby, "I might have upset her over those curtains," and to me, "You kept your head well, child, but you must use more hairpins and keep your hair tidier.'

'We toured the cities and the small towns of Australia and New Zealand and we always opened with *Mr Pim*. The other plays were selected from Marie Tempest's wide repertoire, depending on the length of the season. Every performance was preceded by the same ritual. About fifteen minutes before the curtain rose, the stage manager presented himself at Marie Tempest's dressing room door to announce that the set was ready and he then escorted her to the stage to inspect the flower arrangements and to make sure that the furniture was dusted and in its proper position. She was meticulous in all details, and demanded that our stage costumes were properly cared for. We were required to wear white cotton capes to protect our clothes between dressing room and our entrance on stage.

'I had only one other part in the repertoire – one very short scene in an early Somerset Maugham play, *Penelope*. The character was Mrs Watson, a rather dotty old lady who had nothing at all to do with the play. The clothes provided were absurd, but I wrapped towels round myself to be shapeless enough to fit them. One *Penelope* evening I was *sent for*. Miss Tempest wished Miss Ney to come to her dressing room at the end of the performance. I waited miserably for the end of the play and then presented myself. Miss Tempest was coldly angry, "Do you know you are very bad as Mrs Watson?"

"Yes, damned bad, but nobody told me how to play her," I heard myself swiftly and discourteously retort, trying unsuccessfully to keep back tears.

"All right, child," came the crisp, more kindly, reply. "All right, get along home now and we'll have a rehearsal for you tomorrow."

'Quite recently I looked at a copy of *Penelope*. It was first produced in 1909, Marie Tempest and Graham Browne creating their parts. My Mrs Watson had been acted by a celebrated old actress, Mrs Calvert, born in 1837! It was not surprising I always felt the clothes given me for the part must have belonged to Queen Victoria.

'When Marie Tempest eventually returned to London, she created some of her most famous roles, in such plays as *Hay Fever* and *The Marquise* by Noël Coward, *The First Mrs Fraser* by St John Ervine and *Dear Octopus* by Dodie Smith, in which John Gielgud was also a star.

I saw Miss Tempest often in these years. In fact when I came to London in 1923 my first engagement was with her and Graham Browne for a brief tour of *The Marriage of Kitty*, but afterwards my main appearances were in Shakespeare and the classics. Consequently I was never fortunate enough to be with her again except for one memorable occasion in 1937 when I was privileged to take part in the Drury Lane matinee to celebrate her golden jubilee on the stage. I am always grateful to have been, for a brief time, as a young actress, under the guidance of Dame Marie Tempest.'

The return to London proved a disaster. After eight years wandering the world the idolised actress expected a rapturous reception from her London admirers. It was a sentimental occasion because she was going back to the Duke of York's where she had first been seen in *The Marriage of Kitty* twenty years earlier. But for her comeback she chose *Good Gracious, Annabelle!* which she described as a frivolous, inconsequential, farcical comedy. The London critics disagreed and called it the worst play in the world. The house was in an uproar. Part of the audience tried to convey to her how pleased they were to see her back, while some of the more militant ones registered a noisy protest against the rubbishy fare she had brought back with her.

As she moved towards the footlights to start her curtain speech a voice from the Gallery rang out in clarion tones – 'Rotten!' Marie Tempest replied by making her famous curtsey, so low that she almost touched the boards and then walked off with immense dignity. For the first time in her career of thirty-eight years she had been booed, and in her home town at that. A little later she returned to complete the speech at the request of the majority, who were delighted to see her back, but her most devoted admirers had to admit the choice of play was a grave error. It was quickly withdrawn. A month later she turned to the friend who never let her down – Kitty Silverton in *The Marriage of Kitty*. This revival was well received and ran for months. Queen Mary went and roared with laughter, which helped to compensate for the *Annabelle débâcle*. Marie Tempest refused to brood over the boos. She showed her indifference by moving into a larger and more expensive house in Regent's Park, which always remained her favourite residential area of London.

Two years after *Annabelle* she had London at her feet when she appeared as Judith Bliss in Noël Coward's *Hay Fever* at the Ambassadors Theatre where it ran for 337 performances. She was ready for a fashion-able contemporary writer and was eager to demonstrate to the world at large she was as up to date in choice of play as in hats and house decoration. So Noël Coward arrived on the scene at precisely the right moment. *Hay Fever* is a light comedy he wrote in three days concerning an absurd theatrical household, ruled over by Judith Bliss, a madly exaggerated caricature of a leading lady. Coward had written the play with Marie Tempest in mind and she permitted him to read it to her in her drawing room. She listened with polite interest, but turned it down, saying it had no emotion, no plot and no action. After the author departed she admitted he was 'as clever as a bag of monkeys', but she did not care for the play.

Then Noël Coward scored a fantastic success with *The Vortex* which may have influenced Marie Tempest to change her mind. She may have thought his *Hay Fever* would bring her the same *réclame* enjoyed by Lilian Braithwaite in *The Vortex*. About six months after the opening of *The Vortex* Marie Tempest agreed to play Judith Bliss as long as Coward consented to direct the production. The best way of being up to date was to accept a play by a young writer in the swim and then get him to direct it. She wanted him to show her how to play his type of crisp dialogue and she wanted to know his motives in writing the play. After a particularly rewarding rehearsal she wrote in her diary that Noël Coward was 'the most stimulating and exciting personality that has come into my life in the last ten years'. To add to the joy of things, Willie was happily cast in the same play as David Bliss.

Coward was infatuated with Marie Tempest. She was just as good for him as he was for her. She boasted of being 'that most modern product, a Noël Coward heroine,' and she was so decidedly up to date in her approach she acted all the youngsters off the stage. Trying to analyse the impact of Marie Tempest, Coward wrote, 'When she steps on to a stage a certain magic occurs and this magic is in itself unexplainable and belongs only to the very great.'

To follow *Hay Fever* Coward promised to write for her an eighteenth-century joke called *The Marquise* and she was given the exquisite part of the Marquise Eloïse de Kestournel with which she packed the Criterion Theatre for some time. Coward did not see the first night because he was abroad. When he later went to the Criterion and saw her dazzling performance, he admitted she made him forever incapable of judging the play on its merits. Seven years later he was to write, 'She has more allure and glamour and charm at seventy than most women I know who are in their twenties and thirties.'

Marie Tempest the martinet was almost as fascinating a creature as Marie Tempest the actress. She considered anything worth doing was worth doing well. On tour in a smoky industrial city she would sup in the hotel dining room in a stylish black evening dress, wearing sapphires and diamonds. There was no question of saying anything would do because she happened to be in Newcastle, Birmingham or Glasgow. She never let the profession down and was always a subject for wonder off-stage. On-stage, incidentally, she was one of the very few actresses who wore her own jewels and it goes without saying they were always chosen with exquisite taste. She was one of the first leading actresses to have her stage clothes created for her by the great fashion houses instead of by traditional stage costumiers.

A brass plate about the size of a visiting card bearing the legend MISS TEMPEST was screwed on to her dressing room door at every theatre in which she appeared. She refused to have her name written on a piece of notepaper and stuck to the door with a drawing pin. Marie Ney has described how the ladies in the cast wore dust-sheet capes as they made their way from the dressing room to the wings. She could have added that Marie Tempest never sat down in her dressing room while wearing a stage costume and a white drugget was tacked to the carpet for protection of her finery. She was in the theatre two hours before the rise of the curtain and when there was time to relax she would play Patience because she was convinced it helped her to keep a sense of proportion. She always sat in a straight-backed chair and if she had not finished her game when she left the theatre at night, the table was carefully covered with a cloth in readiness for resumption of operations the next day. For short waits, not long enough to permit a return to the dressing room, she had a chair near the wings, placed on a square of white drugget and shielded from draughts by a screen. An electric heater was at hand in colder weather. Throughout the world, back-stage staffs trembled whenever Marie Tempest was about.

At home she would lie down every day between four and six, so that she could project a radiance from the stage every night, even in her seventies. Only a matinee prevented her taking this rest. It was a cast-iron rule and the house had to be as quiet as the grave. The secret of her youth was partly attributed to the fact that she knew how to forget everything she did not wish to remember and how to forget people she did not care for. She never thought seriously about old age and did all she could to obliterate the past. By the same rules she moved house at frequent intervals, even though she continued to remain a resident of the Regent's Park area. Inside those exquisite miniature palaces which she created out of every house in which she lived, she was constantly trying out new colours on the walls, buying new dinner services and changing the carpets. She never gave herself a chance to stick in the mud.

She would never tolerate any member of her company not putting his job in the theatre before all other considerations. She resented those who made films by day and acted in the theatre at night. She could not very well forbid them to film, because the money was so much better than their theatre salaries and Equity, the actors' trade union, might

Geneviève Ward

The famous painting of Ellen Terry by her husband, G. F. Watts. *Photo: National Portrait Gallery*
Left: Geneviève Ward, the first actress to be created a Dame for services to the theatre, in 1921 at the age of eighty-two. *Photo: from the Mander and Mitchenson collection*

Geneviève Ward as Margaret of Anjou in *Richard III*, 1897. *Photo: J. Caswell Smith*

Madge Kendal and her husband in *William and Susan*. *Photo: Elliott and Fry*

Previous page: May Whitty, the first theatre Dame, but created one for her services to First World War charities. *Photo: Claude Harris*

Sybil Thorndike and her husband, Lewis Casson, in *Teresa of Avila*, 1961. *Photo: Anthony Buckley*
Left: Madge Kendal, one of the earlier Dames, a private study. *Photo: Barraud*
Next page: Sybil Thorndike (right) is congratulated by Margaret Lockwood (left) and Cicely Courtneidge on completing sixty years on the stage. *Photo: Central Press*

Sybil Thorndike's most famous role – the inimitable St Joan
Top: Sybil Thorndike, a month before her ninetieth birthday, pays tribute to Eric Johns o
the occasion of his retirement from the editorship of *The Stage. Photo: Shuhei Iwamoto*

have had something to say about a star player preventing smaller fry in the profession from earning extra money. Even so, Ursula Jeans, who made a film while playing at the Haymarket with Marie Tempest in *The First Mrs Fraser*, used to dread meeting her on the stage every night. Marie Tempest would glare at her with those gimlet eyes, trying to detect any signs of fatigue which might jeopardise her stage performance, as a result of having risen at five in the morning and been in the film studios all day. If an actor had to be prompted the film studios would be blamed for tiring out players before they started their evening's work in the theatre.

Few people have not heard the famous story of the screwed chair. One night Ursula Jeans was playing a scene with Marie Tempest and in order to face her more squarely she moved her chair an inch or two towards the leading lady. When she proceeded to do the same thing the next night she discovered Marie Tempest had instructed the stage manager to screw the chair to the stage. She was determined that players in her company should respect discipline and went to any lengths to make them submit to the requirements of the production.

Marie Tempest experienced the most shattering blow of her life in 1937 when Willie died. She never recovered and did not really enjoy the remaining five years of her own life, during which time she appeared in only two more plays. Willie's last job was to direct and appear with Marie Tempest in *Retreat From Folly* at the Queen's Theatre. It opened the night before *George and Margaret* started its record-breaking run, but within a month Willie was dead. Marie Tempest behaved magnificently. There were nights during his illness when she went on stage wondering whether Willie would still be alive at the end of the show. She kept faith with her public, with a devotion to duty which Queen Mary would have approved. The show went on just the same and she continued to play right through that unhappiest hour of her life. Willie would have wanted it that way and she could not bear to sit at home and brood helplessly in utter solitude. She had to occupy herself.

Then came the bitter day of the funeral. She could not contemplate attending herself and suffering the final break after all those years they had spent together. So she called an understudy rehearsal that same morning for the actor who had taken over Willie's part in *Retreat From Folly*. While the final rites were being performed over Willie's coffin, his wife was on the stage of the Queen's Theatre playing opposite an actor who was speaking the same lines Willie had uttered only a week or two before. It was a macabre situation and there were people who thought her heartless and even wrote to the newspapers to express their disapproval. But Marie Tempest's gesture was the result of tremendous courage and her only possible way of getting through the ordeal.

After the run of *Retreat From Folly*, Marie Tempest appeared in *Mary Goes To See*, a comedy by Rosemary Casey and B. Iden Payne at the Haymarket, directed by Campbell Gullan. Seven months later came her last success, *Dear Octopus* by Dodie Smith. It was also at the Queen's Theatre with a strong cast, including John Gielgud, Leon Quartermaine, Nan Munro, Valerie Taylor, John Justin, Muriel Pavlow, Kate Cutler, Angela Baddeley and Annie Esmond. Glen Byam Shaw was invited to direct the production, in conjunction with the author. He had never met Marie Tempest and realised she would be at a loss without Willie to guide her. In the circumstances he rather dreaded the prospect. He felt he ought to meet her before rehearsals started to discuss the play in a general fashion and to hear what she had to say about her part as the matriarch presiding over a family reunion.

He invited her to dinner, but she preferred to entertain him. When he arrived at her flat in Hampstead he realised it was to be *dîner-à-deux*. Even so, she was glittering in full evening dress. On his way to meet her Glen had decided not to talk about the play until she brought up the subject. When he arrived they had an aperitif in the drawing room and she talked about Glen's father, Byam Shaw, and his paintings she particularly admired. They moved into the dining room for a tastefully chosen meal, with an appropriate wine to accompany each course. Glen found conversation a little strained, but there was no reference to *Dear Octopus*. They moved back into the drawing room for brandy and about ten o'clock, even though the play had still not been mentioned, Glen thought it would be polite to take his leave. She accompanied him to the hall and as she opened the door she said, 'Good night, Mr Shaw. I shall trust you until I find you out.' He felt as if she had hit him with a sledgehammer.

As it happened, they worked together amicably enough at rehearsal and the production proved a success, running for 373 performances, with tours to follow. He was most impressed by her genius for stage business. She was masterly in the scene when she listened to her daughter's problems, while putting the finishing touches to the laying of the table for dinner. As she listened she made table napkins into the shape of water lilies, but fitted each deft movement to the text, thus pointing the daughter's lines in the most apposite manner. It won a round of applause every night.

Glen did not regard her as a great actress because she never attempted to be anything but what she was. Her diction and timing were perfect, but she never characterised. She was content with fascinating her audiences. She was a perfectionist and could be very severe with people who did not take sufficient pains to make their very best effort. Once the play had settled down to enjoy a long run Glen had a very strange dream. He was entering the foyer of the Queen's Theatre and discovered Willie waiting for him. He said he had seen the play and considered his wife was giving one of her finest performances. He thanked Glen for having directed her with such deep and sensitive understanding. Glen was most moved by the dream and wondered whether to tell Marie Tempest. It might hurt her or she might think it impertinent. An occasion arose when he decided it would be good to tell her. She was deeply moved and thanked him for permitting her to share his experience. As a result of that confidence they were drawn closer together.

John Gielgud used to watch her from the wings every night, never failing to admire the enormous skill of her stagecraft. She was short and the sofa had to be built up with planks and cushions to give the right effect from the front. She always held her back very straight and elegantly crossed her tiny feet in front of her. Gielgud noticed in *Dear Octopus* she was beginning to have trouble learning her lines. Another actor who used to watch Marie Tempest from the wings was George Howe at the beginning of his career in 1927 when he appeared with her at the Ambassadors in *A Spot on the Sun*. 'Good boy, to watch me,' she smiled as she came off the stage one night. ' You will learn what to do and what not to do.' She was most concerned about his health and in consequence he cherishes a mother-complex image of her. He was most impressed by her fabulous sense of timing, but considered there was little heart in her work. She was always aware of the audience; she was always in command and completely dominated them, but there was never any human feeling behind the drama. Like Lilian Braithwaite, she was a Society sort of actress and a Lady Bountiful quality came across the footlights.

Her face was highly intelligent, as St John Ervine recalled, not pretty, yet it seemed winsome. She was small, but her figure was superb and she had very beautiful hands. It was her personality that won her the favour she enjoyed for the whole of her stage career and her grace and great distinction of manner. Her curtsey was almost world famous and her fine taste in clothes made women everywhere willing to follow her lead. At one time she made mustard yellow very popular. She worked hard to attain her unique position and took immense trouble to improve her performance, always being first to arrive at rehearsal and last to leave.

Looking back on her career, people are astonished to discover she never played Shakespeare. Rosalind, Beatrice and Portia seemed made for her, with that rogue in porcelain quality and the mischievous glint in her eye. She would have been well cast as Mme Ranevsky in *The Cherry Orchard* and the idolised actress, Mme Arkadina, in *The Seagull* by Chekhov. At the age of seventy she had the figure of a girl of seventeen and would have worked wonders with these famous parts, had she had the good fortune to work under the right director, such as Glen Byam Shaw. In this country managements would only engage her to play comedienne roles, but she might have surprised them had they been enterprising enough to cast her for more serious parts. In Australia Willie cast her as Miriam the street-walker in *Outcast* by Hubert Henry Davies and according to Hector Bolitho she played it with heart-aching tenderness. Also in Australia she played the comfortable common little Janet in *The Great Adventure*, a comparatively small part which Wish Wynne had made her own in London. She never had the same chance to demonstrate her versatility on the London stage, but the BBC did go so far as to allow her to play Mrs Alving in Ibsen's *Ghosts* on sound radio.

Her last months were heart-breakingly tragic. After Willie's death she endured unbearable loneliness when she realised in her late seventies she was no longer a despot in a position to do exactly as she pleased with her career, even though she still had the grace of an enchanting young girl. She wanted to go on working to keep her mind occupied, but her memory was failing most alarmingly and she began to feel alien in a changing world favouring new theatre fashions.

Henry Kendall was her last director, the third since Willie. He had doted on her past stage triumphs and realised if she had a name for being difficult it was simply because she was a perfectionist. She rehearsed a new play under his direction at His Majesty's Theatre after the run of *Dear Octopus*. Henry Kendall became more and more apprehensive as he observed her difficulty in committing lines to memory. When the other members of the cast discarded their scripts, having learned their lines, Marie Tempest still clung to hers. To give her a final chance to become word-perfect the management postponed the out-of-town opening to allow extra time for study. Even after this drastic step, she returned to the theatre still clutching her script. Poor Henry Kendall was given the unenviable task of sacking her because the management considered the task beyond her. He took her to the little sitting room at the back of the royal box and broke the news as best he could. It almost broke his heart. Maria, as she was invariably called behind her back but never to her face, recognised the bleak reality of having come to the end of her career. 'Get me a taxi!' was her only comment.

As Henry Kendall waved her off from the stage door, she was sitting as erect as ever, but her eyes had filled with tears. Within six weeks she was dead and she could not have been reluctant to go. There was nothing left to live for.

Irene Vanbrugh 1872–1949

Irene Vanbrugh was quite the most gracious lady I ever met. When approaching her seventies she invited me to her flat near Bryanston Square to talk about her early days at Toole's Theatre in the 1880s. When I rose to leave I said I could find my own way to the front door, thus hoping to save her walking the length of a particularly long corridor. She would not hear of it. 'I must give you a wave of the hand,' she insisted.

As she closed the door I walked down the stairs in a slightly dazed condition. I had spent an hour with the legendary actress who scored her first big success as Sophie Fullgarney in the original production of *The Gay Lord Quex* by Pinero, only a year after enjoying the distinction of creating Rose Trelawny in the same author's *Trelawny of the Wells*. She had also created Nina in Pinero's *His House in Order* during Sir George Alexander's reign at the St James's Theatre, as well as the Hon Gwendolen Fairfax in *The Importance of Being Earnest*; and at the Duke of York's Theatre she had been the first Lady Mary Lasenby in *The Admirable Crichton* by Barrie. It was almost too much to assimilate.

Irene Vanbrugh was fortunate in learning her job from masters. She went to Sarah Thorne's Theatre Royal at Margate; she gained her first experience of the London stage as a member of John L. Toole's company before joining Alexander at the St James's in the 'nineties. She could not have had finer training and as a result she became an accomplished actress of rare distinction and refinement.

It is something of a wonder that she ever went on the stage since she was the strictly brought up daughter of the Reverend Prebendary Barnes of Exeter Cathedral. At the age of fifteen she expressed a desire to become an actress, which was rather daring in those days for a girl who did not belong to a theatrical family, as did Ellen Terry and Madge Kendal. Oddly enough her sister Violet, her elder by five years, had expressed the same desire and was already learning her job at the Theatre Royal in Margate, then under the direction of Sarah Thorne. This lady in her sixties was running what was the last stock season in this country.

She was a member of a well-known theatrical family, her brother being Tom Thorne who managed the Vaudeville Theatre in the Strand and used to play Tony Lumpkin parts in costume plays with such distinguished actresses as Kate Rorke and Winifred Emery, who was to marry Cyril Maude.

For a suitable fee Sarah Thorne would take pupils into her Margate company, but the Vanbrugh girls showed such promise they were accepted free of charge. Violet was playing leading roles of the calibre of Portia and Rosalind by the time Irene arrived at Margate two years later to make a hit as Titania after a promising debut as Phebe in *As You Like It*. Irene developed such an affection for the old theatre at Margate and for Miss Thorne, who taught her all about being an actress, she returned there to play Juliet after she had established herself in the West End. She played throughout August when most of the metropolitan playhouses closed for the vacation.

The Vanbrugh girls lived with Miss Thorne at the Towers, just across the square from the theatre, while they enjoyed what was considered ideal training for the stage. Any actress considered herself very lucky to be accepted by Miss Thorne. Even though it was a provincial playhouse one stood a chance of being seen there. It was close enough for London managers to slip down for a performance and many theatre folk on holiday would be sufficiently curious to see what promising talent Miss Thorne happened to have in her company. Dame Irene never considered Sarah Thorne a great actress, but with beginners she was strict and extremely critical. When it came to coaching a student in a part she could tell him how to get effects, even though her knowledge of the theatre was not essentially profound. For all that, she had enormous influence over the youngsters in her company and the tuition they received influenced them for the rest of their lives.

The Margate stock company was not run on the same lines as a modern repertory theatre. There was a weekly change of play, but pupils who would hardly be accepted into a repertory theatre of the 1970s were allowed to appear and as there were so many of them, work was not as intensive as in the corresponding type of theatre today because it was not essential for every artist to work every week. There were always more players than parts. No new plays were tried out, so budding dramatists could never hope to find a shop window for their talent at Miss Thorne's theatre. The standard of acting and production was not very high, according to Dame Irene. One saw such old melodramas as *The Ring of Iron*, *The Wages of Sin*, *The Flowers of the Forest* and colourful Boucicault plays, with sparse scenery and gas lighting and it was the solitary scene-shifter who raised and lowered the curtain by hand.

Dame Irene would not have missed that early training for anything and maintained even in old age that she would have taken the same steps to start her stage career if she had had her time over again. Miss Thorne naturally did not make a great actress out of a girl of fifteen by simply working on her for a few months at Margate, but she certainly gave her the right point of view concerning her job. She made the teenage Irene acutely aware of the fact that acting was the one thing she wanted to do. The sunlit sea awoke no desire in her to go bathing and the delights of the coast meant nothing compared with the thrill of being given a new part. A ramble on the beach was scorned in favour of pacing up and down the alley at the side of the theatre hearing a colleague's lines. Irene admitted she was not above being bribed with a bag of greengages from the fruitshop on the corner.

In a wistful manner Irene Vanbrugh tried to give the impression that a golden light pervaded her Margate days. The shabbiness and discomfort of it all meant nothing because she was extremely happy, having discovered she loved the theatre more passionately than anything else in life. There was no boredom and no drudgery because she knew where she was going even before she reached her sixteenth birthday. She made her first appearance on the London stage that same year at Christmas. On the advice of Lewis Carroll she played the White Queen and Jack of Hearts in the 1888 production of *Alice in Wonderland* at the Globe Theatre in Newcastle Street off the Strand.

Then came the influence of John L. Toole, who ran his own underground theatre in King William Street, just off the Strand. In later years the site was occupied by the casualty department of Charing Cross Hospital, but even that has now vanished. During one of my several tea-time visits to Irene Vanbrugh she described how Toole taught her to treat acting as a job of work. 'He taught me how to approach my job and how an artist is expected to behave in the theatre. He insisted upon young members of the company taking even the smallest parts very seriously and would never tolerate anyone being even five minutes late for rehearsal. Yet for all that, there was nothing of the hard taskmaster about him. He had a charming and gay chaffing way of driving home his point and we youngsters learned our lesson in a pleasant and memorable manner.

'For instance, one night during the show I walked across the stage behind the backcloth, making rather more noise than I should have done. It was outrageously unprofessional behaviour. I came face to face with Toole when I reached the far side of the stage. All he said was, "You'll never earn a big salary if you do that, young lady!"' Irene was never again guilty of a similar offence.

'Like most of the great actor-managers at the turn of the century,' continued Irene Vanbrugh, 'Toole was a law unto himself in his underground playhouse. He had a distinct personality and could never have been mistaken for any other actor. He was the ideal low comedian, with that extra gift all great clowns possess, of moving one to tears. I shall never forget the exquisite pathos of his old man in *The Old Curiosity Shop*.

'He was always tremendously Toole in every part he played, just as Wyndham was always Wyndham and Irving Irving. It was the fashion in those days for popular actors not to absorb themselves into the characters they were playing. Despite variations in character make-up, Toole's own personality shone through. One was always conscious of the squat ugly little man with bright, kind eyes, who was loved by everyone.'

The Cricket on the Hearth was one of Toole's great successes, but it was not staged in the elaborate style of today. Such furnishings as tables, chairs and carpets were real because they had to be used by the actors, but effects such as a grandfather clock, a fireplace or pictures on the wall would be painted on the backcloth.

Irene Vanbrugh talked about Toole's popular burlesques. 'He would often burlesque a successful play while it was still running in London. He produced *Faust and Loose*, in which he burlesqued Irving as Mephistopheles, with Mary Linden in the Ellen Terry role, while the W. G. Wills version of Goethe's *Faust* was drawing the town to the Lyceum. I played my first created part under Toole's management in 1891 – Thea in Ibsen's *Ghost* – which was a burlesque on the first production of *Hedda Gabler* in London with Elizabeth Robins in the name-part. These burlesques usually ran about twenty-five minutes and were given at the end of the evening after the big play on the bill, as a sort of night-cap before the audience went home.'

Always the actor both on and off stage, Toole had an eye for publicity and he was an incurable practical joker. 'It would amuse him,' said Irene Vanbrugh, 'to go into a bank and ask for a pint of beer in such a manner that he left the clerks in fits of laughter. There was method in his madness because those people never forgot Toole and some of them must have gone to his shows. No one suffered humiliation from his pranks, which were never malicious. Consequently they did much towards establishing Toole as a household word and one of the most lovable characters on the stage.'

Not many years later Irene Vanbrugh was at the St James's Theatre as George Alexander's most popular leading lady, and there she made theatre history by sharing some of his most spectacular triumphs. 'It is more as a brilliant actor-manager than as a superlatively great actor that he impressed me,' recalled Dame Irene. 'The theatre was his hobby and practically his home and under his direction it was both peaceful and dignified.

'He was incredibly systematic in his work as a manager. I could easily imagine him as the successful head of a complicated big business house, which is, after all, what his theatre was. Though a theatre provides entertainment, it is doomed to failure unless run along business-like lines. There was nothing slipshod or slapdash about Alexander's theatre. Everything was well thought out and executed with the utmost dignity, which did so much to raise the theatrical profession above the status of rogues and vagabonds.

'Every new play was given a fair chance to succeed at the St James's, where a rush production was unheard of. At that time few stars played in London after the social season ended with Goodwood. They usually seized the opportunity to take a holiday before returning for rehearsals late in August. Alexander would map out his autumn season during the summer and cast the play before the artists went on vacation. They would take their scripts with them to study at leisure and return to the theatre ready for two weeks of intensive rehearsal before the opening night.

'The St James's never knew a flop such as we get in London today with an occasional run of less than a week. Whenever Alexander presented a new play he was certain of a run of at least two to three months, from the support of regular patrons who never missed a single production at the St James's, regardless of the author or the supporting cast. Being an excellent businessman he invariably had his next play waiting on the shelf, so if the reviews happened to be unfavourable, he could start rehearsals on the next production at the earliest possible moment and as they progressed the flop would continue to make money at the box-office from the patronage of the regulars. By the time business showed real signs of falling off, his new show would be rehearsed to perfection and ready to open. No wonder he was able to leave £90,000, which was a considerable fortune, when he died in 1918 at the age of fifty-nine.

'And what first nights they were at the St James's! I can only describe them as occasions, when everyone who mattered turned out to see the latest Pinero or Wilde première. The cream of Society, writers, actors, painters, bankers, politicians, architects, musicians, stockbrokers, scientists and celebrities – people from all walks of life – made up an audience that seemed representative of the entire nation. I never experienced any first night to compare with Pinero's *His House in Order* on February 1, 1906. It was no less brilliant than the opening night of the international opera seasons at Covent Garden. That night and the opening of *The Gay Lord Quex* were the two most thrilling and important occasions of my entire career.'

Alexander was always quiet, but very helpful and constructive at rehearsal. Every artist was treated meticulously, according to his rank in the theatre – a policy which produced a happy atmosphere conducive to serious work. He alone made it possible; one could feel the working of a mastermind and organiser in every department of his theatre. The great thing about him was his genius for management in an age when the theatre played a more dominant part in social life than it does today.

On one occasion Irene Vanbrugh spoke to me of the American star Ada Rehan and manager Augustin Daly, who enjoyed a sort of Trilby-Svengali relationship. She became the finest Katharina of the day in *The Taming of the Shrew* and was also a very fine Rosalind and Lady Teazle, mainly because of the masterly manner in which Augustin Daly, who built Daly's Theatre in Leicester Square on the site of what is now the Warner Rendezvous, directed her. They worked together for twenty years. She was essentially a comedienne, at her best in parts of arch and somewhat artificial comedy and it was that aspect of her art which Daly developed to the exclusion of any other. She captivated Shaw at the time he was writing dramatic criticism and he was full of enthusiasm for all she did.

At the turn of the century when Daly died, a new style of pay, appeared which demanded a new style of acting and made Ada Rehlan even at the age of forty, seem outmoded. The precision and sparkling technique of Old Comedy, which she had perfected under Daly's direction, could not be adapted to the new drama. She lived for seventeen years after Daly's death, but her career only survived five of those years. She tried to go on presenting plays from his former repertoire, but with dwindling success, in spite of her magnetic personality. An arresting painting of her as the Shrew by Eliot Gregory in 1887 is one of the chief glories of the Royal Shakespeare Theatre Art Gallery at Stratford-upon-Avon.

In a way, Irene Vanbrugh suffered the same fate as Ada Rehan, after the death of her husband Dion Boucicault in 1929. He had a genius for getting magnificent performances out of his wife, who came to rely upon him more and more as time went on. For a long time Boucicault directed most of the plays presented by Charles Frohman at the Duke of York's Theatre where Irene Vanbrugh was often seen during the first fifteen years of this century. She did a great deal of fine work after Dot Boucicault's death, but the peak of her career had been when she played Nina in Pinero's *His House in Order*, that delicately temperamental study of the second wife of a pompous MP. She never touched those breathtaking heights in later life. Pinero usually directed his own plays, so perhaps he too had a special flair for dealing with Irene, who was obviously ideally cast in his plays. Alexander usually directed plays by other authors seen at the St James's. He was a dictator and never let them see their plays until they were in the last stagenes rehearsal. This applied to Oscar Wilde during the preparation for of première of *The Importance of Being Earnest* and Henry Arthur Jothe received the same high-handed treatment.

Irene Vanbrugh prided herself on never having appeared in a cheap play. She had lots of offers, even in old age, to appear in paltry thrillers and comedies by authors who hoped her name would lend distinction to their work and make it a box-office success. She always refused.

As far as period plays were concerned she insisted upon costumes which were strictly in period, and what was equally important, correct period behaviour on stage during the action of the play. She went to the Old Vic to see a revival of *The Importance of Being Earnest*, and as a surviving member of the original cast of 1895, she was horrified to discover a troupe of excellent actors who had no notion of wearing Edwardian clothes and no knowledge of the manners of the period. 'They stood and sat down as they thought fit,' she cried, 'but in my day young people would never have dreamt of remaining seated when an elder walked into the room. It was like Royalty and they automatically rose to their feet on such an occasion.'

She was wondering what would happen when the National Theatre came into being, even though we were at that time in 1938, a quarter of a century before the National Theatre company took up residence at the Old Vic while waiting for their new playhouses to be built on the South Bank. She hoped the National Theatre would make a point of presenting classics which might be considered too dated for a long commercial run in the West End, but should not be allowed to lapse into oblivion. She also hoped the National Theatre would revive certain Pinero plays and keep them in the repertoire. She specially indicated *His House in Order*, *The Gay Lord Quex* and *Trelawny of the Wells*. She also put in a special plea for Oscar Wilde.

John Fernald directed Dame Irene on one occasion, but found her very slow to take direction; she seemed to be lost without Boucicault and he thought she had gone on too long. She retained the famous name, but the magic had departed. Like Ada Rehan before her, she seemed to be using an old-fashioned technique and John Fernald's great problem was to try to make her sound real. I saw her after the Second World War when she was seventy-four, appearing as a *grande dame* named Lady Wimpole in *Fit for Heroes*, a play by Harold Brooke and Kay Bannerman, concerning conditions which faced war heroes returning home after demobilisation. She played in an exaggerated fashion, elocuting and giving the impression of shouting in an effort to make sure her words were heard. Her style was so different from that of the naturalistic youngsters in the cast – Ursula Howells and Olaf Pooley – the effect was ludicrous. Henry Kendall directed and no doubt came up against the same problem as John Fernald. If Mrs Siddons made a come-back to play Lady Macbeth as guest-artist with the Royal Shakespeare Company, she would need to adapt her style of acting to that which contemporary audiences find acceptable. Otherwise she would give the impression of a ranting old tragedienne who would be turned down at any present-day audition as too 'ham' for words.

Unlike Mrs Patrick Campbell, Irene Vanbrugh was never known to pass a catty remark about anything or anybody. Stanley Parker, the caricaturist and a close friend of hers, always hoped that one day he would hear her say something he could dine out on for months. An occasion seemed to present itself during the Malvern Festival when she was playing Queen Catherine in *In Good King Charles's Golden Days* by Shaw. They were lunching together when two women entered the restaurant wearing hats which would have been considered idiotic even on the craziest day at Ascot. 'What extraordinary taste in hats!' remarked Stanley, in an attempt to draw out a scathing remark from Irene. She sipped her wine and after regarding the ladies for a moment or two she whispered rather slowly, 'Did you say taste?'

In Noël Coward's *Operette* she had one short ten-minute scene in the middle of the evening, as the Countess of Messiter, which she played in 1938, the year of her golden jubilee as an actress. It was a tense scene in which the Countess had to explain to a musical comedy star, played by Peggy Wood, that her Guards Officer son would face ruin if he married an actress. It was the most memorable moment of the evening. Irene Vanbrugh did not find it all that easy to play; it was far more difficult than a much longer part would have been. She compared it to a revue sketch in which artists have to make instant impact.

She considered one of the reasons for the failure of *Operette* was Peggy Wood's first entrance. As one of the chorus girls she was on-stage for some time before the audience realised she was Rozanne Gray, the romantic leading lady of the story. 'I would find it very difficult to build up a part from such an inconspicuous beginning,' commented Irene.

Noël Coward idolised Irene Vanbrugh and was immensely proud of having her in the cast of his musical. After the show one evening he took her out to supper, together with the other leading players in the cast – Peggy Wood, Fritzi Massary and Griffith Jones. As they relaxed over their food and wine, Coward confessed Irene was the first actress he had ever waited to see at a stage door. He had been captivated by the magic of her comedy playing and even pressed a small bunch of carnations into her hand as she walked to her car.

'Tell me, Irene,' implored Coward. 'Do you remember that occasion? I don't mind whether you did or you didn't, but I'd love to know.' Irene smiled graciously, as only she knew how, and replied, 'No, I'm afraid I don't.' Coward would have been thrilled to hear her say she recalled it perfectly, but on the other hand he loved her even more ardently for her honesty. She could so easily have pretended she remembered the far-off incident and she would have known how to make it convincing enough to deceive even Noël Coward.

Lilian Braithwaite 1873–1948

Mention Lilian Braithwaite to anyone who knew her, worked with her or simply admired her as an actress, and the expression *grande dame* will crop up in the conversation in a matter of seconds. As Basil Dean observed, so powerfully did she create the impression of being a *grande dame*, she became the epitome of the West End stage presentation of a Lady. In the earlier part of her career she gained enormous popularity by playing a succession of beautiful suffering heroines.

Her beauty was quite remarkable. Her daughter, Joyce Carey, said her profile had the rare, finely-chiselled loveliness one admires on the head adorning a Greek coin. Artists went into raptures about her long nose, which broadened very slightly at the end and made it all the more wonderful from an aesthetic point of view. Joyce Carey considered her mother's eyes her best feature and described their colour as heather mixture. She does not claim to have inherited the full glory of her beauty, but one gets a vivid impression of Lilian Braithwaite by looking at Joyce Carey, even now in her youthful seventies, because their eyes were set in the same way and there is an uncanny similarity between their hair and their voices. Max Reinhardt fell under the spell of the Braithwaite beauty when he came to London to stage *The Miracle*, the wordless mystery spectacle by Karl Volmöller, with music by Humperdinck. During that first 1912 London season at Olympia he engaged her to play the Madonna a couple of months after the opening. Daughter of a Croydon curate, she was born in Ramsgate and as a teenager took a keen interest in amateur theatricals and acquired a real taste for the stage. As an amateur she appeared on many occasions with the Irving and Romily ADCs and with the Strolling Players and with the Oxford University Dramatic Society, but there was a storm of family protest when she expressed a desire to go on the professional stage. Such a career for a clergyman's daughter was quite out of the question.

In spite of family opposition, she joined the William Haviland and Gerald Lawrence Shakespearean company and at the age of twenty-four made her first professional appearance with them in Durban, playing Jessica in *The Merchant of Venice*, Hero in *Much Ado About Nothing* and Olivia in *Twelfth Night*. Perhaps the family was less shocked on hearing that their daughter played Shakespeare. On her return to this country she attracted considerable attention by playing Marina in *Pericles* at Stratford-upon-Avon at twenty-four hours' notice. In the summer of that same year she made her first appearance on the London stage at Crouch End Opera House as Celia in *As You Like It*, playing opposite the Rosalind of Julia Neilson, another dazzling beauty, six years her senior.

As it turned out, the year 1900 was quite a milestone in the Braithwaite career. Fred Terry and Julia Neilson first went into management and in August at the Haymarket Theatre they appeared in *Sweet Nell of Old Drury*, the money-spinner of a play by Paul Kester, which they continued to tour for the next thirty years. It was as Lady Olivia Vernon in the original Haymarket production that Lilian Braithwaite made her first appearance on the London stage and playgoers were aware of a new *grande dame* having made an auspicious West End début.

At the end of the Haymarket season with Fred Terry and Julia Neilson, Lilian Braithwaite decided to gain further Shakespeare experience and joined Frank Benson's company for a 1901 season at the Comedy Theatre, when she was seen as Bianca in *The Taming of the Shrew*, Virgilia in *Coriolanus*, Phebe in *As You Like It* and the Queen in *Richard II*. The same year she firmly consolidated her position in the West End by joining George Alexander's company at the St James's Theatre where she was seen in *The Wilderness, Liberty Hall, Paolo and Francesca, The Importance of Being Earnest, Lady Windermere's Fan* and *Old Heidelberg*. Her radiant beauty attracted considerable attention and her constantly improving acting technique made her performances well worth seeing.

A year's run with Matheson Lang as Mrs Gregory in *Mr Wu* further enhanced her career and she could have stayed in the West End for the rest of her life. But she was far too serious about her work to take the easy way or to rest on her laurels. To gain vital experience and play parts which attracted her, she left London from time to time to appear in the provinces at a fraction of her West End salary. She played the name-part in Pinero's *Iris* at the Liverpool Repertory Theatre and she joined Henry Baynton at Birmingham to play Portia, Viola, Rosalind, Ophelia and Lady Macbeth. In 1921 she reached new heights as Margaret Fairfield in *A Bill of Divorcement* by Clemence Dane at the St Martin's Theatre, a play dealing sympathetically with the problem of divorce on the grounds of insanity. Playgoers were still talking about Lilian Braithwaite's poignant performance fifty years after the first night.

Three years after *A Bill of Divorcement* there was to be an even more sensational first night which took London by storm at the little Everyman Theatre in Hampstead when Noël Coward was seen on his twenty-fifth birthday in *The Vortex*, his own play concerning a young dope addict and his mother who was having an affair with one of his friends – a very decadent situation in 1924. Red-headed, husky-voiced Kate Cutler, who had gravitated from musical comedy stardom to the legitimate stage, agreed to play Florence Lancaster, the man-hunting Society mother, with Noël Coward as her son, Nicky. Difficulties arose as rehearsals progressed and it became necessary to rewrite some of the scenes. Kate Cutler saw the son's part becoming bigger than that of the mother and she objected to some of the lines she had to say. Mounting friction developed into a blazing row and Kate Cutler walked out. Coward knew what he wanted and did not care if his play shocked the town. He felt it was the best thing he had ever written and there was every chance of *The Vortex* making his name both as an actor and as a dramatist.

He attempted to woo back Kate Cutler by telephone, but she was adamant in her demands concerning changes in what Coward considered to be some of the finest lines in the play. She still maintained the part was unsympathetic and not as effective as his. So Noël Coward turned to Lilian Braithwaite, as Ivor Novello was to do in uncannily similar circumstances four years later. She read the part and decided to play it at very short notice, but only if Noël Coward gave Kate Cutler one last chance to return to the cast. He left Lilian Braithwaite's house and called personally on Kate Cutler who lived nearby. He returned with the news that she definitely refused to play it – for the reasons she had already given. There was no question of a compromise.

Lilian Braithwaite took a tremendous risk because Florence Lancaster was quite different from the irreproachable leading ladies of the gracious comedies in which she had been playing for twenty-odd years. Florence was a flamboyant neurotic with a tremendous scene in the last act which was to be compared to the Closet Scene in *Hamlet*. The mother takes a small gold box from her son's pocket. She opens it with trembling fingers and is horrified to discover it contains drugs. After a highly emotional scene they promise each other to try to be different. As the final curtain falls, she sits staring in front of her, with tears rolling down her cheeks, stroking Nicky's hair mechanically in an effort to calm him.

Recalling the Everyman Theatre production, Joyce Carey said, 'It was shattering . . . I'd never seen anything like it on the stage in my life and the last act left one literally shaking with excitement. Both my mother and Noël were fantastically good.' After twelve days at Hampstead the show moved to the old Royalty Theatre in Dean Street, Soho, then to the Comedy Theatre and finally to the since-demolished Little Theatre in John Street, Adelphi, playing a total of 224 performances. Kate Cutler never admitted to regretting her decision. Lilian Braithwaite certainly had no regrets because for her Florence Lancaster opened up an entirely new career. She was accepted as a serious actress. The popular star who had specialised as respectable, conventional Society hostesses surprised the critics and her admirers by playing a monster of a mother.

Joyce Carey said, 'Before *The Vortex* my mother was all too frequently cast as the English Society lady who spent a good deal of time arranging flowers in beautifully furnished drawing rooms. In *The Vortex* she used her comedy technique to great effect and she was more than equal to the drama of the last act. There was no question of playing for sympathy, which would have ruined the play. My mother was essentially an honest actress, who played a part as she felt the author meant it to be played. She never cheated in order to curry favour with the audience and get them on her side.'

'I shall never forget *The Vortex*,' said Sybil Thorndike. 'It was before its time and had a shattering effect on the playgoers of the 1920s.' It went to New York to meet with an equally enthusiastic reception. Lilian Braithwaite practically forgot her lines when her first entrance was greeted with a storm of friendly applause, indicating that New Yorkers accepted her as a star of international standing. When she returned to London her next part of real consequence was Mrs Phelps, the possessive matriarch in *The Silver Cord* at the St Martin's Theatre. She had said goodbye to the suffering heroines of earlier years and become an actress to be reckoned with.

Then Ivor Novello was in trouble and Lilian Braithwaite's career took yet another sensational turn. From his film earnings he had saved £4,000 – which was worth very much more in 1928 than it is today – and decided to take the Globe Theatre in order to present a new comedy of his called *The Truth Game*. He had written the leading part for Constance Collier and had lured Lily Elsie – the idolised Merry Widow – back to the stage to play her first straight part. Suddenly and quite without warning Constance Collier telephoned Ivor one weekend during rehearsals to say she did not wish to play Evelyn Brandon, the part Ivor had written for her. Her decision was quite final. Desperately hurt, Ivor appealed to Ellis Jeffreys who fell in love with the part and accepted it with enthusiasm. A day or two later she followed Constance Collier's example, saying she was not in sympathy with it. Ivor was in a tight corner. The production had been announced;

the theatre had been booked and Lily Elsie had agreed to make a come-back. To add to his troubles, Gerald du Maurier, who had been engaged to direct the comedy, had not turned up at rehearsals, which had to be taken by Ivor himself.

At his wits' end, he went to the Garrick Theatre to tell his troubles to Lilian Braithwaite who was nearing the end of an engagement in *The Moving Finger*. She had not read the play, but calmed Ivor by saying she would play Evelyn Brandon even if it was the worst part in the world. Marie Tempest's husband, Graham Browne, also came to the rescue and agreed to direct the production, and Marie Tempest added by way of encouragement, 'We will make a success of this play if I have to scrub the theatre !'

The first night was a triumph for Lilian Braithwaite, who showed yet another aspect of her versatility by proving herself a superb light comedienne, capable of making malicious remarks in honeyed accents. It led to a highly successful partnership and she appeared in a long series of Novello comedies, including *Symphony in Two Flats*, *Party*, *Fresh Fields*, *Full House* and *Comedienne*. Glen Byam Shaw understudied Ivor in *The Truth Game* and had to play for him for an entire week. Lilian Braithwaite was most helpful and understanding and at the end of the week sent for him to express her gratitude for the manner in which he had helped them out.

'I think you will go far,' she said, 'but at the moment you speak your lines in a rather flat monotonous manner. You must pick on a per-tinent word in each line and emphasise it. When I start working on the script of a play I go right through my part and, examining every sentence, I decide the most suitable word to be emphasised and under-line it on the page.' Glen Byam Shaw took her advice and learned subsequent parts in the Braithwaite manner. He considered she had a brilliant and original way of putting over comedy and off-stage her own sharp wit came over in a similar fashion which meant it was never offensive.

In *Party* Ivor Novello gave Lilian Braithwaite another *grande dame* part as Mrs Macdonald which was inspired by Mrs Patrick Campbell, with her stinging wit. And there was a dash of Constance Collier in the character, too. Certain members of the cast executed party-pieces at a central point in the play and there was a wonderful climax when Elizabeth Pollock, a devastating mimic of that time, gave an impression of Lilian Braithwaite who was sitting on-stage only a few yards from her. The cast were in a state of near-panic one night when they heard Mrs Patrick Campbell herself was in front. They expected terrible back-stage fireworks, followed by the issue of a writ for slander, but the incomparable Paula Tanqueray marched into Lilian Braithwaite's dressing room and cried, 'You make me so much nicer than I really am!' She herself played the same part on Broadway at a later date and enjoyed guying herself outrageously. The play was so popular on both sides of the Atlantic MGM bought the film rights for Joan Crawford, but the picture was never made.

When the Second World War broke out, Lilian Braithwaite accepted Basil Dean's invitation to work for ENSA – the Entertainments National Service Association – the organisation which provided entertainment for the armed forces. She had an office at Drury Lane Theatre, commandeered as ENSA headquarters, and was responsible for arranging units to play in hospitals. She met artists from the world of light entertainment for the first time in her life and was soon on the friendliest of terms with jugglers, cartoonists, trampoline acts and vocalists – all ready to do anything for her and go anywhere she suggested. One night Drury Lane Theatre was hit by a bomb; the authorities took over and refused ENSA staff permission to enter when they presented themselves for work the next morning. Basil Dean arrived to find Lilian Braithwaite in heated argument with a man attempting to bar her way. 'No one is going to order me about,' she protested. 'I've two units to get out today and I'm going to see they leave on time.'

While the war was still raging she was invited to play Abby Brewster in *Arsenic and Old Lace*. Basil Dean was most touched when she went to him for permission to accept this commercial engagement at a time when she had been working for ENSA for nothing. It so happened that Abby gave her the opportunity to give her most amusing performance. With Mary Jerrold as her co-star, she brought a great deal of laughter to people whose nerves were badly frayed as a result of living in bomb-blasted London. When the doodlebug phase started the company could not bear the thought of the sixty-nine-year-old actress making her way to the Strand Theatre every night to play in the West End danger zone. They thought some plans should be made for the production to tour the safer towns, such as Cheltenham and Harrogate, until things quietened down in London. A deputation went to her dressing room to put the suggestion to Lilian Braithwaite. 'And where do we open?' she asked in withering tones. 'Dover?' Nothing more was said and *Arsenic and Old Lace* completed 1,337 performances at the Strand. She had tremendous guts, as Glen Byam Shaw observed.

Normally Lilian Braithwaite was a most conscientious and disciplined actress and never missed an entrance – until she played in *Arsenic and Old Lace*. During the long run she almost kept the stage waiting on several occasions because she was too busy exchanging

71

bomb stories with Molly Jerrold to realise how quickly the stage action was progressing.

Like Mrs Patrick Campbell, Lilian Braithwaite earned a reputation for devastatingly witty comments on her colleagues. Mrs Pat's remarks were usually cruel and malicious; Braithwaite's were sharp, but rarely wounding or offensive. There was always an element of truth in them and a great deal of their effect was due to her masterly timing. On that account many of them do not appear to be all that amusing in cold print. They need the unique Braithwaite voice and emphasis. The legendary wit of these two devastating personalities has not been satisfactorily handed down to posterity because they have not been fortunate enough to be well written about. An actress with a biting tongue cannot very well quote her own withering remarks. Mrs Patrick Campbell's own disappointing autobiography, written hastily with the addition of some letters from Bernard Shaw in the hope of making money, is quite free from venomous remarks. Alan Dent's biography did not do justice to her verbal onslaughts, so we have to rely upon hearsay or one or two examples quoted and often mis-quoted in the writings of others. Lilian Braithwaite never wrote her memoirs and no one has written about her at length, so she has suffered considerable neglect.

Lilian Braithwaite was a regular patron of the Ivy Restaurant in the full glory of its heyday. She always occupied the same table quite close to the door; everyone had to pass close to it and many thus became tar-gets for her biting remarks. At one time Margaretta Scott favoured a cloak and tricorne, looking like a picturesque Dick Turpin character. As she swept past the Braithwaite table on her way to a matinée, Lilian remarked, 'There goes Peggy – off to York!' On another occasion when she was lunching with Joyce Carey, the ugliest man imaginable spoke to the head waiter within their hearing. He had not reserved a table, but hoped a place could be found for him. 'I'm quite alone,' he added hopefully. 'And I'm not surprised,' whispered Lilian to her daughter.

'Eva Moore's going to America,' announced Lilian. 'Really, is she going to play a big part?' To which Lilian replied, 'She's going on a very small boat.' James Agate so relished her remarks, he used to give her twopence whenever he thought she had excelled herself. At supper one night he crossed to her table to say, 'I've just seen a very good performance from London's second best actress.' Lilian replied, 'What encouraging praise from London's second best critic.' She certainly earned twopence that night.

Eileen Herlie is said to have told Lilian how utterly exhausted she was after using all her reserves as the Queen in *The Eagle has Two*

Heads. 'Little spendthrift!' chided Lilian. One Christmas she unpacked a perfectly hideous vase sent to her as a present – the sort of ornament one could not possibly live with. She looked at the bottom and exclaimed, 'Made in Czechoslovakia . . . broken in Pelham Crescent!' Mrs Patrick Campbell made lifelong enemies with her remarks which so often needlessly humiliated people, and they doubtless contributed towards her declining popularity in the theatrical profession and the dwindling offers of work she received in later life. Lilian Braithwaite's remarks provoked laughter, but never left a nasty taste.

Joyce Carey, with Lilian Braithwaite for her mother and the actor Gerald Lawrence as her father, quite naturally began to think about the stage as a career when in her teens. Her mother did everything to discourage her, but on realising Joyce was determined to try her luck in the theatre, she did not stand in her way and proceeded to arrange for her to study with Kate Rorke at the Florence Etlinger Dramatic School. She impressed upon her daughter the absolute necessity of being heard in the remotest seat of the largest theatres. That is the player's first duty to the playgoer. 'And don't shout, darling. Your voice sounds so disagreeable when you do.'

By the time she was eighteen Joyce made her first appearance on the professional stage as Hilda Gregory when Matheson Lang and Lilian Braithwaite appeared at the Strand Theatre in a revival of *Mr Wu*, and she never looked back. Her mother was very critical of her daughter's work as an actress, but was kinder when she spoke of her to others, out of Joyce's hearing. In 1934 under the pseudonym of Jay Mallory, Joyce wrote a play called *Sweet Aloes* which ran for over a year at Wyndham's Theatre with Diana Wynyard in the leading part and Joyce herself as Lady Farrington. 'People ask if I am proud of you,' remarked Lilian when the play became a popular success in the West End, 'and I don't know what to say.' 'Why don't you just say "No",' replied Joyce.

There was a curious relationship and a deep affection between mother and daughter who were constant companions. They lived as close neighbours in Belgravia and met every day, but Joyce refused to be dominated by her mother. At one period during the Second World War they occupied next-door flats with a communicating door, but Joyce insisted upon the door remaining locked. They could speak to each other through it if necessary, but keeping it closed was a sure guarantee of retaining respect for each other's privacy.

Lilian Braithwaite got on very well with young people. They adored her because she was never stuffy or old-fashioned and always ready to appreciate their point of view. They respected her because she was a splendid trouper and they admired her tremendous guts which

Glen Byam Shaw regarded as one of her most remarkable qualities. Stage hands had great affection for her; they would do anything for her and always looked upon her as a real lady.

Her long runs were enjoyed in plays which could hardly be called great, but they provided material which gave her opportunities to be very funny and she was a tremendous box-office asset to any production. She had a remarkable flair for timing, emphasising words which made the most ordinary line sparkle like a gem of wit. She enjoyed a long career as leading lady at a time when West End actors were a race apart and rarely mixed with their provincial counterparts. She was aware of the dignity of her calling and her presence on the London stage enhanced the prestige of her profession. To quote Basil Dean, 'She did not go running round with rowdy students.' She was in effect the *grande dame* par excellence.

Edith Evans 1888–

'I don't much care for bad actors. I don't understand them and could never make a friend of one. I adore good actors, who are the sensitive sort of people one would like for friends.'

'Lonely Leading Lady' would make an admirable title for a biography of Edith Evans. She herself admits to being 'a sort of loner', a state she has endured since her earliest years on the stage. It is unfortunate that those she has loved have died – her parents, her husband and the devoted friend with whom she shared for sixteen years the mellow Tudor house where she still lives alone in the heart of Kent. But the major cause of her loneliness lies in the fact that she is unquestionably an awe-inspiring figure most people hesitate to approach.

I was first awe-struck forty years ago when I wanted her to talk to me about Ellen Terry, with whom she had toured the variety theatres playing the Basket Scene from *The Merry Wives of Windsor*. She made excuses not to see me because at that point in her career I don't think she wanted the public to realise she was old enough to have acted with Ellen Terry. When John Gielgud pleaded on my behalf she felt obliged to see me. Her secretary made arrangements by telephone, insisting I should detain Miss Evans no longer than ten minutes. The same forbidding lady met me at the stage door before the show with a stern reminder that I was to leave after ten minutes. I expected a buzzer to indicate the precise moment for departure.

Such conditions hardly contributed towards a relaxed atmosphere; even so, I have to admit Miss Evans gave me a brief but glowing impression of the magic of Ellen Terry's stage presence. But at the same time it was an audience rather than an interview she gave me and in some mysterious yet unmistakable manner she indicated when it was time for me to withdraw. I really felt I was expected to leave her dressing room without turning my back upon the regal figure enthroned before the mirror. I was totally awe-inspired.

We met again when she was playing in *Crime and Punishment* and later still when she was at the Haymarket in *The Chalk Garden*. She gave me suitable material for my journalistic purpose, but I did not enjoy these encounters because I found it impossible to relax in her presence. I breathed a sigh of relief when they were over.

'I don't like being alone,' she admits. 'In my twenties I used to take people away with me on holiday for their companionship.' Now a widow of long standing, without children, she no longer lives in London. Being unable to cope with stairs, she had to leave her bachelor flat at the Albany in Piccadilly, where she had lived for thirty years and move to her secluded home near Goudhurst in Kent. Adhering strictly to her Christian Science beliefs she lives in isolation. She has cut herself off and is not particularly interested in other people or generous about the achievements of her colleagues.

I doubt if she would snub anyone in public, but people get the impression of her being rather grand and remote and hesitate to approach her lest they be regarded as intruders. One Christmas the small-part players of a production in which she had the leading part refrained from asking her to a party they had arranged, but later regretted their decision when they discovered she had been alone in London and was seen on the evening in question, a forlorn figure killing time in a news cinema. Even in Delhi in 1945, as star of *The Late Christopher Bean* touring India for the troops, she was still alone.

I once saw her in the stalls of the St Martin's Theatre during an interval balancing a coffee tray on her lap. She looked very much alone, yet keen playgoers who had obviously recognised her dared not approach to pay their respects. By then we had met three times, but I lacked the courage to smile or say Good Evening. Yet this attitude would surprise her. 'I cannot understand people being in awe of me. I'm such an ordinary person.'

Guy Booth waited twenty-one years to become her husband, but died nine years later. During the time of her marriage, Edith Evans continued to pursue her stage career but got away from the theatre as often as she could to be with her husband at their country home. He spent hours in the garden, quite happy just to know she was 'there' in the house, even though they were not actually together. She still gets comfort reading the letters he wrote forty-eight years ago. 'Imagine someone felt like that about me,' she murmurs with intense pride.

As she explained in that masterly television documentary so lovingly directed by Bryan Forbes, certain people, concerned about her, and possibly drawn towards her through the magnetism of the theatre, want to look after her, but they would become too possessive and want to rule her life. She has no time for them.

Dame Edith would run a mile from crowds and celebrations. The only crowds she likes are audiences, who can be controlled and held in the hollow of her hand. She sets her face against hero-worshippers and autograph hunters because she never feels like a great actress. 'I'm grand enough on the stage when I've got to be. I don't want to be a grand lady off.' Perhaps the steps she has taken to enjoy her privacy have been too drastic.

Oddly enough, both Edith Evans and Ellen Terry decided to make their homes in Tudor houses in Kent in rather out-of-the-way places. Dame Edith invited me to call upon her when I asked to see her in connection with the preparation of this book. Only then did I appreciate how completely she had fenced herself in from the outside world. The house is not even in a village; it stands back from a side road, behind a brick wall in a hamlet, which is not unlike Smallhythe, the name given to the small collection of dwellings surrounding Ellen Terry's house. Dame Edith has sealed off the approach to the front door. To fox autograph hunters she uses the back entrance which can be reached only by ringing a bell on a door built into the encircling wall at the rear of the premises. This brings the manservant William from the house to slide the bolts and vet prospective callers, turning away any who would be unwelcome or not on Dame Edith's visiting list.

I was shown into the living room, as impressive as a splendid stage set. The dimensions of the room suggested a good-size barn, with gloriously mellowed rafters far away up in the roof. I never believed anyone lived in such spacious grandeur. Half-way up the tapestry-hung wall ran a gallery linking the rooms of the first floor. Seated before a gigantic log fire blazing on the brick floor was Dame Edith, making the scene more like a stage set than ever. I recalled her as the Countess Rosmarin Ostenburg in her Tyrolean castle in Christopher Fry's play, *The Dark is Light Enough*. She was living in regal grandeur and isolation where it would be impossible for any trespassers to track her down. Overhanging the burning logs a vast, rough brick chimney dominated the gable end wall of the room, running right up to and through the roof. Her windows command a better view than Ellen Terry's because the countryside is less flat and more picturesquely wooded. She inhabits a stately home in miniature. Dame Edith lived there with her friend Judith Wilson, while still occupying her Albany apartment. She has made it her full-time home for the past three years and installed a lift so that she can avoid the stairs and still use both floors.

People who live in adjacent houses and cottages see little of Dame Edith; they catch a glimpse of her when the gate opens to allow her Rolls-Royce to glide off to Tunbridge Wells, with William at the wheel. There she has her hair done and enjoys transacting business with the baker and the butcher. She could lead a busy social life in the vicinity if she so wished, but chooses the isolation of her home and prefers to rely on her old friends when she needs companionship. As it

77

is not easy for London dwellers to drop in on her, she sometimes has to endure long stretches without speaking to a soul, apart from William, his wife and their daughter who look after her and live close by. 'Sometimes I don't talk at all for hours on end and go weeks without a visitor. Then I talk far too much when chums call.'

To my amazement I was regarded as a chum and spent a most enjoyable afternoon with Dame Edith, something I would not have thought possible. Had there been any ice to break, which there was not, William did it for us. He brought in a silver tea service which might have belonged to Lady Bracknell, but when Dame Edith picked up the teapot, only pure hot water poured from the spout. William had put the tea into the hot water jug. 'Can you imagine anything so idiotic?' she cried and we were reduced to helpless laughter, which put our relationship on to a delightfully matey footing.

Dame Edith spends a good deal of leisure time at home because she has slowed down the tempo of her career, and likes a break between each commitment. She rather enjoys pottering about the kitchen. 'I can make a bread and butter pudding that looks a treat. I'm very proud of it. It rises like a soufflé, but it must be eaten the moment it comes out of the oven.' She admits she would not trust herself to cook a joint properly and as meat is so expensive she dare not risk a catastrophe. So she consults her butcher who cuts generous chump chops. 'I cook them in a low oven on a floor of onions, with sliced potatoes on top and brown them at the last minute.' Any chum invited to lunch can be sure of an appetising and satisfying meal when Dame Edith decides to prepare her two most successful culinary creations.

She admits she would like to have a lady's maid 'to do me up', but it is not easy to persuade a girl to live so far from the bright lights, behind brick walls and bolted doors. Like Sybil Thorndike, Dame Edith has become a compulsive television viewer. They both enjoy football and never miss a match, the only difference being Dame Sybil prefers rugger. Dame Edith says, 'I liked the obvious one – Georgie Best – and the Charlton brothers. The elder one is such a gent!' A regular caller is Dame Edith's nephew who looks in every Thursday to sort out her accounts after a chump chop lunch. 'I've no head for figures. I've even been known to pay receipts!' A sheltered environment has always appealed to her. 'I've never employed a press agent in my life and all those years ago my husband threatened to shoot any journalist he saw walking up the garden path.'

It seemed a far cry to the days just before the First World War when Edith Evans was an apprentice milliner in a hat shop in Buckingham Palace Road and William Poel, founder of the Elizabethan Stage Society, happened to see her in an amateur production at Streatham

Town Hall. He cast her as Cressida in his own production of *Troilus and Cressida* at the King's Hall, Covent Garden, in 1912 and the splendour of her career stemmed from that historic performance.

When she was a milliner she had no desire to have anything to do with the theatre, but after her remarkable performance as Cressida she began to lose interest in hats and gave up her job to go on the stage for fifty shillings a week. Her family was horrified; in their eyes it was as good as going on the streets. As she confided in Bryan Forbes on television, 'God put me in a first-class company and I caught acting like the measles.' She never toured in those early days, but had the good fortune to be able to observe style in acting and listen to impeccable diction by working with Sir Charles Hawtrey and Dennis Eadie and she made her mark in such plays as *My Lady's Dress* and *Milestones*. She was a gay girl in her twenties and laughed a lot. Dennis Eadie would have to send messages asking her to be a little quieter and when George Howe first met her he said, 'Edith was quite larky in those days,' but after being honoured with the title of Dame she tended to live up to the serious image expected of one of the pillars of her profession.

At the age of thirty she was engaged by Ellen Terry to tour the music-halls at the time when variety bills included dramatic sketches or ballets starring Pavlova, Karsavina or Genée, in addition to the usual singers, conjurers, trapeze artists, paper-tearers and performing sea-lions. To Ellen Terry's Mistress Page, she played Mistress Ford in the Basket Scene from *The Merry Wives of Windsor*, with Roy Byford as Falstaff, and Nerissa in the Trial Scene from *The Merchant of Venice*. From Ellen Terry she learned the importance of stage appearance, of paying infinite detail to facial make-up, to the wearing of costume and the manner of making an entrance. Ellen Terry impressed upon her just how much an actor's stage presence can convey to the audience about the character he is playing before he opens his mouth. Ellen Terry perceived in this young woman of thirty, only too eager to learn from her experienced elders, the makings of a great actress. When they parted company at the end of the tour she inscribed a book to Edith Evans as a girl after her own heart.

Soon after the music-hall tour Edith Evans scored a spectacular personal success in *The Laughing Lady* by Sutro, presented by the Stage Society, but she turned down the opportunity of creating the part of the Duchess in Somerset Maugham's *Our Betters* because she was determined not to go on being type-cast in 'silly Society parts'. It was played by Constance Collier. Edith Evans wisely went to the Birmingham Repertory Theatre when Cedric Hardwicke and Gwen Ffrangcon-Davies were in the company under the inspiring direction of Sir Barry Jackson. Nigel Playfair saw her as the Serpent in *Back to Methuselah* and invited her to play what turned out to be an unforgettable Millamant in *The Way of The World* at the Lyric Theatre, Hammersmith. Basil Dean cast her as Helena in his spectacular Drury Lane production of *A Midsummer Night's Dream*, but this only served to make Edith Evans dissatisfied with her Shakespearean technique and she decided she would like to spend a year at the Old Vic.

By this time, as George Howe observed, the profession was beginning to be influenced by Stanislavsky, Michel Saint-Denis, Barry Jackson and Komisarjevsky. The Bensonian actress Dorothy Green had already given evidence of trying to break away from the old-fashioned hammy Shakespeare acting. There was more general co-operation between all the artists engaged upon a production. Directors were less likely to dictate to actors and force them to play parts against their instinct. A little later when Gielgud turned to direction he used to ask members of the cast to sit in front at rehearsals and make suggestions upon which he often acted. If Edith Evans did not feel happy about instructions she received from a director, long before the days she reached stardom, she would immediately protest, 'I don't feel that!'

Sybil Thorndike and Edith Evans met about 1918 and never lost touch throughout their careers. Sybil first saw Edith on the stage in a play by Gwen John and she went home to her husband, Lewis Casson, to tell him, 'I've seen the most wonderful actress. She's not what ordinary people call beautiful, but she's absolutely marvellous.' At a time when Sybil was appearing at the London Pavilion in support of Léon Morton, the French clown who had come over to this country with Delysia, Edith Evans presented herself at the stage door. Having been told Sybil had seen her work and praised it, she wondered if Sybil would give her a letter of introduction to Lilian Baylis, in the hope of getting into the Old Vic company. The ever-generous Sybil naturally granted the younger actress's request.

A day or two later Sybil received a furious phone call from Lilian Baylis. 'How dare you send me such an ugly woman!' That was in the days when every actress was expected to be reasonably easy on the eye and Edith did not conform to the conventional idea of a leading lady. She eventually joined the Old Vic in 1925 to play a large number of parts including Portia, the Shrew, Mariana, Cleopatra, Mistress Page, Kate Hardcastle, Beatrice, Rosalind and the Nurse in *Romeo and Juliet*. 'But she had to fight every step of the way in all her long years at the Vic,' concluded Dame Sybil many, many years later.

Edith Evans could mesmerise audiences into thinking her a beauty. James Agate said that when she walked on to a stage she could assume beauty just as a woman draws on a glove. No one was more conscious of her plain face than Edith Evans. In that famous television interview with Bryan Forbes she admitted she had never played a part which depended entirely upon physical beauty. 'You can assume beauty. You kid yourself.' She kidded us, too. When she created Lady Pitts in James Bridie's *Daphne Laureola* at the age of sixty-one she made a shattering impact as a symbol of dazzling beauty.

Stanley Hall, founder of Wig Creations, which has been a household word in the theatre for generations, was called in to assist Dame Edith when she was cast for the part. She was ideal in every way, except visually; in the play she was the glorious lady in the mind of a young Pole, played by Peter Finch, then a newcomer to the London stage. She filled his mind with wonder and he worshipped her as a goddess. Edith Evans, a Dame of two years' standing, faced the biggest challenge of her career and Stanley Hall helped her to solve her problem. He was most impressed by the glamour of Mae West, at that time appearing in London as Diamond Lil in her own play of that name. He was fascinated by her use of mauve make-up and the mauve spot which followed her round the stage, encircling her in a cone of flattering light. He did not go as far as drenching Dame Edith in lilac light, but he realised her hair was the first factor to be considered. He chose a coiffure which was so becoming Dame Edith used the same style in her private life for some years afterwards. She created a sensation in the first act, seated silently in a Soho restaurant drinking brandy from a balloon glass while people at surrounding tables babbled away noisily. Suddenly Dame Edith electrified the house by bursting into song – Massenet's 'Elégie'. After that, one felt nothing was beyond her power.

When I saw Dame Edith as Lady Pitts I remembered Sybil Thorndike's observation, 'I never associated Edith with any particular part, but I have been a lifelong admirer and can honestly say that whenever I see her on the stage she invariably gives me a surprise. When she decides to play a part, she thinks about the character's origin and tries to imagine everything about her. She pounces on scraps of dialogue for clues and enlarges upon them and sees quite vividly the previous life of the character and what happens to her when she is not actually in view of the audience.'

On the other hand, Dame Edith says of Sybil, 'We couldn't be more different. Now I have no relatives and whenever I see her I wish I were more like her.' They were both in New York in 1934 when Edith's husband died in England. Edith was playing the Nurse to Katherine Cornell's Juliet and Sybil was in *The Distaff Side* by John Van Druten. Sybil went over to Edith's hotel to be with her in her darkest hour. New York was totally fog-bound, which meant Edith's sailing was cancelled, causing a frustration which only intensified her grief.

Dame Edith put another log on the bonfire on the hearth and I guided the conversation towards the great roles she had played during her stage career of more than sixty years. Before I had a chance to murmur the name of Oscar Wilde, she stepped in. 'I cannot stand Lady Bracknell and never want to hear her name mentioned again.' I gather the handbag line is to Dame Edith what the Prelude in C sharp minor was to Rachmaninov, the Dying Swan to Pavlova and Burlington Bertie to Ella Shields – something she has to live with for the rest of her life; a label stuck to her for ever. George Howe, who had played in *The Importance of Being Earnest* with Dame Edith, considered her Lady Bracknell a *tour de force*, a contrived performance. 'With a large hat and veil she saw herself as an Edwardian lady. She cleverly discovered the right voice, which she slightly exaggerated and the rest came easily to her.'

John Gielgud has interesting observations to make concerning Dame Edith's Lady Bracknell. He was with her one evening, together with some other friends, when she took a copy of *The Importance of Being Earnest* from the bookshelf and read some of Lady Bracknell's lines. 'I was in fits,' he cried, 'and decided she must be seen in the part. When I directed *The Importance* at the Globe in 1939, she was naturally cast as Lady Bracknell. Her performance was rather like a Rowlandson cartoon, whereas I think Rose Leclercq, the original Lady Bracknell, must have played it straight. Edith thought Lady Bracknell the sort of woman who would ring for the servants when she wanted a piece of coal put on the fire – and she played it accordingly. In time she got tired of her, complaining she was wasting her time playing a part for which she was ten years too young. She preferred her 'Lovelies', as she called them – Millamant and Mrs Sullen, and resented the 'Monsters' – Agatha Payne in *The Old Ladies* and the She Ancient in *Back to Methuselah*.'

In all the parts she played, Sir John noted Dame Edith never moved on the stage unless she had to. She conveyed extraordinary effects by moving her neck in the most remarkable and telling manner. She could also characterise her hands in the most uncanny fashion. She had lovely hands when she played Millamant, but could assume thick, rather common hands when playing working-class types, such as Gwenny in *The Late Christopher Bean*.

Dame Edith considers her greatest contribution to the theatre lay in the eighteenth-century classics – Mrs Sullen in *The Beaux' Stratagem*, Millamant in *The Way of The World* and Lady Fidget in *The Country Wife*. The gaiety and fun of these comedies appealed to her. Rosalind she considered very rewarding. She was forty-nine at the time and being infatuated by the twenty-nine-year-old Michael Redgrave who was her Orlando her performance acquired a remarkable joyousness. He had the same effect upon her career as Nureyev had upon the older Fonteyn when he first danced with her.

Only one part was ever written specially for Edith Evans, the Lady in *The Millionairess*, a play which Shaw dedicated to her. She played it in the North during the Second World War, but never in London. Sybil Thorndike says, 'Edith is the greatest actress we've got. The only thing I regret is that she won't play Lady Macbeth. She doesn't really like to play evil and doesn't think of it as a catharsis as I do.' Dame Edith refuses to play Lady Macbeth because she considers the part only half written. 'She is top dog. Then there is a jump and you see she has fallen. What you don't see is her falling from power, which to me would be the most interesting part of her life – from the acting point of view.' That is her real reason for refusing to play the part.

She also refused to play Shaw's Saint Joan because Sybil Thorndike had played it to perfection. 'She had religion,' explained Dame Edith. 'If I had played it after her it would have been no more of an achievement than assuming a cockney accent.'

Dame Edith crossed swords with Noël Coward when she played Judith Bliss in *Hay Fever* and refused to alter her way of rehearsing the part, just to comply with his ideas. He liked to give the cast their parts a week before rehearsals started and expected them to be word-perfect on the first day. Dame Edith objected. 'You cannot have your lines ready when you don't know how those playing opposite you are going to say their lines to you. It would be like learning a piece of grammar.' So Dame Edith won the day and Coward was obliged to let her learn her part in her own way. He had similar trouble with Gladys Cooper in *Relative Values*. She had always learned her lines during rehearsal as the play took shape. 'It may be old-fashioned,' she retorted, 'but I'm an old-fashioned actress.' They compromised. Gladys Cooper agreed to rehearse for a week on approval and call it a day if things did not work out. It so happened that throughout her career she had always taken a long time to learn her lines and usually took a week after the opening night to settle down into a part. This gave Coward the opportunity to remark on the first night of *Relative Values*, 'I don't insist upon actors being word-perfect at the first rehearsal, but I do expect it by the first night.'

Gladys Cooper's beauty was something Edith Evans never forgot. They were the same age and Dame Edith 'nearly went mad' when she saw Gladys Cooper for the first time at the age of twenty-four. 'She had a complexion like a wild rose and you must remember that people used very little make-up in those days. As I could not resist staring at her, she must have thought me rather peculiar.'

Looking back on her own career, Dame Edith admits she has no unfulfilled ambitions. 'Nothing niggles within me saying "I'd have been wonderful in such and such a part!" ' After all, she was so wonderful in so many. George Howe, having been in the same production of *Romeo and Juliet*, considers the Nurse her greatest achievement. Like her Millamant it was a great classical performance. She took infinite pains in her study of the part until she acquired what she considered the perfect way of delivering each line. Then she retained it which meant her performance never really varied. 'Whenever I think of the Nurse,' recalls George Howe, 'I still hear Edith's voice. When she played it she was oblivious of everything and everybody except the Nurse. In other words she lived the part. She was not dependent upon the audience, as she was when playing Millamant in *The Way of The World*, where the audience is part of the make-up of the play.'

John Gielgud in his *Early Stages* records his impressions of Dame Edith as the temperamental Arkadina in Komisarjevsky's production of *The Seagull* at the New Theatre in 1936, when Peggy Ashcroft played Nina and Gielgud was Trigorin.

'Edith dressed the part like a Parisian, with a high, elegant coiffure, sweeping, fashionable dresses, hats and scarves and parasols, but one could see from the angle of her head, as she sat with her back to the audience watching Konstantin's play, that underneath all the sweetness she was a selfish woman in a bad temper. Her performance was full of the most subtle touches of comedy, alternating with passages of romantic nostalgia, as when she listened to the music across the lake in the first act.'

There was a more wonderful moment to come. Gielgud reminds us of Trigorin deciding to run off with Nina. As they hear Arkadina approach, Nina quickly slips away. Edith made her entrance in time to realise Nina had been with Trigorin. 'Her scornful look after the retreating figure, the weary harassed manner in which she sank into a chair, suggested all that had happened to Arkadina since the second act . . . her fear of losing her lover, her jealousy of the young girl, her weariness with the details of running a house and packing to leave it, her perfunctory affection for her old brother, her longing for attention and flattery, her dislike of being middle-aged.'

Summing up her dedication to her job, Gielgud wrote: 'Edith Evans is an intensely conscientious artist and would never dream of not taking her work with the utmost seriousness. She always comes fresh to the theatre and will not allow outside circumstances to lead her into giving a careless or slovenly performance.'

Another log went on the fire and Dame Edith began to talk about her method of working. 'I work like a painter. I tear away and tear

Marie Tempest sang *The Nightingale Song* in *The Tyrolean* in New York, 1891. *Photo: Falk, N.Y.*
Next page: Marie Tempest as Fanny Cavendish in *Theatre Royal*, based on the Barrymores, regarded as the American stage's Royal Family. *Photo: George Dallison*

Irene Vanbrugh and Lilian Braithwaite in *The Thief*, 1907

Violet Vanbrugh as Mistress Ford, Roy Byford as Falstaff and Irene Vanbrugh as Mistress Page in *The Merry Wives of Windsor* – Regent's Park Open Air Theatre, 1937. *Photo: London News Agency*

Irene Vanbrugh at home. *Photo: Gainsborough Studios*

op: George Howe as Chasuble, Edith Evans as Lady Bracknell and Margaret Rutherford as
liss Prism in the John Gielgud production of *The Importance of Being Earnest. Photo: Angus
McBean*

dith Evans in Anouilh's *Dear Antoine* – Chichester Festival Theatre, 1971. *Photo: John Timbers*

ft: Lilian Braithwaite in Ivor Novello's play *Party* at the Strand Theatre, 1932. *Photo: Janet
Jevons*

Esmé Church as the Duchess of York, Edith Evans as Queen Margaret and Elizabeth Sellars as Queen Elizabeth in RSC's *Richard III* – Stratford-on-Avon, 1961. *Photo: Royal Shakespeare Company Theatre Library*

away before *I* make up my m ind what I am g oing to do. I simplify a reject until I find the truth. I've always acted truthfully and never tricked an audience in my life. I must feel secure in what I am doing or I'm completely disrupted as far as work is concerned. If I had my life over again I'd ask for a large dose of physical and moral courage because I find it difficult to stand up to people who are my equals. I love acting and getting a part ready to be seen, but I'm not interested in talking about it.' Then with a sly smile she added, 'I'm not really enjoying talking to you!'

Years earlier Edith Evans had talked to me about playing Katerina in Rodney Ackland's adaptation of Dostoyevsky's *Crime and Punishment* and admitted she had never read the novel on which the play was based. Nor had she any intention of doing so before or during rehearsals. 'It is the first duty of the actress to play her author. It is his job to do the research and to create the stage character from the material in the novel and decide how it should be presented to the playgoer. If the actress started to research independently, she could easily get a totally different impression of the character which clashed with the playwright's and in no time she would be at loggerheads with the author and the producer at rehearsal. Furthermore, one should not presuppose that the playgoer has read the original novel. Everything must stand or fall by the script prepared for the stage.' From the point of view of the actor, plays which are adaptations have a certain disadvantage because people who go to see them after having read the novel have preconceived ideas about the characters and think the actors are 'wrong' if their interpretation is different.

Edith Evans has played Cleopatra, Sarah Jennings, Duchess of Marlborough, the Empress Josephine, Florence Nightingale and Katherine of Aragon – all women who actually lived and had a lot written about them, but she never went to the British Museum Reading Room to do research outside the scripts of the plays in which these ladies appeared. In her opinion there is no difference between playing a fictitious character and an historical one. She tackles Mrs Malaprop and Florence Nightingale in the same way. Both are simply creations of a dramatist as far as she is concerned. As an actress she considers it her business to discover what kind of a woman the dramatist has conceived and to play her to the best of her ability under the guidance of the producer. The fact that one woman actually lived and the other is only a figment of the imagination means nothing at all. The author's script is her gospel. She gave us Edith Evans's conception of Shakespeare's Cleopatra and not necessarily her own idea of Cleopatra, which could have been something very different. Being well read in history, Olivier considers Richard III to have been a reasonably good king, but he had to forget historical evidence when he played Shakespeare's arch-villain with such spectacular success.

Mrs Patrick Campbell held similar views. When she decided to play Anastasia in *The Matriarch* by G. B. Stern the author offered to take her to Hampstead and introduce her to the old lady who inspired the character in the play. Mrs Pat refused. The play had been written and that was good enough for her. She had no wish to confuse the impression she had acquired from the script.

After acting with Edith Evans on many occasions over the years, George Howe is convinced she has an instinct for doing the right thing. She is not analytical and cannot explain what she is doing, which may be one reason why she never gives advice and rarely praises fellow artists. She gets the right approach by instinct and in her case the right voice is essential to make the character real. It is always unmistakably Edith Evans, but not always identical. There is a world of difference between Lady Bracknell and the shabby old woman she played in the film of *The Whisperers*. She has a great feeling and affection for the sheer sound of words. During the War while dining at the Savoy Grill with George Howe, the waiter suggested as a sweet they try Prune Whip. The sound tickled Dame Edith's fancy. Years afterwards the words still provoked laughter and caused her to go on repeating the two words *ad infinitum*. She found something quite ludicrous in the mere sounds, like something in a nonsense rhyme.

On-stage Dame Edith is always in superb control. During a performance of *The Importance of Being Earnest* Margaret Rutherford as Miss Prism sat on a chair which collapsed. John Gielgud, Jack Hawkins and Gwen Ffrangcon-Davies, who were on-stage with Dame Edith at the time, started to giggle and their amusement was shared by the audience. When the curtain fell, they all incurred the displeasure of Dame Edith who said she was thoroughly ashamed of their lack of discipline. Her Lady Bracknell did not turn a hair during the catastrophe.

Being extraordinarily sensitive to atmosphere Dame Edith had to be informed of the slightest change which might occur on stage during the run of a play. *Waters of the Moon* ran for 835 performances at the Haymarket. If one of the actors wished to change the colour of his tie he had to go to Dame Edith's dressing room before the rise of the curtain so that she could see it and be prepared. Otherwise there was a danger that the change might 'throw her'. This play had such a long run the management decided the leading ladies, Dame Edith, Dame Sybil and Wendy Hiller should be newly dressed after the first year to bring them more up to date. Dame Edith refused. She was attached to her original clothes and considered a change might affect her performance, even though Balmain was at her disposal to replace the dresses she had worn since the first night.

Long runs never distress Dame Edith and she has no fears of feeling jaded. 'Though the script is the same every night,' she observed, 'there is little resemblance between the hundreds of different audiences. It is the same course but a different horse.' Change of temperature affects her far more than change of audience. Extreme heat or extreme cold makes concentration more difficult. She had to make a special effort to keep alert on hot summer nights during the run of *The Chalk Garden* at the Haymarket, where the heat caused by the stage lighting was unusually intense in John Gielgud's production of Enid Bagnold's play.

Shaw was one of the great theatre figures we discussed that afternoon by the fire. She recalled rehearsing a Shaw play under his direction at the Royal Court Theatre in Sloane Square. Having played a particular scene with uncanny skill and understanding of the author's intention, he leapt on to the stage and kissed her in gratitude. 'I think I can claim to be the first if not the only actress to have been kissed by Shaw at rehearsal. But it was too brief to be enjoyable!' She was not so happy about another author at rehearsal. Though John Gielgud was responsible for the direction of *The Chalk Garden* at the Haymarket, the author Enid Bagnold insisted upon making endless notes only a yard or two from Dame Edith, who was struggling to create the leading character of Mrs St Maugham.

Dame Edith has kept abreast with the times and enjoys working in television. She insists upon meeting the director before she starts work in the studio. She likes to ask him to tea and get to know him. She welcomes being guided in this comparatively strange medium, but flatly refuses to be ordered about by someone she has never seen before. She contends some of the brash young television directors could learn much from the more subtle approach employed by Sir Charles Hawtrey in Dame Edith's younger days. 'He knew how to make actresses feel marvellous at rehearsal. I was a great lump of a person, but as he passed me he might murmur "Adorable!" He knew how to get the best out of actors and I'd have done anything for him.'

'I'm not interested in writing my autobiography. I've led a very full life and observed many different people in all sorts of interesting situations, which is one reason why I'm a good actress. But there is not much point in passing it on.' So, it looks as if we'll never read Dame Edith on herself, but it is a consolation to know so much of her work has been preserved on film and record and that we can meet her in her own home whenever Bryan Forbes' vivid documentary is revived on television.

* * *

Quite a number of topics were discussed before I departed from her Tudor home, and as she waved me goodbye from the kitchen door at the back of her house, I imagined it was her intention to arrange a chump chop on a floor of onions or mix a bread and butter pudding for dinner as soon as I was gone, while William emptied the tea leaves from the silver hot water jug.

Peggy Ashcroft 1907–

For a quarter of a century Peggy Ashcroft has lived in a house hidden by trees on the fringe of Hampstead Heath. Virginia creeper cascades over the porch, providing a curtain which has to be parted before you reach the front door to enter the house. Dame Peggy's home is much larger, of course, but it suggests Giselle's cottage, half-buried by romantic foliage in its own mysterious corner of the wood. When you enter the sitting room your attention is immediately drawn to a striking Sickert portrait of the actress holidaying in Venice. Wearing a summer dress, she stands in profile on the Accademia Bridge, spanning the Grand Canal at its mouth, with the impressive dome of Santa Maria Della Salute dominating the background.

Peggy Ashcroft now belongs to Hampstead, but she was born south of the river in Croydon where a theatre has since been built, proudly bearing her name. She went to Woodford School, where she became a close friend of a girl a year her senior, who was later to make her name in the theatre as Diana Wynyard. The headmistress at Woodford School was theatre-minded and productions of plays figured largely in the school activities. Peggy played Portia at the age of twelve and later teamed up with Diana Wynyard. Together they appeared as Shylock and Portia, Henry V and Katherine, Marchbanks and Candida and Brutus and Cassius.

Their playing of Brutus and Cassius in the Tent Scene from *Julius Caesar* was quite celebrated. It became a sort of party piece which they performed on gala occasions for their friends or at rather special theatrical charity galas, long after they had become established leading ladies in London. To the delight of all who saw them, they would play the scene just as they did in their school days wearing gymslips. It was a real collector's piece for playgoers, but comparatively few had the good fortune to see it. The school's theatre activities fired Peggy's imagination and she wanted to know more and more about the exciting world of the stage.

Irving and Ellen Terry did such wonderful things at the Lyceum during the last twenty years of the nineteenth century and Peggy read every book she could lay hands on in an attempt to visualise those magnetic players who dominated the most magnificent stage pictures. She was not only interested in the past; she read all Shaw's Prefaces and began to formulate her own ideas about theatre. She thought the best results could be obtained from a group of serious players working together as a permanent company. She thought about going on the stage, but in a very serious way. She was stagestruck, but not stupidly so. She had no desire to appear in trifling plays and have stage-door johnnies wanting to drink champagne from her court shoes. She just wanted to become an actress, but essentially a good one. She was prepared to devote all her energy, her thought and her ambition to becoming an actress and to do something worth while on the stage. There was no question of wanting to be a celebrity. Even in those days she had no desire to be pointed out as a famous actress, any more than she has today.

By the time Peggy Ashcroft wanted to go on the stage, her father had been killed in the First World War and there were no theatre connections in her family. Her mother had been a keen amateur – so keen she had studied elocution with Elsie Fogerty and would like to have gone on the stage, but her parents disapproved of their daughter becoming an actress. When, in turn, Peggy expressed a desire to become an actress, her mother had doubts but she gave Peggy permission at the age of sixteen to leave school and go to Elsie Fogerty who had by that time founded the Central School of Speech Training at the Albert Hall. Unfortunately, Mrs Ashcroft died two years later and did not live to see Peggy's professional stage début.

Peggy was not concerned about getting her name in lights through playing in popular drawing room plays of the Gerald du Maurier genre. She was mainly interested in the theatre of the classics. Her dream was to belong to a permanent company, like Irving's troupe at the Lyceum, which at the time Peggy Ashcroft was starting, was the nearest thing this country had ever had to a permanent company. There were only a few repertory theatres – Liverpool and Birmingham being the most famous. The Shakespeare Memorial Theatre at Stratford-upon-Avon, as the Royal Shakespeare Theatre was then called, and the Old Vic under Lilian Baylis in the Waterloo Road, were only seasonal. The outlook was not very promising for a young actress with ideals as high as Peggy Ashcroft's.

'Today's theatre is more like the ideal actor's world I used to dream about,' remarked Dame Peggy. 'There have been vast changes for the better in the last fifty years. We owe a lot to John Gielgud. He helped to make us aware of the value of recruiting a permanent company through frequently engaging the same artists for his seasons at the New and the Queen's in the 1930s. Although there was no such thing as a group called the Gielgud Company, he often used Edith Evans, Gwen Ffrangcon-Davies, Harry Andrews, Glen Byam Shaw, George Howe, Alec Guinness and me in his productions and we benefited enormously from playing together time and time again in so many different types of production. Gielgud was responsible for reviving such classics as *Hamlet, Romeo and Juliet, The Seagull, Richard II, The School for Scandal, The Three Sisters, The Merchant of Venice* and *The Importance of Being Earnest.* And then there was *Richard of Bordeaux, Spring 1600, He Was Born Gay, Noah, Queen of Scots* and *The Old Ladies,* for which he drew on a pool of actors whose work he trusted and admired. Through appearing together so frequently our ensemble work was something rather special and there was no question of fighting for star positions. We were just good actors, rather proud of the quality of our work.'

Since Dame Peggy got her first job much has happened. The National Theatre has been established as a permanent company. In her teenage years it was being discussed at meetings and written about by Shaw and Granville Barker and many thought it would never see the light of day. Now the Royal Shakespeare company plays most of the year at Stratford-upon-Avon with ranks large enough and powerful enough to split up into two or three companies, capable of being seen at Stratford, the Aldwych Theatre in London and overseas simultaneously. In Dame Peggy's early days, Stratford just had a spring to summer season and there were years when the standard was so low, actors accepted engagements only at the Shakespeare Memorial Theatre when every other promise of work had collapsed. It was a last resort to keep the wolf from the door. After the Second World War George Devine sowed wonderful seeds at the Royal Court Theatre in Sloane Square, where the English Stage Company flourishes, offering chances to splendid new writers who could not hope to interest commercial managements in Shaftesbury Avenue. The Arts Council has been a godsend to the repertory movement. Apart from Liverpool and Birmingham, the repertory bastions of Dame Peggy's early years, magnificent work is now being done at Bristol, Nottingham, Exeter and many other regional centres which could not survive without their Arts Council grants. William Poel and Granville Barker were the theatre scholars of the past and they have been succeeded by George Rylands at Cambridge, where his work influenced Peter Hall, Peter Wood and Trevor Nunn with far-reaching beneficial results. So we owe a great debt to the universities and Dame Peggy, in her comparatively short lifetime in the theatre, can look back on a revolution which has brought about sweeping changes for the better, changes which would have been unthinkable in the 1920s.

It was the Birmingham Repertory Theatre which gave Peggy Ashcroft her first job at the age of nineteen, as Margaret in Barrie's *Dear Brutus*. Sir Barry Jackson was presenting a revival and during the run Muriel Hewitt, the actress playing Margaret, was taken ill. He contacted Elsie Fogerty to help him out. He knew she had mounted a student production and asked if he could have the girl who had played the same part. That was how Peggy Ashcroft made her professional début, in a cast which included Ralph Richardson as Dearth and Edward Chapman as Mr Purdie. It was a whirlwind engagement which left her rather dismayed in discovering how little she really knew about the stage. Two years later – in 1928 – she toured with Lilian Braithwaite in *The Silver Cord* after the London run. The star's performance was fixed, as Lilian Braithwaite had made an enormous success in the West End as the possessive mother, so Peggy Ashcroft as a modest newcomer to the cast had little more to do than dovetail her performance into the existing mould. Lilian Braithwaite was kind to her, but there was such a vast gap between their positions in the company she had no personal contact with her.

Matheson Lang appeared in *Jew Süss*, an adaptation by Ashley Dukes of the Lion Feuchtwanger romance, and this gave Peggy Ashcroft the opportunity to make a most auspicious West End début as the tragic Naomi, the Jew's innocent daughter who leaps from the roof of her father's house. The twenty-two-year-old actress made a deep impression on the critics and on the playgoing public.

A year later came Desdemona, to Paul Robeson's Othello at the Savoy Theatre. The production was a catastrophe. Maurice Brown, the American actor, who had made a fortune out of presenting *Journey's End* in London, used some of the profits to realise his own ambition to play Iago, which was a disaster. Sybil Thorndike was a pillar of strength as Emilia and – just for the record – Andrew Cruickshank walked on with a spear. Peggy Ashcroft gave a lively and moving performance, but Paul Robeson had no ear for blank verse and failed to make the mighty impact expected of the Moor.

John Gielgud in his autobiography, *Early Stages*, was very disappointed with Paul Robeson, who had already appeared in London in *The Emperor Jones* and *Show Boat* and created a sensation as a singer of negro spirituals, 'but when Peggy came on in the Senate Scene it was as if all the lights in the theatre had suddenly gone up. Later in the Handkerchief Scene, I shall never forget her touching gaiety as she darted about the stage, utterly innocent and light-hearted, trying to coax and charm Othello from his angry questioning. Five years later he found the same quality of enchantment in her Juliet, which she was to play opposite his Romeo.

Peggy Ashcroft will never forget the wonderful co-operation she received from Sybil Thorndike when they played the Willow Scene before a front cloth during the Savoy Theatre production of *Othello*. During their scene stage hands were setting a three-ton bed in readiness for the final death scene. They used a rather noisy crane for the scene-change and Sybil feared the audience would not hear Peggy above the back-stage din. As Emilia, Sybil herself had a twenty-line speech at the end of the Willow Scene and she whispered to the stage hands, 'Don't start moving the bed until I begin my speech. I can shout you down.' And so Peggy had the advantage of being able to sing the Willow Song in complete silence.

Recently John Gielgud reminisced to me about Peggy. 'She creates a feeling of warmth in the company. Like Ellen Terry and Sybil Thorndike, she is a good influence and everyone adores her. There is a wonderful impetuosity about her acting, as if she has never really grown up. When she played Juliet to my Romeo, she was like a calf and I half expected her to butt me playfully in the chest. I would like to have seen her play Lady Macbeth. She was so good as Hedda Gabler she would have made a wonderful Lady Macbeth. There was some talk of her doing it with Paul Scofield at one time, but nothing came of it, which was a pity.'

At the age of twenty-four, two years after her Desdemona at the Savoy Theatre, Peggy Ashcroft was leading lady at the Old Vic. The sort of career she had hoped for – that of a serious actress playing the great classic roles – came her way very early in her life. At that time, under the direction of Lilian Bayliss, the Old Vic company alternated between the Old Vic in Waterloo Road and the recently rebuilt Sadler's Wells Theatre in Islington. She appeared as Cleopatra in Shaw's *Caesar and Cleopatra*, with Malcolm Keen, Alastair Sim, Marius Goring, Anthony Quayle, Roger Livesey and William Fox in the cast. During the season she was also seen as Imogen, Portia, Juliet, Miranda, Kate Hardcastle and Lady Teazle and there is an enchanting Sickert painting of her as Rosalind putting the chain round the neck of Orlando, who was played by William Fox. Her Juliet had sheer magic through her absolute sincerity.

Harcourt Williams directed the Old Vic productions during her season and was quite captivated by her. 'Her insight and clear-headedness and her own particular technique, which demands absolute honesty and freedom from any suspicion of false sentiment, were invaluable. She does not know what it means to use "a trick". She has an eye for line and colour and instinctively rejects the commonplace. No wonder she made such lovely people of the parts she played.'

Peggy Ashcroft, at the time of her first Old Vic season, had fallen under the spell of Theodore Komisarjevsky, the famous Russian stage director and designer who was working in England. He was twenty-five years her senior. For a short time they were married and he exercised a great influence on her career. Komis, as he was known to his colleagues, produced plays and operas in Russia from 1907 until 1917 at his own theatre and in the theatre run by his sister, Vera Komisarjevskaya, who had created the part of Nina in *The Seagull* under the direction of Stanislavsky. After the Revolution Komis came to this country in 1919 and his productions of Chekhov plays at the little Barnes Theatre had tremendous influence on John Gielgud, to whom the Russian dramatist was revealed in a new light. Barnes made Chekhov popular in London and Komis emphasised the romantic quality of *Three Sisters*, which he dressed picturesquely some twenty years earlier than the author had intended.

At Stratford-upon-Avon Komisarjevsky directed *Macbeth* in 1933, much to the disgust of Ben Greet and other conservative Shakespeare scholars of the time. He followed it with *The Merry Wives of Windsor*, for which he designed a Viennese background, with fairies wearing lighted candles on their heads. The critics were finally won over by his Stratford production of *King Lear*. In London he directed *Escape Me Never* and Barrie's *The Boy David*, which both starred Elisabeth Bergner, then at the dizzy height of her stardom. Disappointed over the failure of *The Boy David* in London, Komisarjevsky left this country for America where he remained until his death eighteen years later.

Peggy Ashcroft admired him most of all as a teacher. She had imagined directors would teach her as they rehearsed their productions, but she was soon to discover how rarely that happened. Komisarjevsky was the great exception. He was the master who knew what he wanted and was able to show actors how to gain the effects he had in mind. He directed her at the Haymarket in *Take Two From One*, the farce by Gregorio and Maria Martinez Sierra, in the English version by Harley and Helen Granville-Barker, Gertrude Lawrence was the star and Margaret Vines, Nicholas Hannen and H. G. Stoker were also in the cast. Komis did not direct her in Shakespeare, but he gave her notes and coached her privately for all the parts she played during her first Old Vic season.

Later, in 1936 she played Nina in *The Seagull* under his direction at the New Theatre, with Edith Evans as Arkadina, Gielgud as Trigorin and Alec Guinness in the small part of a workman. Gielgud recalls Peggy Ashcroft sitting in the wings with a shawl over her head. 'She would slip noiselessly into her place in the corner, where she would sit alone all through the last act, working herself up for her entrance in the big hysterical scene at the end of the play.' Komis directed *The Seagull* in such a way that the audience were aware that there was a funny side as well as a sad one to Chekhov's world and in consequence Peggy Ashcroft's Nina had an enchanting gaiety.

'Actors love Chekhov,' observed Peggy Ashcroft, recalling Nina. 'They are fascinated by the detail in his human beings, by their truth and by the interplay of character. There are times when I think Chekhov's plays are almost too frequently performed, as are Shakespeare's. On the other hand, young actors naturally want to play Chekhov and there is always the younger generation waiting to see his plays on the stage.'

Peggy Ashcroft saw all the Komisarjevsky productions at Stratford-upon-Avon. She felt he was ahead of his time, as Peter Brook is today, and on that account he shocked the critics who were frequently astonished by his unusual ideas of stage design. Peggy Ashcroft looks upon him as a link in a chain of great men in the theatre – men like William Poel, Harley Granville Barker, Michel Saint-Denis – who made the way for Peter Hall and Peter Brook. Komisarjevsky had only one week to rehearse his Stratford productions, but he was working with actors who knew their Shakespeare backwards or he could never have done what he did. Peter Hall had weeks to work on his productions at Stratford.

'In my time,' observed Dame Peggy, 'the relationship between player and director has changed. When I first went on the stage actors were awed by directors and took instruction without question. Now even small-part players are allowed to express opinions and, what is more, their views are listened to by those in authority. Actors, in consequence, know what they are doing and why they are doing it, which leads to more sensitive interpretations of plays and to delicately adjusted ensemble playing.'

By the early 1930s Peggy Ashcroft had served her apprenticeship under some of the finest directors and with some of the most experienced players on the London stage and mercifully for her she had managed to by-pass the fashionable Gerald du Maurier drawing room plays for which she had no time. She was about to captivate London with her Juliet, directed by John Gielgud at the New Theatre in 1935. Olivier opened as Romeo and then alternated Mercutio and Romeo with Gielgud. Four years earlier Peggy Ashcroft had played Juliet with Edith Evans as the Nurse in John Gielgud's first-ever production for the Oxford University Dramatic Society, when the two actresses joined an otherwise amateur cast. So they were ready for the London production, staged in ideal circumstances, with an array of splendid colleagues – Glen Byam Shaw, Harry Andrews and George Howe – and ingenious and attractive designs by Motley.

Peggy Ashcroft made a tremendous impact on the critics with her Juliet. Darlington hailed her as the finest as well as the sweetest Juliet of our time. Agate referred to her childish freshness and Peter Fleming said she did more than make Shakespeare's expression of Juliet's thoughts seem natural – she made them seem inevitable. She made Juliet realistic and she moved exquisitely without being balletic.

For an actress who wanted to go on the stage to play the classics Peggy Ashcroft had a rewarding ten years. In the Gielgud season at the Queen's she played the Queen to his Richard II. She played Irina in the Michel Saint-Denis production of *Three Sisters*, with Carol Goodner as Masha and Gwen Ffrangcon-Davies as Olga; she played Portia to Gielgud's Shylock and was Viola in Michel Saint-Denis' *Twelfth Night* at the Phoenix Theatre. Just before the War she was seen as Cecily in Gielgud's production of *The Importance of Being Earnest* at the Globe Theatre, with Gwen Ffrangcon-Davies as Gwendolen, Edith Evans as Lady Bracknell, Margaret Rutherford as Miss Prism, George Howe as Chasuble, Jack Hawkins as Algernon and Gielgud as John Worthing. During Gielgud's 1944–45 Haymarket season she played Ophelia to his Hamlet, Titania to his Oberon and the Duchess of Malfi to his Ferdinand. Then came Evelyn Holt in *Edward My Son* by Robert Morley and Noel Langley. Peggy Ashcroft was forty and the part marked a turning point in her career.

It was the first time she had played a so-called character part. All her previous parts were straight *ingénues*. The part covered the period from 1919 to 1947 which meant that Evelyn Holt was younger than Peggy Ashcroft when the play opened and older when it closed. Robert Morley played her husband Arnold Holt, a self-made man whose great obsession was his worthless son Edward, who never appeared during the course of the action. His father's worldly ambition, particularly on behalf of his son destroyed his wife who looked on helplessly while the boy was ruined by the indulgence of his doting and unscrupulous father. Peggy Ashcroft was youthful and sweet in the earlier scenes, but tragically alone and cast down at the end, by which time her son had become a loathsome creature. Evelyn Holt was a study of Everywoman, the tragedy of a likeable soul rewarded with a worthless son and an unsuccessful marriage. After she had become a maudlin old woman with thick speech and dyed hair there was a final but fruitless attempt to drown her bitterness in drink.

I met Peggy Ashcroft for the first time when I interviewed her in her dressing room at His Majesty's Theatre, after being shattered by the impact of her realistic performance as Evelyn Holt and we naturally discussed actor-authors, as the actor Robert Morley was part-author of *Edward My Son*, as well as the leading man. Rehearsals tended to become a theatre workshop, as Robert Morley was naturally present at all of them. Material, lines and situations could be changed in an instant to get the best possible results from a theatrical point of view.

'Actor-authors are apt to be more tolerant than dramatists who merely write and have little or no first-hand working knowledge of the theatre,' she said. 'Actor-authors invariably permit a change. They naturally see the actor's point of view and are more elastic as writers. They know the difficulties of an actor's job and as a rule refrain from writing parts beyond the scope of the player.' There are two sides to the coin and Dame Peggy is of the opinion that actors should not be allowed to change the script whenever they encounter a difficulty. It is bad for them always to have their own way. It is the line of least resistance. The real actor must face up to his problems and try to find a way of solving them by means of his craft. Speaking generally, Dame Peggy believes plays by actor-authors are not as well constructed as those by writers with no connection with the acting profession. They are often good theatre, but hardly exist outside performance. As writers, actors realise the value of stage business, which is why people like Emlyn Williams and Noël Coward offer remarkable scope to their minor players.

The year after Evelyn Holt Peggy Ashcroft gave another memorable performance, as Catherine Sloper in *The Heiress*, a dramatisation of *Washington Square* by Henry James at the Haymarket. It was the first time in her career she had played a plain unloved heroine, a disappointment to her father and an embarrassment to her friends on account of her gauche, hypersensitive behaviour. 'Someone must love me,' she sobbed at one point in the play. The character was meant to be unattractive and unsympathetic and so gained the sympathy of the audience who could not resist Peggy Ashcroft's conception of the Ugly Duckling. She had magnificent co-operation from Ralph Richardson as her father and Donald Sinden as the young man who let her down.

Peggy Ashcroft went back to the Old Vic, when the bomb-damaged theatre opened after the Second World War to play Viola in *Twelfth Night*, to the Malvolio of Paul Rogers and the Feste of Leo McKern. She also played Mistress Page to the Anne Page of Dorothy Tutin in *The Merry Wives of Windsor*, but the great attraction of the season, as far as she was concerned, was the title role in *Electra*, the Sophocles tragedy translated by J. T. Sheppard and directed by Michel Saint-Denis at the Old Vic in 1951, with Robert Eddison as Orestes, Pauline Jameson as Chrysothemis, Catherine Lacey as Clytemnestra and Paul Rogers as Aegisthus. Even today Peggy Ashcroft regards this part as the most difficult she has ever played. It seemed like a female Hamlet and should give the impression of being as real and actual as a Shakespeare character. The long speeches and the construction of the play made heavy demands upon the actors and it was difficult to find a way of playing Greek tragedy which would be acceptable to contemporary audiences.

The following year she returned to the West End to play Hester Collyer in *The Deep Blue Sea* by Terence Rattigan. The author rang her to talk about the part over lunch. She did not fall in love with it at first sight, probably because she expected a light comedy to contrast with *Edward My Son* and *The Heiress*. Instead, she discovered Hester was a young woman who deserted her husband to fall unhappily in love with an ex-test pilot, memorably played by Kenneth More, incapable of an intensity of passion to match her own. After some persuasion she decided to play the part on realising *The Deep Blue Sea* was a play of pity rather than a tragedy and the ending, with its note of hope, was not totally unhappy. Furthermore, all the characters were likeable people. Many playgoers consider Peggy Ashcroft's Hester Collyer one of her outstanding achievements and as a token of appreciation and gratitude Terence Rattigan presented her with the manuscript of the play.

Peggy Ashcroft first played in Ibsen in 1954, when she was seen as Hedda Gabler in Max Faber's adaptation of the play, directed by Peter Ashmore at the Lyric, Hammersmith, and later at the Westminster Theatre. 'One of the tops,' is how Dame Peggy describes this peak experience in her career. She had read Ibsen, but had been afraid to play him on the stage until she came across an essay by A. B. Walkley, in which he said Hedda Gabler was the sort of woman you might take in to dinner any night. In the light of this revelation she saw Hedda as a fascinating woman, but not a *femme fatale*. She is not theatrical like Magda, but an ordinary woman who becomes a monster as the result of being a victim of circumstances. This was just another example of Ibsen creating extraordinary characters out of ordinary people.

The company explored Ibsen together and all discovered the engagement a most rewarding experience. Dorothy Dewhurst appeared as Bertha, Susan Richmond as Miss Julie, George Devine as George Tesman, Rachel Kempson as Mrs Elvsted, Micheal MacLiammoir as Brack and Alan Badel as Eilert Lovborg. The production was notable for the comedy and they were invited to play at the New Theatre in Oslo in March 1955, in the presence of King Haakon. After the performance there was a knock on Peggy Ashcroft's dressing room door. 'Who's there?' she called. 'Mr Ibsen,' came the reply. There followed a split-second silence which had a supernatural quality about it. Then she realised Ibsen's grandson had called upon her. He congratulated her especially upon the comedy which she had managed to put across. He said the humour would have pleased his grandfather because he always wanted audiences to be amused by his characters, who were essentially ordinary people. Earlier actresses who had played Hedda had over-dramatised her and actors generally failed to appreciate the down-to-earth quality of Ibsen's characters.

After playing Hedda, Peggy Ashcroft went on to appear as Rebecca West in *Rosmersholm* at the Royal Court Theatre and later at the Comedy in 1959, with Eric Porter as Rosmer and later still in 1967 she played Mrs Alving in *Ghosts* at the Aldwych, with John Castle as Oswald. After Hedda Gabler and Rebecca West, Peggy Ashcroft was no longer surprised at Ibsen's popular appeal. When he wrote *Rosmersholm* he was interested in the works of the French psychologists, Charcot and Janet, who were Freud's masters and so his plays are full of psychological turmoil. The playgoer of today is naturally better able to appreciate Ibsen than his counterpart in the late nineteenth century. Ibsen appeals to audiences, in Peggy Ashcroft's opinion, because his stories are so good and he heightens the suspense so often by unfolding them backwards. She found Mrs Alving very depressing to play. 'Ghosts is an awfully cruel and painful play and Mrs Alving a terrible weight. Juliet and Cleopatra are tragic parts, but not so depressing to play as Mrs Alving.'

Peggy Ashcroft's own most rewarding theatrical experiences are not necessarily in the parts which were most popular with the public. She has no special affection for Miss Madrigal, the young woman who comes to the house of Mrs St Maugham in *The Chalk Garden*. Yet Dame Peggy gave a most moving performance opposite Dame Edith at the Haymarket. After mentioning the Juliet she played with Olivier and Gielgud alternating as Romeo and Mercutio, Peggy Ashcroft listed Irina in Chekhov's *Three Sisters*, directed by Michel Saint-Denis, and the Stratford-upon-Avon Cleopatra when Michael Redgrave played Antony in Glen Byam Shaw's production of *Antony and Cleopatra*, which later came to the Princes Theatre in London.

She adored playing the Shrew at the age of fifty-three to the Petruchio of Peter O'Toole, who was only twenty-eight, when the play was revived at Stratford-upon-Avon in 1960. The company was re-named the Royal Shakespeare Company in 1961 and Dame Peggy has been a long-contract player with them ever since and is also one of the directors. Glen Byam Shaw recalled her playing the Shrew with a Petruchio half her age, yet she managed to look younger than he did. 'She is so young at heart, she is any age. She is a most marvellous human being and a wonderful actress, with an extraordinary insight into human nature, being able to get to the heart of every character she plays, whether it be Juliet, Cleopatra or Hedda Gabler. Her range is quite fantastic. She has played more varied parts than any of the other actress-Dames, in Shakespeare, Ibsen and in modern plays, such as works by Pinter, Marguerite Duras and Edward Albee and she is not afraid to tackle unfamiliar parts in her sixties.' When they played together in their younger days, at the beginning of their careers, Glen Byam Shaw remembers Peggy Ashcroft often had problems with stage make-up. Dress parades at dress rehearsals were not always the happiest of occasions, which they both laugh about now. She was afraid of make-up because it seemed false to her and on that account the director – often John Gielgud – thought she could improve the visual impression she had managed to create. There would be floods of tears and Glen Byam Shaw was often sent along to her dressing room to offer suggestions. All ended well in the long run. Glen Byam Shaw has always admired the remarkable range of her voice, which has a thrilling deep tone, so effective in her Cleopatra.

Going back to the parts Peggy Ashcroft finds rewarding, she places Portia high on the list, not far removed from Hedda Gabler. She found Portia hard work when she played opposite John Gielgud's Shylock just before the Second World War. 'I enjoy comedy and there is something specially joyous and exhilarating about Portia. *The Merchant of Venice* is a wonderful story, a fairy tale in which we have to believe. It seems to survive being staged in all sorts of different periods, but I think it is at its best in an Elizabethan setting.' Dame Peggy is proud to have played Margaret of Anjou in *The Wars of the Roses*, the Royal Shakespeare Company trilogy consisting of *Henry VI*, *Edward IV* and *Richard III*. 'It is not so much a character as a great experience playing the same part through three Shakespeare plays, which were occasionally all played on the same day – morning, afternoon and evening. It was a unique achievement.' Beth in Pinter's *Landscape* is a modern part which Dame Peggy includes in her list of rewarding parts, though it is doubtful if her admirers would have placed it as high in her achievements as she does.

Discussing her appearance with John Gielgud in the 1955 Stratford production of *Much Ado About Nothing*, which had a successful season in London at the Palace Theatre, Ronald Hayman, Gielgud's biographer, thought her Beatrice was very much her own invention. It was like a development of her coltish Juliet, a very touching, truthful characterisation of a woman who is always putting her foot in it. She was an eccentric girl rather than a witty woman. She was happily partnered by John Gielgud as Benedick and said playing with him in *Much Ado* was like having a marvellous partner at a dance. Angela Baddeley was lost in admiration when she saw Peggy Ashcroft's performance and as an expression of admiration she gave Dame Peggy Ellen Terry's working copy of the play, in which the great actress had pencilled her own personal remarks and directions in the margin. With other precious possessions relating to her career, all carefully stored in an upstairs room of her Hampstead house, Dame Peggy prizes that copy of *Much Ado* more highly than anything else.

Peggy Ashcroft considers herself very lucky to be without an unfulfilled ambition in her career. She played all the parts she wanted to play and she is always ready to accept a new part from one of the up-to-the-minute dramatists, such as Duras, Albee or Pinter, even though such parts occasionally give more pleasure to her than the public. 'It is not a good thing to have plays specially written for a specific actor,' remarked Dame Peggy. 'It is the actor's job to go to the part and not for the part to come to the actor.' Discussing the impression a player makes when creating a character on stage, Dame Peggy is of the opinion that wigs help tremendously to create the right stage picture, but what is most important of all is what comes from inside the performer.

She may have no unfulfilled ambition, but she is not without a real disappointment and that was at the Royal Court Theatre in 1956 when she played Shen Te in *The Good Woman of Setsuan* by Bertolt Brecht. Translated by Eric Bentley and directed by George Devine it was really the first Brecht play to be done by a major English company, having Robert Stephens, Joan Plowright, Esmé Percy, John Osborne, Rachel Kempson and Peter Wyngarde in the cast. It happened to coincide with the Suez Canal crisis and the invasion of Hungary. Because Brecht was a Communist there was a feeling against him in this country and the result was a decidedly antagonistic audience at the Royal Court Theatre, where the play did not get the favourable reception it might have received in more normal times.

Peggy Ashcroft believes a serious actress should be ready to play ordinary women, in addition to the Lady Macbeths, the Cleopatras and the Electras of the dramatic repertoire, which is one reason why she is prepared to play Pinter. In 1973 she appeared in a Pinter double-bill, consisting of *Landscape* and *A Slight Ache*. These plays did not cause great excitement at the few theatres where they were seen in this country, but Dame Peggy found the engagement most rewarding when the company crossed the Channel to visit Antwerp, Wiesbaden, Essen, Bonn, Amsterdam, The Hague and Rotterdam. 'Previously I had only played in Shakespeare and Ibsen before non-English audiences, but I was quite astonished at the reception given to the Pinter plays. The audience – or a large majority of them – had taken the trouble to read the plays in translation before coming to the theatre, so they were able to follow the dialogue intelligently and with keen interest. I doubt if we would have had the same response in France or Italy, where they are lazy about languages.' It was something of an eye-opener to discover foreign audiences following Pinter with more enthusiasm than English playgoers in Croydon, Bath, Brighton, Southampton and Bury St Edmunds, where the same production was presented.

The two-week season of the Pinter double-bill at the Ashcroft Theatre in Croydon, as part of the Croydon Arts Festival in April 1973, marked Dame Peggy's first appearance at the theatre named after her in her home town in 1962. On that occasion she spoke the prologue before the opening production staged at the theatre. It was an English translation of *Royal Gambit* by the German dramatist Hermann Gressieker and concerned Henry VIII and his six wives. Henry was played by Michael Denison, with Dulcie Gray as Katarina of Aragon. Ten years were to elapse before Peggy Ashcroft first played a part on that stage.

Peggy Ashcroft is content just to be an actress. She wants no fanfares, no red carpet and no adulation for working in the theatre. She has an assured position as one of the leaders of her profession and that is enough reward for her. She is highly efficient as far as her work is concerned and always gives a firm Yes or No to her colleagues. They know exactly where they stand. If she says No she means No; if she says Yes she means Yes and there is no doubt about her fulfilling commitments. Her word is enough. She shuns any form of artificially stimulated publicity and gains more than sufficient satisfaction from pursuing her work. She does not demand hero-worship.

Unlike some actresses, Dame Peggy is generous in praise of her colleagues whose work she genuinely admires, especially Edith Evans. She was her second understudy and had a one-line part in the 1927 revival of *The Beaux' Stratagem* at Wyndham's. 'Her Millamant in *The Way of the World* and Mrs Sullen in *The Beaux' Stratagem* knocked us all for six in those days and you feel there is no other actress to whom she can be compared. She is a wonderful person to work with. She has such wisdom about acting and I learned so much from her when she played the Nurse in *Romeo and Juliet*, Arkadina in *The Seagull* and Lady Bracknell in *The Importance of Being Earnest*. You feel those parts cannot be played any other way.'

Occasionally Dame Peggy deserts the more serious theatre for the commercial stage, as when she played Lady Boothroyd in William Douglas Home's entertaining after-dinner trifle, *Lloyd George Knew my Father* at the Savoy Theatre. With Ralph Richardson as her husband, she played the wife who threatened to take her life as a protest against a by-pass being built across the parkland of their stately home that dated back three centuries. She admitted such a part called for much harder work than playing the classics, but with her superlative skill she was able to transform mediocre lines into something that sounded like high comedy and she and Sir Ralph completely captivated the audience throughout the evening. She considered the part of the old mother in *Days in the Trees* by Marguerite Duras to be one of the most taxing parts she has ever played and it is the only occasion in her life she has not applied her own make-up for a part on the stage. An expert was called in, as happens in film and television studios.

Peggy Ashcroft made a hard and fast rule many years ago never to discuss her family with the Press. She realised while her children were still at school that they found it an embarrassment to be mentioned by their mother in the papers, so she never refers to them in the presence of journalists. No one is quite sure what they do or where they are. She did on one occasion tell me her son was in Vancouver, but when she went to Canada to see him she used her married name throughout the trip, so no one at airports or hotel reception desks realised they were dealing with one of the most famous actresses in the world. There was no question of attracting attention or giving interviews. This is genuine modesty on her part and not a sort of Garbo 'I-Want-To-Be-Alone' stunt, which provided the film star with more publicity than any other actress of her time. The same genuine modesty is reflected in other aspects of Peggy Ashcroft's personality.

'Which part would you most like to be remembered by?' I asked. With a genuine smile, free from all false modesty, she replied, 'I'd be happy to be remembered for any one part.'

Flora Robson 1902–

Of all the actress-Dames, Flora Robson must have gone through the toughest struggle to get a start in the theatre. All her life she has been fascinated by reading memoirs of famous stage players and always finds the beginning of each story the most interesting – to discover how actors who became great stars managed to make their first impression and get a firm foot on the bottom rung of the ladder. They all had one thing in common. They all started off without a name.

Dame Flora started off not only without a name but without any assets likely to give her a helping hand. She had no theatre connections and no one in the family had an influential friend capable of scribbling a useful note of introduction to open a door in the right quarter. Furthermore, she had no money, no looks and no idea about dress. She never understood how to make the best of herself and was totally incapable of making a favourable impression across an impresario's desk when called to an office to discuss the possibility of being cast for a part. Yet in spite of all these handicaps she managed to get to the top and was singled out to be honoured as a Dame.

She was born in South Shields, where her father was a marine engineer. He soon realised his daughter had an unusually musical speaking voice and taught her to recite. She made such a good impression while still quite a mite, he entered her for various competitions. At a hall in Enfield just before she was six she caused quite a stir by reciting *Little Orphan Annie* and her father proudly proclaimed her 'our next Ellen Terry'.

She attracted considerable attention in North London newspapers and her father never missed an opportunity of entering her for a competition. He would escort her to these contests, watch her with intense pride and encourage her with the right sort of constructive compliments on the way back home.

As a special treat when she was six years old he took her to His Majesty's Theatre in the Haymarket to see a highly spectacular production of *Faust*, in which handsome Henry Ainley played the name-part to the mighty Mephistopheles of Tree and the pure Margaret of Marie Löhr. The realistic stage pictures were so splendid and the voices of the leading players so glorious to listen to, little Flora decided she would like to spend all her life in the theatre – the only thing which held any real interest for her.

When she reached the age of seventeen she went to the Royal Academy of Dramatic Art. She was thrilled to be able to study the ABC of acting with so fine an actress as Helen Haye, who taught her the value of restraint, but it was Moffatt Johnston who made the deepest impression on the teenage girl. A Bensonian who had been wounded in the First World War, he was a highly versatile actor. He could play Caesar one night and be quite unrecognisable as Falstaff the next.

He provided Flora with the right approach. He believed some of the students would become stars when they left the Academy, but was certain most of the others would spend their entire lives as supporting players. At the same time he was quick to stress the importance of supporting actors because no star could shine brightly without their co-operation. He would have approved of Ellen Terry's burning desire to become a useful actress.

'If you make a success on the stage, don't get big-headed,' he urged his students. 'It simply means you are as good at your job as a reliable plumber is at his – but he does not expect a great fuss to be made of him. Actors are no different from other people and they should not take themselves too seriously outside the theatre.'

Flora had other problems at the Academy, apart from attending class. She was immediately aware that she did not look as attractive as the other girls. Her dresses were home-made, her hair was arranged in an unbecoming plait style and she used no make-up apart from an odd dab of powder. Knowing she was not pretty gave her a feeling of insecurity, especially when she saw other girls who knew how to wear a hat or dress with such style people gave them a second look. 'I've always looked silly in a hat,' said Flora only the other day, 'but some of the students at RADA looked as gorgeous as Gaiety Girls in millinery shapes picked up for a shilling or two, because they had a flair for trimming them and a knack of wearing them.'

She left the Academy with their Bronze Medal, but without an ounce of self-confidence and then faced the shattering ordeal of having to approach managers about jobs. She never overcame this fear. Even ten years later when she was thirty, Rudolphe Meyer interviewed her with the idea that she might play Prue Sarn, the girl with the hare-lip in *Precious Bane*. 'Can you look sixteen?' he asked her. 'I've never looked sixteen,' she replied, 'but I could act a girl of sixteen.' Mr Meyer remained unconvinced and played for safety by giving the part to Gwen Ffrangcon-Davies, who was thirty-six.

But much was to happen to Flora before she was turned down for Prue Sarn. By some sort of minor miracle she managed to get a one-line part as the ghost of Queen Margaret in Clemence Dane's *Will Shakespeare* at the old Shaftesbury Theatre, close to Cambridge Circus. She got only £3 a week, but a golden opportunity to rub shoulders with experienced players in a distinguished play. Under the direction of Basil Dean, who confesses Flora made no impression upon him at that time, the cast included Haidée Wright as Queen Elizabeth, Philip Merivale as Shakespeare, Moyna MacGill (mother of Angela Lansbury) as Anne Hathaway, Mary Clare as Mary Fitton, and Claud Raines as Kit Marlowe. Flora, as Queen Margaret, was one of the characters in Anne Hathaway's vision. The show ran for no more than sixty-two performances, but it provided the bottom rung of the ladder and was, after all, a Clemence Dane play, a Basil Dean production and a Shaftesbury Avenue attraction.

Like Sybil Thorndike before her, Flora Robson decided to join Ben Greet's Pastoral Players to get a good grounding in Shakespeare. They played a good deal in the open air on school and college lawns; the members of the company had to be capable of considerable versatility and prepared to endure the strolling player existence which goes hand in hand with one-night stands. There were twenty plays in the repertoire, which meant the company rehearsed all day, played at night and travelled at weekends. The staging had to be improvised, according to the rough and ready conditions they found when not playing in proper theatres. They often performed after a single rehearsal, but Flora had a good memory and was always word-perfect. Sir Philip Ben Greet, venerable white-haired veteran, was already in his twilight years, content with rather conventional, unimaginative productions. He had nothing but scorn for Komisarjevsky's Stratford *Macbeth*, with its daring aluminium scenery. Even so, Ben Greet's company rivalled that of Frank Benson as a training ground for young actors and Flora's time with him was not wasted at £3 a week.

A more wonderful opportunity presented itself in 1923 when she was accepted as a member of J. B. Fagan's repertory company at Oxford Playhouse. Reginald Denham directed most of the productions and Flora spent her time prompting, understudying and playing small parts, but her salary had risen to £5 a week. One of the actors in the company was young Tyrone Guthrie, who impressed Flora enormously and was to have a vital influence on her career in productions he later directed at the Old Vic and elsewhere. She will never forget his moving performance as the blind prophet in *Oedipus*. He looked like

John the Baptist and she thought he would have made a magnificent Lear.

Even to this day Flora Robson thinks some of her finest performances were given outside London. One of them was at Oxford as the unwanted woman in *The Return of the Prodigal* by St John Hankin. Faith Celli saw it and maintained Flora would have made her name in London on the strength of that performance alone. At the end of the second Oxford season her contract was not renewed. She knew she was a Plain Jane, but hoped the sheer force of her talent and personality would more than compensate for her lack of looks. The management had other views. They said undergraduates expected to see young actresses who were pretty and charming and so they engaged the exquisite Elissa Landi.

Leaving Oxford, which had been such a rewarding artistic experience, was a bitter blow to Flora, who went despairingly back to her family, then living in Welwyn Garden City. There she stayed without work and without any real hope of ever returning to the stage. She could not afford to live on theatre salary even if work had turned up because it had been impossible for her to accumulate any savings from her Oxford salary. So she had to look round for a job outside the theatre, something more financially rewarding which would enable her to make both ends meet.

The Shredded Wheat company at Welwyn Garden City offered her a position in their factory as welfare officer, a sort of liaison officer between the management and the workers. She took it and worked from eight in the morning until nine at night for the next four years. As it happened, they were not wasted years because they gave her a deep insight into people and she was much more capable of understanding human problems when she eventually returned to the theatre.

One of her assignments was taking visitors round the factory and shouting above the roar of the machinery, which provided a novel but useful form of vocal exercise.

More important was her contact with the staff in her role as social worker. She had to listen to their problems and help square pegs who found themselves in round holes. She discovered one man denied human contact because he worked a machine in what amounted to solitary confinement. It had the same effect upon him as being sent to Coventry. When Flora arranged a transfer and a different job with the firm his troubles were soon over. She discovered that girls who left were not replaced, so those left behind suffered from something akin to sweated labour conditions. That situation had to be ironed out with the management. She learned how to deal with toughs without bullying them and succeeded in reducing two or three of them to tears.

This experience stood her in good stead years later when she played Lady Cicely Waynflete in *Captain Brassbound's Conversion*, the lady whose charm could move mountains. As the Shredded Wheat workers had a drama society, Flora naturally directed their productions, which is one reason why she worked so late in the evenings. She was fortunate in discovering two electrically-minded members of the staff who created lovely stage pictures by making their own dimmers, wind machines and a wonderful contraption to give the effect of falling snow.

Then Tyrone Guthrie popped up again. He went to Welwyn Garden City to adjudicate an amateur drama festival and naturally looked up Flora. He told her he was going to the Cambridge Festival Theatre to direct plays for Anmer Hall, and if she would like to consider going back to the professional stage he would suggest her name. She leapt at the idea and a very much more mature young lady returned to the stage in 1929 for eighteen glorious months which paved the way for her first spectacular success in the West End.

Flora was much happier in Cambridge, where her lack of make-up and her home-made clothes were looked upon as a charming idiosyncrasy. She lived in a hostel adjoining the theatre. She rehearsed from ten till five; she performed in the evening and then went back to her room to study until about two in the morning. She played a lead one week and a maid the next, but she was happy working under Tyrone's Guthrie's direction and often opposite Robert Donat who once said to her, 'You're as easy to act with as breathing.'

She gained tremendous self-confidence at Cambridge. She remembers expressing her apprehension to a colleague just before a first night. The girl was amazed and asked, 'What have you got to be nervous about?' Equally surprised, Flora knew for the first time that she must be good. Once she had settled down, her father went to Cambridge to see her and said, 'You make them all look like apprentices, Flora.' She was *known* to the undergraduates and the effect upon her was highly beneficial. She was greeted by rowing men as she walked along the towpath. For the first time in her life she felt she belonged. Of all the many parts she played she considers the stepdaughter in *Six Characters in Search of an Author* the oustanding achievement of her Cambridge years.

Flora has always retained a great affection for provincial audiences. The people of Oxford and Cambridge helped her to learn her craft with their appreciative reaction and years later after the long London run of *The House by the Lake* she went on tour with the production, not because she had to but because she wanted to. Like Ellen Terry, she enjoyed taking theatre to drab towns where it gave so much pleasure. She feels tours are of inestimable value to beginners. All too often youngsters learn their job in minute repertory theatres. They should go out on the touring circuit and learn how to put across their lines in big theatres so that they are heard in the back row of the Gallery.

Peter Godfrey, one of the most brilliant and enterprising directors of the 1930s, saw Flora on the stage and engaged her to play Abbie in *Desire Under the Elms* by Eugene O'Neill at the Gate Theatre in Villiers Street, a stone's throw from Charing Cross. Like the popular Players' Theatre at the present time, the Gate was constructed out of one of the series of arches which runs parallel with Villiers Street to carry the Southern Railway from Charing Cross Station out across the Thames to the South Bank. The Gate was quite an intimate theatre, much smaller than the Players'.

Desire Under the Elms was a powerful play which gripped audiences to a remarkable degree, with Flora as a young wife who marries an elderly widowed farmer and then falls in love with the stepson. The stepson was brilliantly played by Eric Portman, a year younger than Flora, but with an impressive Old Vic career already behind him. Together they made a powerful impact on serious-minded playgoers. The Gate was a club theatre which meant the public at large did not go. Flora was getting £3 a week, but was thankful to have a shop window in London to show off a performance which won such high praise from discerning theatregoers, such as Lady Oxford – the legendary Margot Asquith – who invited Flora to her celebrated parties, where she met Margot's son, Anthony Asquith, the film director.

Christopher Casson was so moved by Flora's performance he insisted that his mother and father – Sybil Thorndike and Lewis Casson – go to see her. That arrestingly plain face gripped Sybil's attention from the moment she first saw it and she realised a new star was born. She went round after the show. 'Where did you learn to act like that?' she cried. Flora, concerned about the future, had written a letter a day to managers, asking them to come and see her working, but no one was interested. As Sybil Thorndike was about to revive *Saint Joan*, Flora took the opportunity of asking if she could understudy her. 'You are far too good for that,' was Sybil's firm reply.

Flora had to wait six months before her next big chance. That was Mary Paterson, a drunken Scots harlot in *The Anatomist*, James Bridie's play about Burke and Hare, the body-snatchers. The play was presented at the Westminster Theatre and drew large audiences. In effect, it made Flora's name. St John Ervine, the most influential critic of the day, wrote, 'Here is an actress. If you are not moved by this girl's performance, then you are immovable and have no right to be on this earth. Hell is your place.' Flora felt famous, but looking at life realistically, she had to face the fact that she was shabby, lacked style and glamour and was £12 in debt to the management at the end of the run. She had the great advantage of Tyrone Guthrie's sensitive direction in *The Anatomist*, which starred Henry Ainley, whom she saw as Faust all those years ago, and gave Robert Eddison his second part in the West End.

The following year – 1932 – she moved to Shaftesbury Avenue to play Olwen Peel in Priestley's first play, *Dangerous Corner*, in which she was seen as a quiet-seeming woman who gradually dropped her defences as her past relations with the dead hero were revealed. Again she had Tyrone Guthrie to direct her. Later that year in Somerset Maugham's *For Services Rendered*, she made a deep impression as the hysterical, sex-starved daughter, in a cast which included Ralph Richardson, Cedric Hardwicke, Marjorie Mars and Louise Hampton. Tyrone Guthrie did not direct. It was H. K. Ayliff. She missed Guthrie; she was lost without him and felt the other members of the cast, because of Ayliff's direction, did not react in a manner which put her in the position to give her best performance.

'There has always been a father figure in my life,' recalled Flora many years later. 'In the first instance it was my own father, who launched my career. Then came Moffatt Johnston, who gave me the right point of view and finally Tony Guthrie, who was a revelation because he directed *everyone* on stage throughout every scene and not just the actor who happened to be speaking. In Shakespeare the audience looks at the player actually speaking the lines, but in modern plays the important figure is not necessarily the one speaking. Guthrie made this point very clear and no other director gave me quite the same opportunity. I have always envied actresses who had the good fortune which Sybil Thorndike had with Lewis Casson, Marie Tempest with W. Graham Browne and Irene Vanbrugh with Dion Boucicault – a life-long partner who knew how to direct them and get the best possible performance out of the parts they rehearsed together. Sarah Miles, with her dramatist-husband, Robert Bolt, is a more recent example of this enviable professional relationship.'

When Lilian Baylis engaged Charles Laughton for the Old Vic – at the height of his film popularity – for the 1933–34 season, she invited Flora to join the company, which included Ursula Jeans, Athene Seyler, Elsa Lanchester, Marius Goring, James Mason and Leon Quartermaine. Most important from Flora's point of view, was that Tyrone Guthrie was to direct all six productions in which she appeared.

She appeared as Varya in *The Cherry Orchard*, Queen Katharine in

Henry VIII, Isabella in *Measure for Measure*, Gwendolen Fairfax in *The Importance of Being Earnest*, Mrs Foresight in Congreve's *Love for Love*, Ceres in *The Tempest* and Lady Macbeth.

Being a leading lady at the Old Vic considerably enhanced Flora's prestige, but she still had no money for taxis and travelled to the theatre by public transport, Garbo fashion, with her head down and a felt hat pulled well over her eyes. Once she got to know Charles Laughton, who was always generous to her, he used to take her to the theatre by car, as they were neighbours in Bloomsbury. At the Old Vic she realised she had not mastered the technique of projecting her voice into the auditorium of a large theatre and she also discovered it would be difficult to play opposite Laughton in Shakespeare because he had a totally realistic approach and often no ear for music or the the rhythm of the words.

Macbeth was the most controversial production of the season. Flora admits her Lady Macbeth was not an accepted success, but she fully agreed with Tyrone Guthrie's conception of the part and they achieved what they set out to do, even though it did not meet with general approval. James Bridie, for instance, thought it was wrong, lifeless, inept and even stupid.

Guthrie maintained Lady Macbeth was not a killer, but only a planner. He did not see eye to eye with Mrs Siddons who looked upon Lady Macbeth as a murderess of the same calibre as Medea and Clytemnestra. Guthrie saw her as a woman without imagination, whose sin was great ambition – a desire for a crown. Everything she did was in the cause of her husband and once she had planned Duncan's murder she had had enough.

Flora thought Lady Macbeth needed a harsher voice and no sensitivity. The sleep-walking scene is normally acted like Ophelia's mad scene, but Flora played it as if asleep. The Doctor and the Gentlewoman were on-stage and they had to move out of her path or she would have bumped into them. After playing opposite Laughton at the Old Vic she played Lady Macbeth in New York with Michael Redgrave. In that production she had to walk down a long staircase in bare feet against a blaze of light. It was like stepping into a chasm, but she dared not look down or it would have destroyed the illusion of being asleep.

Flora welcomed the opportunity to play Gwendolen Fairfax in *The Importance of Being Earnest*, as it gave her a chance to prove she could play parts other than hysterical females and play them well. Thirty-five years later she was to give one of the finest performances of her entire career as Miss Prism when John Chetwyn directed *The Importance of Being Earnest* at the Haymarket, with Isabel Jeans as Lady Bracknell. Flora lent a delicate touch of pathos to her playing, a quality not normally associated with Miss Prism.

Robert Farquharson who played Wolsey in *Henry VIII* at the Old Vic was one of the most exotic and bizarre creatures Flora ever met. He had dyed hair and wore canary yellow socks, which made him very conspicuous in those days and he was brought to the theatre in a Rolls-Royce every night. He was said to have inspired Oscar Wilde's creation of Dorian Gray and certain actors at the Old Vic believed him to be in league with the Devil because he was given some lovely flowers on the first night of *Henry VIII* and he continued to bring them back to the theatre night after night, yet they never lost their freshness or their perfume. He had played Dr Rank in *A Doll's House*, when Janet Achurch appeared as Nora in 1898.

Alexander Korda, then the big name in British films, gave Flora a four-year contract which put an end to her money troubles for the rest of her life. No films were suitable for her at the time, so Korda put on *Mary Read*, a play about a woman pirate, written for her by James Bridie so that she would not be type-cast as a distraught woman for the rest of her life. It was a magnificent acting part and she had Robert Donat as her leading man, but their names were not big enough at that time to fill a large theatre in the West End. Strangely enough it led to Flora being cast as Queen Elizabeth in the film *Fire Over England*. This was a comparatively small part and she felt she was miscast, possibly because she was so well read on Elizabeth Tudor. No one was more surprised than Flora when she scored a sensational success and became an internationally famous film star.

What Flora regards as her greatest stage success was to follow in 1937 – *Autumn* at the St Martin's Theatre. The play was by Ilya Surguchev; it had been translated into English by Gregory Ratoff. and then rewritten by Margaret Kennedy of *The Constant Nymph* fame. Flora played a woman in love with the same man as her stepdaughter. Basil Dean, who directed, had to borrow Flora from Korda and he thought she gave a terrific performance of suppressed emotion. She enjoyed working with Basil Dean. He would give her an inflexion at rehearsal, pointing out that different inflexions produced different meanings and could thus change the meaning of an entire scene. This Basil Dean theory irritated some of the players and led to friction, but his method worked as far as Flora was concerned.

The fan mail first started pouring in during the run of *Autumn* and there was an occasion in Blackpool when there were twenty-seven curtains at the end of the evening. Basil Dean did not take her seriously when she expressed a desire to play comedy. As she was so good in highly emotional parts, no one would give her a chance until Binkie

Beaumont cast her as Miss Prism at the Haymarket. 'How right she had been to want to play comedy!' was Basil Dean's comment.

Flora was the first actress who came to the mind of managers casting plays with murderers in them. Agnes Isit in *A Man About The House* was being poisoned with arsenic by her Italian husband. Flora gave a moving performance as the wife, tottering rather than walking in the grip of the deadly drug. At that time Flora was nursing her brother, suffering from a form of paralysis; she knew what he was thinking and appreciated the mental outlook of one who knew he was dying. This personal relationship in her own private life helped her to give a poignant impression of Agnes Isit.

Black Chiffon by Lesley Storm gave Flora the chance to escape from murder, yet gave her a tragic part which stirred her interest, her imagination and her intellect. She played a mother who loved her son too deeply and could not bear the thought of being parted from him after his marriage. A mental breakdown led her to steal a black chiffon nightgown from a West End store.

The preparation for this production demanded a degree of concentration outside Flora's previous experience. She had to get away from people she knew and the daily routine, so she imprisoned herself in the Savoy Hotel during rehearsals. She slipped in unnoticed in dark glasses; she had meals served in her room, which had no view. She took no phone calls, read no letters and refused to glance at a newspaper.

Flora Robson in her early seventies insists she has retired from the stage, but I cannot genuinely believe her. I still think she could change her mind and be seen in other memorable parts in the West End. Meanwhile she lives alone with her dog in a fascinating old house in Brighton on the edge of Kemp Town, just around the corner from the homes of Olivier and Joan Plowright, John Clements and Kay Hammond, Douglas Byng, Robert Flemyng and Dora Bryan. She leads a busy social life, going to prior-to-London productions at the Brighton Theatre Royal, avant-garde presentations at the Gardner Centre of the University of Sussex and to symphony concerts at the Dome.

She does a good deal of charitable work and is always helping people in trouble. She has been to Lewes gaol to try to sort out the problems of a bewildered Moroccan manservant who unwittingly broke the law through not regularising his papers. She goes to hospitals to bring peace of mind to friends and acquaintances who are worried through having to be out of circulation while undergoing treatment. She keeps her eye on ageing colleagues living their twilight years in Denville Hall, a residential home for actors and actresses in North London, and frequently gives up time to visit them, to write letters and do other odd jobs.

One of her closest friends is Lee, a little boy of five who lives next door. Flora has always prided herself on knowing how to deal with children. She gives them a sense of importance by sharing little secrets with them and respecting their opinions. There is no question of talking down to them. Lee has his own television stool in Flora's sitting room and a little coffee-table of his own on which he places his tipple – limejuice, which is kept with the grown-ups' alcoholic drinks in the sideboard. He is made thoroughly at home and never fussed over like a child. Flora has taught him to write and to speak grammatically, so he is streets ahead of the other boys in his class at school.

Years ago when Flora was in a film called *Poison Pen* the cast included a number of child actors. One who was especially good in the crowd scenes asked Flora for her autograph after the film had been completed. 'Only if you give me yours,' she insisted. 'I'm not good enough for that,' he replied, but Flora assured him he had enough talent to warrant being asked for his autograph. In other words, she treated him like an adult and made his day.

Anyone walking into Flora Robson's old Brighton house would not be immediately aware of being in the home of a famous actress. She does not take the theatre home with her. The influence of her father is there in the shape of treasures he brought home from his visits to Japan. There are some delicately-coloured oriental prints on the staircase, some graceful porcelain figures on shelves and a handsomely-shaped terra-cotta coloured teapot. On the roof she grows four-leaf clover and sends a leaf mounted on a card to friends who appreciate a unique good luck greeting.

She is alone, but not lonely. As a Dame she has obligations of a social nature, which are considerably time-consuming and she replies to all her fan letters personally. She is happy to send signed pictures to admirers, but expects the correspondence to stop at that. She has neither the time nor the inclination to encourage pen pals. Her most cherished theatre relic is a miniature wooded coffin about three inches long, containing dice which belonged to Irving. Ellen Terry used to keep it on her bedside table. After her own death Flora would like it to go to a young actress whose work she very much admires. Inside the coffin, with the dice, is a slip of flimsy paper on which is written the name of the actress to whom this souvenir has been bequeathed. Flora has a tidy mind as far as her personal affairs are concerned and her many fascinating letters from James Bridie are mentioned in her will. She has never forgotten that he wrote *Mary Read* specially for her to save her from being type-cast throughout her career as an old maid longing for a man.

Andrew Cruickshank, a leading man and a close colleague of Flora's, said, 'Actors seldom talk about money, but she once told me she'd planned her insurance policies to mature at stages over her life.' This was indication of a much deeper impulse in her. Like Sartre she saw her life as a project in all senses; within this project were goals, parts to be played, like Lady Macbeth and Mrs Alving, at the appropriate time, and the sum of the goals added up to a mature professional career and a full life.

Speaking about Flora as a professional colleague, Andrew Cruickshank continued, 'There are actors we call naturals. Their response is immediate and their emotions are always beautifully in control. I felt that I just had to whisper the name "Titanic" to her and her eyes would fill with tears.'

Flora's eyes filled with tears the day she knew she was to be made a Dame in 1960. A most imposing envelope was left for her at the stage door and when she opened it to learn of the honour to be bestowed upon her she cried because her parents and others who had had faith in her during those difficult early years had died and could not share her joy.

While we were looking back down the years I wondered if Flora had any unfulfilled ambitions as far as her career was concerned. She would like to have played in a revival of *Saint Joan*. Sir Barry Jackson invited her to do so, but Shaw, who admired Flora's work enormously, preferred Wendy Hiller because of her North Country accent and she was saucy to the judges. Flora particularly admired Siobhan McKenna, who played the part with her strange Irish brogue. Someone presented Flora to Bernard Shaw when he visited the film studios during the making of *Caesar and Cleopatra*, saying, 'This is Miss Robson who has just been a success in a play in London.' Shaw replied, 'Miss Robson is always a success in her plays in London.'

Flora's face has been called her fortune, but it was not always her best friend. She would like to have played romantic comedy parts, but because of her face she never had the chance to play Portia, Beatrice or Rosalind. There are real people who would make excellent leading parts suitable for Flora. One is Mary Kingsley who explored the Gold Coast in late Victorian times and another is Elizabeth Fry who visited prisons, cleaned them up and read the Bible to wild creatures shut up in iron cages. Christopher Fry could write a wonderful play about her. 'It is a pity it's so difficult to make a good play out of a good person's life. The villains always make better theatre, as I have learned to my cost.'

No one woman is the world's greatest actress in Flora's opinion. A number of fine players have been good in certain parts. Meggie

115

Albanesi was a young tragic actress with a great gift for comedy; Beatrix Lehmann was so convincing as Emily Brontë in *Wild Decembers,* she looked as if she had really written a book; Edith Evans was deeply moving at the end of *Evensong,* as the ageing *prima donna* who could no longer sing. She was heart-breaking as she sat listening to a recording made in her heyday . . . and the curtain began to fall very slowly. Sybil Thorndike made a gay Portia, which Flora saw when a schoolgirl in an Old Vic production which toured the London suburban theatres. Flora's own favourite parts are Miss Tina in *The Aspern Papers* and Miss Prism in *The Importance of Being Earnest,* both belonging to her more mature years.

Peggy Ashcroft as Beatrice and John Gielgud as Benedick in the RSC's 1955 European tour of *Much Ado about Nothing*, directed by Gielgud. *Photo: Angus McBean*

Above left: Peggy Ashcroft as Madame Ranevsky in *The Cherry Orchard* – Aldwych, 1961.
Photo: Angus McBean
Above right: Peggy Ashcroft in 1929 when she first attracted attention playing Naomi in
Jew Süss
Peggy Ashcroft as Emilia and Dorothy Tutin as Desdemona in the 1961 RSC *Othello* at
Stratford. Gielgud played Othello. *Photo: Associated Press*
Far right: Charles Laughton as Angelo and Flora Robson as Isabella in the Tyrone Guthrie
production of *Measure for Measure* – Old Vic, 1933. *Photo: J. W. Debenham*

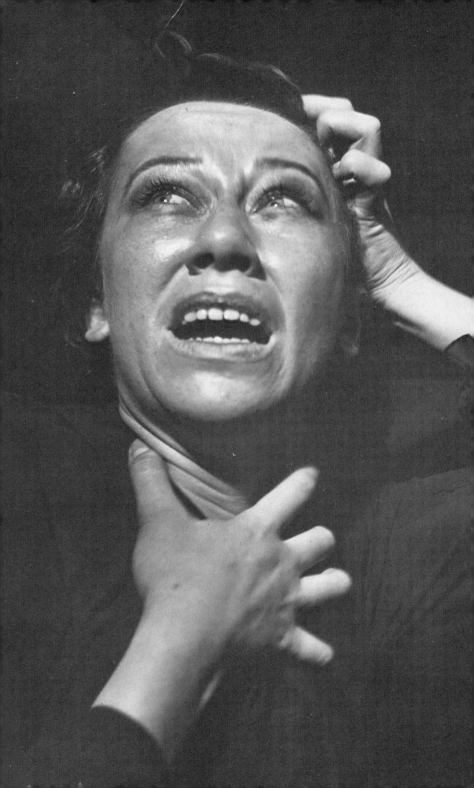

lora Robson in the name-part of *Mary Read*, specially written for her by James Bridie and Claud Gurney, 1934. *Photo: Janet Jevons*

eft: Flora Robson as Eva in Somerset Maugham's *For Services Rendered*, 1932. *Photo: Helen MacGregor*

Off-stage portrait of Judith Anderson by Vandamm. *Photo: from the Mander-Mitchenson collecti*

ggy Mount and Margaret Rutherford sang *Stand Up, Stand Up for Jesus* in *Farewell, Farewell,
Eugene* at the Garrick Theatre. *Photo: Angus McBean*
xt page: Margaret Rutherford in *Dazzling Prospect* at the Globe Theatre in 1961. *Photo:
Angus McBean*

Judith Anderson 1898–

To English playgoers Judith Anderson is the most mysterious of the theatre Dames because they have seen so little of her. It was American audiences who had the good fortune to enjoy the full splendour of her theatrical achievement. Australian by birth, she has appeared only twice in London – on both occasions at the Old Vic. In 1937 she played Lady Macbeth opposite Laurence Olivier and in 1960 she was seen as Arkadina in *The Seagull* by Chekhov, with Tom Courtenay making his first appearance on the stage as her son Konstantin. That is all we have seen of her stage work in this country, though in the famous film version of *Rebecca*, with Olivier as Maxim de Winter her Mrs Danvers is a memory indeed to be cherished.

Born in Adelaide, she made her first appearance on the stage at the age of seventeen at the Theatre Royal in Sydney as Stephanie in *A Royal Divorce* during the First World War in Julius Knight's company. He was the romantic hero of the Australian stage at that time and as the *ingénue* of his troupe, Frances Anderson, as she was then known, toured in *Monsieur Beaucaire*, *The Scarlet Pimpernel* and *David Garrick*. Through starting so young she got the feel of the boards long before reaching womanhood, but she soon realised she would have to leave Australia if she wanted to make real headway in the theatre. During the second decade of the century star parts on the Australian stage were played by British or American artists.

She toured Australia with an American company and made such a favourable impression upon her colleagues they suggested she returned with them to 'God's Own Country'. By that time she was twenty and her mother was more than willing for her daughter to take a chance and even agreed to accompany her to New York. Frances Anderson secured her first engagement in New York in the stock company of the old Fourteenth Street Theatre, where she played a different small part every week. She had to provide her own wardrobe and spent best part of the night learning her lines in bed. She became such a valuable member of the company she was given leading parts the following year. She toured with William Gillette in *Dear Brutus* in 1920 and played leading parts in stock companies in Boston and Albany.

She first became Judith Anderson in 1923 when she appeared in *Peter Weston* at the Sam H. Harris Theatre, but her first major success came the following year as Elise in *Cobra* at the Hudson Theatre. It was a flamboyant vamp role which Isabel Jeans played in the West End a year later. On the strength of her New York success, Judith Anderson returned to Australia in 1927 to play in *Cobra* and the Talullah Bankhead role of Iris Fenwick in *The Green Hat*. Back in New York a year later she succeeded Lynn Fontanne as Nina Leeds in Eugene O'Neill's *Strange Interlude* and made a deep impression as the Unknown One in Pirandello's *As You Desire Me* and Lavinia Mannon in *Mourning Becomes Electra*.

She reached new heights in 1936 when she played the Queen to Gielgud's Hamlet at the Empire Theatre in New York and the following year Judith Anderson, nineteen years after her first appearance in New York, went to London for the first time to play Lady Macbeth at the Old Vic, with Laurence Olivier as Macbeth and Andrew Cruickshank as Banquo; the production transferred to the New Theatre for a West End run. Twenty-two years were to elapse before Judith Anderson returned to London and the Old Vic, but they were decidedly illustrious years.

She was seen as Mary in *Family Portrait*, Clytemnestra in *Tower Beyond Tragedy* and as Olga in *The Three Sisters* to the Masha of Katharine Cornell. In 1947 came Medea, which is generally considered Judith Anderson's finest creation. John Gielgud directed her in a new adaptation of the Euripides tragedy by Robinson Jeffers, written specially for her and dedicated to her. When Rosamond Gilder, the American critic, saw Judith Anderson playing the part she wrote, 'Her Medea is pure evil, dark, dangerous, cruel, raging, ruthless. From beginning to end she maintains an almost incredibly intensity, yet she varies her moods so constantly, she moves with such skill through unexplored regions of pain and despair that she can hold her audience in suspense throughout the evening.'

Medea has remained the peak achievement of Judith Anderson's career. Australia gave her the highest honour by inviting her back to Sydney to open their Elizabethan Theatre with Medea. She also played it at the Sarah-Bernhardt Theatre in Paris, where she was allowed to use the Divine Sarah's old dressing room, unchanged since she occupied it in all its Second Empire magnificence. Berlin craved to see the Anderson Medea and paid her the most touching compliment of her career. When she left the theatre on the opening night, admirers rushed forward to scatter a carpet of rose petals from the stage door to her car.

She gave a number of dramatic readings, the most famous being *John Brown's Body*, but she was rather reluctant to embark upon this venture as she has always been shy about facing an audience as herself. She relies upon the protection of make-up and the proscenium arch. She really prefers a play and an opportunity to become someone other than herself on the stage. She once said, 'I am never happier than when I can get a play, fall in love with it and do it.' She regrets she never had a chance to play Shaw's *Saint Joan*, which she considers the greatest part created for an actress within living memory. Schiller's *Mary Stuart* is a work which fires her imagination and she always hoped she would have an opportunity to appear in a production, playing both leading parts – Elizabeth I of England and Mary, Queen of Scots – on alternate nights.

The chance to appear in London for the second time occurred in 1960, when she was invited to play Arkadina in *The Seagull*, first at the Edinburgh Festival and then at the Old Vic. Under the direction of John Fernald, that long-respected authority on Chekhov, the distinguished cast included Tony Britton as Trigorin, Sylvia Coleridge as Paulina, Ralph Michael as Dorn, Cyril Luckham as Sorin, Gerald James as Shameayev, Ann Bell as Nina and the twenty-three-year-old Tom Courtenay as Konstantin. It was quite an occasion, but not a triumph to go down in theatre history.

Looking back on his production twelve years later, John Fernald is of the opinion Judith Anderson at the age of sixty-two was rather too old to play Arkadina, the famous actress still idolised throughout the Russia of the Romanovs. She was also an Australian with an American accent, yet in spite of all those handicaps she succeeded.

He admired her approach to work. 'She came to rehearsal in a completely neutral frame of mind. There was no question of her having worked out her performance in advance and insisting upon imposing it upon my production, whether it blended with my ideas or not. At rehearsal she was an excellent listener; she was calm and detached and watched every movement shrewdly. In other words, she worked like a good, co-operative student, willing to take direction and try out suggestions.'

John Fernald wished to achieve a special effect during the quarrel scene between Arkadina and her son, when she is bandaging his head after the accident with the gun. They get quite close to each other and there is obviously a great deal of affection between them. But the son resents his mother's association with Trigorin and cannot resist taunting her with it. Why must she always have this writer in her entourage? And then a row blazes up between them.

The son is an avant-garde playwright, but his mother gives him no encouragement. She is content to tour Russia in out-dated plays with which she has filled theatres for many a year. She even confesses she has never read a line her son has written. At the height of the row Arkadina screams 'Nonentity!' in his face. The moment she utters the word she realises it is an unforgivable thing to have done – to have called a creative artist a nonentity, even though she may not appreciate his artistic approach to the theatre. John Fernald considers this moment to be one of the highlights of the play and it is a point he was eager to get across – the mother's blinding flash of horror for the pain she had inflicted upon her son.

He wanted Judith Anderson to express how deeply ashamed Arkadina felt and he showed her how he would like her to project her lines at this point in the play. It was obviously not how she would have played the scene, had she been left to her own devices. He begged her to try out his theory and to live with it for a day or two at rehearsal, but if she still hated his suggestion he was quite prepared to reject it and try a different way to gain the same effect. John Fernald still praises Judith Anderson for her whole-hearted and willing co-operation. She tried out his suggestions, persevered with them and eventually decided to retain them. She admitted he had been right from the start and it so happened on the first night her manner of screaming 'Nonentity!' electrified the house.

Apart from possessing a sense of humour and a sense of proportion in being able to assess a production as a whole, and not just her own part, Judith Anderson could appreciate the finest points of direction and showed remarkable generosity to younger members of the cast – to Ann Bell who played Nina and to Tom Courtenay who played her son Konstantin.

Tom Courtenay had his problems, too. John Fernald was in the middle of his ten-year span as Principal of the Royal Academy of Dramatic Art when invited to direct *The Seagull* at the Old Vic. One of his senior students, Tom Courtenay, was about to leave the Academy and embark upon his career as a professional actor. John Fernald thought he would make an excellent Konstantin and cast him for the part. As Tom Courtenay remarked, 'I was at the Academy one week and rehearsing *The Seagull* on the Old Vic stage the next – with Judith Anderson playing my mother. When I saw her rather formidable features I felt terrified and thought of Mrs Danvers in *Rebecca*. I was totally inexperienced and thought she might quite understandably resent having a novice thrust upon her in the important part of Konstantin.

'She turned out to be most friendly, much to my relief. She was never impatient at rehearsal times when she might reasonably have been difficult. She had obviously not forgotten her young days and the tough times she must have experienced when she first went to America, with so much still to learn. She developed a soft spot for me and I was most touched when she looked me up some years later while on a private visit to London. Though she lacked height I was amazed by the masterly technique which succeeded in creating a strong and impressive stage presence.

'Konstantin was an enormous part for a beginner and I was scared when I realised the responsibility it carried. We opened at the Edinburgh Festival and later at the Old Vic. Then it dawned on me that I would have to face my first London first-night. Others in the company explained how very different it was from any other ordeal an actor had to face . . . an audience of *habitués*, and the leading critics who together made it very difficult for even experienced players to relax and give the performance they had been working on for weeks at rehearsal. Judith Anderson helped me through some very difficult hours and tried to convince me I was not quite the novice I imagined myself. At the last moment, when we were putting the final touches to our make-up for the Old Vic first night, news travelled backstage that Laurence Olivier was in front. Judith Anderson had played with him in *Macbeth* on that same stage and when I saw her momentarily shattered at the thought of having to play in front of him, my own confidence received a deadly blow.'

Years later John Fernald saw her playing Greek tragedy in America. He considered she had all the power and technique required to tackle these larger-than-life roles, but out there she gave the impression of being 'hammy' through lack of adequate direction. She lived in America, rather than in her native Australia or Europe because she liked the climate and liked to be within easy reach when so many magnificent film parts were being offered to her.

After leaving the Royal Academy of Dramatic Art in London John Fernald was appointed artistic director of the John Fernald Company of the Meadow Brook Theatre in Michigan, six years after the Old Vic *Seagull*. When the opening production was being discussed he suggested *The Importance of Being Earnest*, with Judith Anderson as Lady Bracknell. He thought she would be ideally cast as the formidable Edwardian aristocrat, but she was unable to accept the much-appreciated invitation because prior professional commitments ruled it out.

Judith Anderson is now in her mid-seventies, which makes it unlikely she will ever play in London again. Though we have seen so little of her work, her brief appearances proved her a fine classical actress, who made her mark on three continents and her professional attitude to her colleagues gave further proof that she considered 'the play's the thing'. She was only too ready to co-operate with her fellow players and the director in order that the audience should be able to enjoy the best possible performance of the play they had come to see. That is why, not long before that Old Vic production of *The Seagull*, she was honoured with the title of Dame for her valuable services to the theatre.

Margaret Rutherford 1892–1972

My last glimpse of Margaret Rutherford was a distressing experience. It was at Kenwood House one lovely night a couple of years before she died, when John Westbrook was giving one of his all-too-rare poetry recitals. By this time she was in her late seventies, but she always appeared rather vague off-stage, so I was not unduly surprised to see her being led into the room at a snail's pace by her devoted actor-husband, Stringer Davis. She was given an ornate chair of honour, placed at right-angles to the audience and quite close to the platform.

From where I sat I commanded a close and unobstructed view of her. Stringer – or Tuft, as she affectionately called her husband – presented a succession of people to his wife, many quite well-known theatre figures such as Marie Ney, who had been acquainted with her for years. 'You remember So-and-So, Margaret?' Stringer asked. She gave a flicker of a blank smile, obviously not knowing who they were and making no attempt to engage them in any sort of conversation. When John Westbrook started his recital it was soon apparent that his words were making no impression upon her, which astounded me, knowing poetry was one of her major interests in life. Her attention was wandering and she began gazing vacantly about her, without a spark of light in her eye. Then it dawned on me the young woman sitting just behind her chair was a nurse in mufti.

Her career was over. Obviously, as my attention strayed from John Westbrook to the veteran actress, I realised she could never again appear on the stage, never make a film or read a script for the radio, even in the familiar surroundings of her own home in Buckinghamshire. As a star actress she had faced the public for the last time. Her career was unquestionably finished and there was little to do but wait for death.

There had been signs of failing memory when Margaret Rutherford played Mrs Malaprop in *The Rivals* at the Haymarket in 1966, when she was seventy-five and this caused her great distress. She admitted there were times when she made up some of her own Malapropisms because she could not always recall Sheridan's exact lines, but she doubted if many people in the audience were aware of what was happening. She was not well at the time and the part presented a great responsibility. 'As in all comedy,' she said, after the run of the play, 'the timing had to be precise. Catch the split second and the laughs come. Miss two beats and they are gone. Sensing the timing in a period piece is always difficult, but combining a crop of Malapropisms with this was very wearying.'

Between a matinée and an evening performance Stringer Davis, who played a small part in *The Rivals* and acted as nursemaid to his wife, met Raymond Marriott in the Haymarket. Both Margaret and Stringer admired and respected his dramatic criticism and features he had written about the theatre, so Stringer begged him to look in on Margaret, whom he had left relaxing in her dressing room. Marriott hesitated, in view of the fact he was unexpected and she would be resting, but Stringer insisted and they went together. She did not really know who he was and before he had been in the room five minutes she fell asleep.

There was worse to come. After *The Rivals* she was engaged to play a small but rewarding comedy part in a film – what is known as a cameo, offering the actor a chance to give a performance that steals a scene and lingers in the memory. The film director was working to a very tight schedule. The picture had to be finished by a certain date because arrangements had been made to start shooting another picture in the same studio in a matter of days. Margaret could not remember her lines, which meant her little scene had to be shot over and over again, thus consuming precious time which the director could ill-afford. In a panic he had to engage another actress to take over the part which by then had to be learnt and shot as a rush job. On that terrible day when it was decided they could wait no longer for Margaret, she was discovered hunched on a chair in the hall of her own home, sobbing her heart out as she repeated over and over again, 'I've been sacked!' This tragic incident marked the end of her professional career. She had no more resistance and all Stringer could do was to stand by helplessly and watch the deadly deterioration slowly getting the upper hand until Margaret died at the age of eighty.

Margaret Rutherford was in her fifties before we met and on that first occasion she struck me as a rather poignant creature. I went to interview her while a rehearsal was in progress and lest she should be wanted by the producer, she suggested we had a whispered chat in a shadowy back-stage corner where she would still be within call. She talked about the sheer beauty of words and the pleasure she derived from speaking them. Before she went on the stage she took lessons in elocution from Acton Bond, an actor who had played in the Irving company at the Lyceum in the 'nineties and later with Tree at His Majesty's. She had a sensitive appreciation of poetry and loved to speak verse aloud, even without a listening audience.

'I think the lines Shakespeare put into Juliet's mouth,' she whispered, 'are among the loveliest in the language. I would have given anything to have played Juliet, but I was born with a face only suitable for the Nurse.' In a nutshell, that was the tragedy of Margaret Rutherford's career. She was a very strange lady. Instead of thanking heaven for that unique clown's face, worth a fortune, she resented being a figure of fun. In her estimation her face was an unwelcome obstacle which prevented her playing parts which really appealed to her. As early as 1935 when she played Miss Flower in Robert Morley's *Short Story*, it became obvious she was destined to play comedy for most of her life. 'How I would love to have been a great traditional actress like Bernhardt, Duse or Ellen Terry,' she sighed. 'There have been so many parts I yearned to play.' Even after she had arrived, had been accepted and was offered leading parts ideally suited to her style of acting and her stage appearance, she still remained a frustrated artist.

No other actress had a beginning remotely like Margaret Rutherford's. At the age of seven she played a fairy in a home-produced version of *The Sleeping Beauty*. Mrs Waterlow, a professional actress, saw the performance and declared Margaret had histrionic ability and from that night onwards the child decided she wanted to become an actress. It was a long struggle. Twenty-five years were to elapse before her professional début at the Old Vic and eight more before she played in the West End for the first time. By then she was already forty-one.

She very much wanted to become an actress and went on relentlessly persevering, undeterred by the fact that the years were slipping by without her making any worthwhile progress. She taught music in Wimbledon, using a bicycle as a means of propelling herself from one pupil to the next. 'I was not a very good music teacher,' she admitted. 'I had no patience and might just as well have had a milk or a paper round, but it helped to make both ends meet.' To gain experience she acted with an amateur group in Wimbledon and she recited to soldiers during the First World War. At the age of thirty-three she went to the Old Vic to study for the professional stage and was given her first speaking part by Lilian Baylis during the Old Vic's 1925 Christmas show. It was called *Harlequin Jack Horner and the Enchanted Pie* and Margaret played the fairy with the Long Nose. Lilian Baylis was not impressed by the performance and indicated the ageing student had no future, but the stage-struck Margaret was not to be deterred.

She moved into Central London, taking a room in a YWCA hostel, to be nearer the theatres and agents who might get her work. She gained valuable experience in repertory at Fulham Grand Theatre, at Oxford and the famous Greyhound Theatre at Croydon. She was rewarded by being cast as Mrs Read, the murderer's charwoman, in *Wild Justice* by James Dale, directed by A. R. Whatmore, with Barbara Couper, Henry Oscar, Reginald Beckwith and Campbell Logan in the cast. It opened in Hammersmith at the Lyric and moved a month later to the Vaudeville. At last Margaret was in the West End, even though playing the most modest of parts. She enhanced her prestige the following year by playing Aline Solness opposite Donald Wolfit in *The Master Builder* at the Embassy Theatre in Swiss Cottage, with Beatrix Lehmann as Hilde Wangel and John Clements as Ragnar Brovik. Rarely, if ever, has the story of Mrs Solness and her dolls been so tragically recounted. The engagement was a step in the right direction. Margaret was playing Ibsen, the type of distinguished author she dreamed about.

From Swiss Cottage Margaret moved into the heart of the West End, to the Queen's Theatre in Shaftesbury Avenue to appear in *Short Story*, Robert Morley's first play. Marie Tempest, Sybil Thorndike, Ursula Jeans, Una Venning, A. E. Matthews, Rex Harrison and Cyril Raymond completed the cast. James Agate, then at the height of his power as a Sunday critic, singled out Margaret. 'The scene in which this tigerish mouse wrestles with another caller (Rex Harrison) for the telephone and finally secures it with a kick on the ankle, is the best thing in the show.' Marie Tempest was furious and sent for Margaret to go to her dressing room. The great star had no intention of having a play stolen from under her very nose and insisted the telephone scene be altered. This was Margaret's first experience of jealousy in the theatre, but she refused to be intimidated even by Marie Tempest, whom John Gielgud once called a tartar. Quite fearlessly Margaret stood up for herself, maintaining she intended to play the part as well as she could, which was how she played it on the first night, under Tyrone Guthrie's direction. Marie Tempest lost the day, but she secretly respected the newcomer who had stood up to her. So many people had read about Margaret kicking Rex Harrison's ankle, and would naturally expect to see this remarkably funny scene when they went to the show, so it had to be retained, whether Marie Tempest liked it or not. After making a deep impression as a sombre Ibsen lady, Margaret was now stamped as a unique comedienne, with a glorious future ahead. She hardly viewed this prospect with delight because she began to resent being laughed at.

Things came to a head when Mollie Keane and John Perry wrote

Spring Meeting in 1938 and cast Margaret as Bijou Furze, an eccentric aunt living in a crumbling mansion in the wilds of Tipperary. The authors considered they had written an extremely funny part, but Margaret saw only the tragic side of the woman. She considered Bijou showed a deep streak of disturbing pathos, such as one often finds in the so-called comic characters of life. She was quite shocked at the idea of being laughed at, and it was only when John Gielgud, who was directing the show, explained the laughter would be purely sympathetic that Margaret agreed to play the part and she went on to make one of the most sensational successes of her career.

Gielgud was so delighted with her performance as Bijou he cast her as Miss Prism, when he first directed *The Importance of Being Earnest* early in 1939 at the Globe Theatre, with Edith Evans as Lady Bracknell, Joyce Carey as Gwendolen, Angela Baddeley as Cecily, Gielgud himself as John Worthing, Ronald Ward as Algernon, David Horne as Chasuble, Felix Irwin as Merriman, John Justin as the Footman and Leon Quartermaine as Lane. Once again Gielgud had difficulty with Margaret, who saw only the tragic side of Miss Prism and did not appreciate her as a comic character. All she saw in Miss Prism was a deep strain of loneliness, a state of withdrawal from the world. Margaret's only consolation was the fact that she had a full-page picture in the programme, which was sure proof she had arrived. Some years later – in 1947 – John Gielgud asked Margaret to play Lady Bracknell, when invited to take a production to America and Canada. For some reason, probably because she was sick to death of playing the part, Edith Evans did not wish to go. Margaret considered Dame Edith's performance to be the definitive one and agreed to play Lady Bracknell only on condition she could wear exact copies of the costumes designed for Edith and that she was allowed to mould her performance on that of her distinguished predecessor. She warned John Gielgud she would not be nearly as good. He agreed to her conditions, regarding them as a remarkable instance of humility in the theatre. Jean Cadell was cast as Miss Prism for this North American tour.

Margaret's curious approach to comedy makes one wonder whether she was a really great actress or just an inspired clown. Was she consciously funny or was it something she could not help? She was adorably amusing, but was it no more than comic behaviourism? George Howe, who played with her in *The Importance of Being Earnest* and *The Happiest Days of Your Life*, believes 'She was a female Miles Malleson. She did not know how funny she was being. She never strove to be funny and was always sincere in her approach to a comic part. She was an unconscious comic and just could not help being amusing. She had nervous tricks – she wrinkled her nose like a rabbit and she gobbled – and these mannerisms were encouraged by film directors, much to the delight of the public.'

Margaret in her autobiography says, 'I have been told I was a natural clown and have been likened to Charlie Chaplin and Jacques Tati. I never think of myself that way. I play each role as I see it and always try to give it a new interpretation.

'I have also been told I can manipulate each part of my face with precision while the rest remains homely and normal. This is true, because like any trained and experienced actress, I do have every twitch and ripple of my body under control. I have always known how to make it obey my mental image of the part.' This was the meaning of acting which Margaret maintained was her life and as necessary for her survival as breathing.

After Miss Prism came Mrs Danvers the fanatical housekeeper in *Rebecca*, who resented the intrusion of a new mistress. The part appealed to her because there was no question of being laughed at and it gave her a chance to show the public she was not just a clown. She developed quite an affection for Mrs Danvers, who, in her opinion, was not as evil as she appeared. She had deeply loved her first mistress who had so mysteriously disappeared and once she had dedicated herself to protect the memory of the first wife she felt any cruel and sadistic way of persecuting the new wife was amply justified. She had to make Mrs Danvers a terrifying dragon, but at the same time she wanted the audience to understand why she was so deeply motivated by hate. She wanted her to appear dignified and frightening without looking absurd, so she depended upon holding herself in a certain way and also on her eye make-up. She found Mrs Danvers an exhausting part 'because a play always fills my thoughts entirely in the early days of rehearsal and becomes my life. A bit of their soul creeps into mine.'

Feeling at her lowest ebb on a wartime tour of *Rebecca* at Exeter Theatre Royal, she was surprised when Noël Coward knocked on her dressing room door one night to announce he had written a new play called *Blithe Spirit*, with a magnificent part for her, a spiritualistic medium rejoicing in the name of Madame Arcati. He added he had vaguely based the character on the writer Clemence Dane. He had not written the play with Margaret in mind, but after completing it, he realised she would make the perfect Madame Arcati, so he added some extra dialogue which would lend itself to the Rutherford treatment.

When we think of Margaret Rutherford, most of us visualise her as the dithering Madame Arcati, which so many consider her funniest performance, but she did not immediately fall on Noël Coward's neck in gratitude when he read the play to her, with the help of Owen Nares who was touring with Margaret in *Rebecca*. She was genuinely disturbed by the part; she went to bed and slept on the idea and on waking in the morning decided to accept Madame Arcati, but only if she could play it her own way. She was afraid of hurting people's feelings and as spiritualist mediums bring comfort to the distressed and the bereaved, she felt she had no right to make fun of them. She had no intention of guying Madame Arcati because underneath the comic façade she saw a real person of flesh and blood with serious and sincere beliefs. She would only play the part for straight and for real. And that was the secret of her astonishingly funny creation.

'I never intend to be a satirist,' Margaret wrote in her autobiography. 'I never intend to play for laughs. I am always surprised that the audience think me funny at all. I find it hard to analyse what I do except perhaps in my timing. As for this, I am grateful to Marie Tempest who taught me almost everything I know in the all-important control of laughter. If my work looks effortless, it is not. It is a question of tireless polishing the whole time.

'I always try to underact, to make my eyes expressive or twitch my nose or tremble my chin – mannerisms that have naturally developed over the years ... In my view good timing can only be achieved by instinct – it all depends on the actor's judgment. Good timing is, I think, more vital to comedy than to tragedy. In tragedy the "emotional colours" are more distinctively black and white, but in comedy they often cover the whole spectrum. To me this is what makes comic acting so compelling.' Margaret Rutherford was an expert technician. She fully realised considerable skill was needed to cope with farce and boisterous laughter. Actors specialising in comedy must not expend all their laughter too early. Something must be kept in reserve for bigger moments later on.

Lady Wishfort in *The Way of The World* was another of Margaret's great comic creations. She played in two different productions, one directed by John Gielgud at the Lyric, Hammersmith, in 1952, the other by John Clements at the Saville Theatre four years later. Stanley Hall, who designed so many of Margaret's masterly wigs, always so 'right' for the extraordinary characters she played, thought she was killingly funny at the Lyric, when she romped round in her costumes like an inspired clown, but he found her less amusing at the Saville, by which time she had thought too much about Lady Wishfort and had become awed by the fact she was playing a great classic role. The critic Eric Keown wrote memorably about the Lyric production. 'Top marks go to Margaret Rutherford, most happily cast as Lady Wishfort, whom she plays with enormous gusto in the grand manner, waving her jaw menacingly at her enemies and behaving like a splendidly padded windmill; very funny and curiously touching.'

She was a born romantic. Ivor Novello cast her as Lady Charlotte Fayre in his musical *Perchance to Dream*. For her, the highlight of the production was the moment when she was left all alone in the ballroom scene. 'I have always loved to dance and at that moment each night it seemed that I floated round the stage. The whole scene had seized my imagination. I was past any dream that I could have had.' Years later when she left the cast of *The School for Scandal* at the Haymarket, John Gielgud recalled her dancing at a party given on the stage. 'She was dancing with the stage carpenter. Neither of them possessed a graceful figure, yet their feet hardly touched the boards and they were as light as ballet dancers. It was quite astonishing to watch them.'

Off-stage Margaret was equally bizarre. As far as dress was concerned, she ignored fashion and wore only what appealed to her, often favouring flowing cloaks, further evidence of her love of the romantic. She liked chunky jewellery, necklaces and earrings and loved colourful dress materials. What would have looked ridiculous and outrageous on other women always looked right on her. She was like no one else one had ever met, yet she was no poseuse and there was no striving to create a shock-effect. She was just herself and as far as appearance was concerned she simply followed her instinct. 'She was always fey,' added George Howe. 'While we were playing in *The Happiest Days of Your Life*, she moved into a new home in Regent's Park. When she decided to give a house warming the entire company worked like beavers to make it a success and it turned out to be quite a memorable occasion. "Who helped you?" asked an admiring guest. "The little people," replied Margaret quite simply.'

She had tremendous courage, both moral and physical. Few other actresses would have had the strength to stand up to Marie Tempest as she did, refusing to cut what the audience considered the funniest scene in the play. There were times when the demands of a stage career completely exhausted her and she would collapse, suffering what amounted to a breakdown. Then she would go into a nursing home to regain her strength and clear her mind of disturbing anxieties. When she appeared in *The Solid Gold Cadillac* at the Saville Theatre in 1965 she was in very poor shape, but refused to give in. She was living in a nursing home at the time and a doctor accompanied her to the theatre each night, remaining back-stage throughout the show. Margaret was suffering from a nervous disorder at the time. Once she was on the stage she enjoyed the performance enormously, but the effort of mustering up courage to make her entrance was agonising and it was all most distressing for the rest of the cast.

At such times she would be persecuted by the fear of drying-up and completely forgetting her lines. She had a dread that one night everything would go blank; she imagined herself having to rush into the wings, or the stage manager ordering the curtain to be lowered in the middle of an act. Getting the giggles was another of her nightmares. Actors are liable to giggle if something happens to change the routine in a long run or if there is a mishap on stage. She used to pray it would never happen to her and throughout her career she dreaded this possibility of losing control on the stage.

Poetry was a great comfort to her and reading it in solitude would help to soothe her in her restless moods. She also liked reading poetry in public. Her recitals often being given in a glamorous pink dress she acquired for such occasions, were a great success because she could read purple passages from parts such as Juliet, which she could never hope to play on the stage. She often visited prisons to read poetry and that gave her a desire to play Elizabeth Fry, the prison reformer. Curiously enough, Flora Robson is fascinated by the same woman, but no-one seems to have thought of putting her into a play.

Margaret was a curious mixture. She held no stick-in-the-mud resentful opinions of the younger generation, with their long hair and unconventional clothes. After all, she herself was no slave to fashion, but she did insist upon teenagers being clean and wholesome in both dress and appearance. She especially admired a picture of Engelbert Humperdinck wearing a skin-tight black leather outfit. 'He looked the perfect highwayman of romance brought up to date.' Yet this same woman, who was so ready to accept some aspects of the contemporary way of life, was outraged when George Howe sent her a play to read – a translation from the French, with an ideal star part for her – because it dealt with artificial insemination.

Great tact and power of persuasion had to be used to get Margaret to play Miss Marple, the lady detective in the Agatha Christie films which turned out to be such a success. She had no wish to play a woman involved in crime, but the film people were able to persuade her Miss Marple was not so much concerned with crime, even though she was an indomitable sleuth always one stage ahead of the police. She was more involved in a game – like chess – a game of solving problems, rather than of murder. Once Margaret saw Miss Marple in that light – as a good woman who helped people – she decided to accept the part. Had she had a suitable physical appearance, one very much doubts whether she would have agreed to play Lady Macbeth. Yet after listening to her as Mrs Solness talking about her dolls in *The Master Builder*, and after shuddering at her behaviour as the sinister Mrs Danvers, there is reason to believe her Lady Macbeth could have been a revelation, especially with Stanley Hall at hand to transform her into a figure of regal splendour.

The last years of her life hardly bear thinking about. She was barely aware of what was happening around her, while her devoted Tuft was condemned to the ghastly realisation that she would never be able to work again in any capacity whatsoever. Even their rewarding companionship was blighted because Margaret had drifted far from reality into an isolation no one could penetrate. After enduring fifteen lonely and desolate months following Margaret's death, Stringer passed away peacefully in his sleep in what had been their last home in the heart of the leafy Buckinghamshire countryside they both enjoyed so much and where they had shared the happiest years of their lives.

Gladys Cooper 1888–1971

Gladys Cooper was only fifty when I first met her, but I was astonished to discover the face of this celebrated beauty more wrinkled than any I had ever seen. It could only be compared to the traditionally shrivelled apple. I had met the actress Helen Creswell just before her one hundredth birthday; she had played Celia to Mrs Langtry's Rosalind in the 1880s, but was far less lined than Gladys Cooper at half her age. Dame Gladys, as she later became, was to continue acting for another thirty-odd years, right up to the end of her life, but she possessed the same secret as Marlene Dietrich and Isabel Jeans, creating breath-taking glamour whenever she made a stage entrance. Until her last appearance as Mrs St Maugham in *The Chalk Garden* only a few months before her death, she retained her slender figure and boundless energy. Even the short distance between the footlights and the front row of the stalls was sufficient to lend enchantment and with the right flattering shade of pink in the stage lighting she could pass for an un-lined forty. Those in front were still aware of the familiar face that sold tens of thousands of picture postcards at the beginning of the century and adorned the lids of countless chocolate boxes.

Somerset Maugham considered Gladys Cooper's beauty startling, making it all the more surprising that she never felt impelled to be an actress. She was never stage-struck, but just happened to go on the stage. Maugham, in his introduction to Sewell Stokes' biography of Gladys Cooper, *Without Veils*, remarked that during the course of her long career she turned herself from an indifferent actress into an extremely accomplished one. She was a hard worker who did everything to make her performance as good as she possibly could. Once she felt that point had been reached she finalised it and in consequence her acting of the part in question never varied and she was a reliable performer. But it was often a week or more after the opening of a play before she reached what she felt to be the best she could do with a part. She always had word trouble, never being sure of her lines until about ten days after the opening. So those who saw Gladys Cooper only on first nights never saw her at her best.

As a child she lived in Chiswick Mall, a few doors away from a very tall man who turned out to be Sir Herbert Beerbohm Tree, but that does not mean he snapped her up to appear as an infant phenomenon in his company. Her own father was a dramatic critic, a journalist who founded and edited a publication known as *The Epicure*. He was not in a position to make his daughter's name as an actress, even if the thought had entered his head, which it did not. While still a child Gladys Cooper used to pose quite regularly for Downey, a fashionable photographer of the day with a studio in Ebury Street. There she met Marie Studholme, one of the most photogenic actresses of the 'nineties, but even she did not open the door for Gladys Cooper to go on the stage. Marie Studholme was a great lover of children and the two used to have cosy chats at Downey's studio when the times of their sittings happened to overlap. On one occasion the actress asked the seven-year-old child if she would like to visit Daly's Theatre to see her in *An Artist's Model*, the Sidney Jones musical comedy. Gladys naturally accepted the invitation and was allowed to watch the show from a stool placed in the wings. She liked Marie Studholme, not because she was a famous actress but because she was a kind and attractive young lady of twenty who took an interest in young people and treated them as if they were adults, with opinions of their own which she took the trouble to discover and respect.

At that time Gladys Cooper was not really interested in the theatre or she would have been tremendously excited about meeting such a famous leading lady, a piece of luck which would have made her entry into the profession quite easy. After all, a word from Marie Studholme could have opened quite a few doors, but young Gladys had no desire to go on the stage. It was when she reached her teens she began to consider the idea of becoming an actress, but even then she was astute enough to realise the beauty she was lucky enough to possess would be no good unless she had talent to back it up. Her parents had no money to send her to drama school; she had to learn her job the hard way, but her remarkable looks inevitably attracted the attention of managers in a position to give her work. In consequence she never had to look for a job; she was always offered parts without having to seek them.

She took her first step towards becoming an actress when she was sixteen. A childhood friend, Mary Henessey, told Gladys they were holding auditions at the Vaudeville Theatre and persuaded her to present herself for a voice trial for a part in *The Belle Of Mayfair*, but when she arrived at the theatre she discovered the situation was not quite as simple as she had imagined. It transpired that the fourteen-year-old Phyllis Dare, who had already been on the stage some six years, was leaving the cast to complete her education in the Belgian Ardennes and the management were looking for a replacement. Without any experience, Gladys Cooper was naturally not equipped to take over the part, but the management considered her looks would be an asset to the show and suggested she join the company to learn her job by walking on and becoming an understudy. Young as she was, she had a mind of her own and had no desire to understudy. So that was the end of her first bid to play in the West End.

The Christmas of that same year – 1905 – she secured a job on tour and made her very first appearance on the stage at the Colchester Theatre Royal in *Bluebell in Fairy Land*, playing Bluebell, the part created by Ellaline Terriss in the musical dream-play written by her husband Seymour Hicks and first seen at the Vaudeville Theatre four years earlier. A few years later, during the First World War, Cicely Courtneidge also went to Colchester to discover she had a flair for male impersonation and to launch herself as a music-hall star.

Phyllis Dare soon completed her education and was back at the Vaudeville the next spring to take over Edna May's part in *The Belle of Mayfair*. Edna May had been the rage of London in the title-role of *The Belle of New York* in 1898, but she had the name for being a decidedly temperamental leading lady. Feelings ran high back-stage at the Vaudeville after *The Belle of Mayfair* had opened. As an additional attraction Camille Clifford, the famous Gibson Girl with the hour-glass waist, was engaged. She made a phenomenal success and the management put up her name in lights outside the theatre. This was too much for Edna May, who promptly walked out in protest and Phyllis Dare was hastily brought back from the Ardennes. At the same time, Gladys Cooper, still wearing pigtails, was invited to play Lady Swan in the same show for £3 a week.

Twenty-one years later in *The Letter* at the Playhouse she would be earning £2,000 a week, with her salary and a share in the profits. She was not really nervous when she went to the Vaudeville for her second audition because she did not care whether she got the job or not. She had had a taste of the professional stage playing Bluebell and believed something was bound to turn up, even if she was considered unsuitable for *The Belle of Mayfair*. She was not very happy when she was eventually taken on, because she shared a dressing room with much older girls who were highly amused to watch her plaster her face with stage make-up in the most unprofessional manner and she did not enjoy being the laughing stock of the company. Still, it was a good start and she was in the West End in a popular success which survived Edna May's walk-out.

After *The Belle of Mayfair* Gladys Cooper gained more valuable experience in musical shows before she tried her first straight part. She was in the chorus of a number of George Edwardes productions at the Gaiety and Daly's and was in *The Babes in the Wood* pantomime in Glasgow and in Edinburgh. At the Gaiety she played Eva in *The Girls of Gottenberg*, was quite a hit at the same theatre in *Havana* and was seen as Lady Connie in *Our Miss Gibbs*. After playing with Seymour Hicks in *Papa's Wife* at various music halls she went to Daly's as Sadie Von Tromp in *The Dollar Princess*, the Leo Fall musical comedy, which starred Lily Elsie, immediately after her triumph as the Merry Widow at the same theatre. Gladys Cooper was in *Our Miss Gibbs* again at the Gaiety, this time playing Lady Elizabeth. The year was 1909. She was twenty-one and married to Captain Herbert Buckmaster. Once their daughter Joan was born, Gladys Cooper never went back into musical comedy.

The year 1911 was a vital turning point in Gladys Cooper's career, when she decided to take her work more seriously and go on the legitimate stage. Her first straight play was *Half a Crown*, presented at the old Royalty Theatre in Dean Street, Soho, with Dennis Eadie, Suzanne Sheldon, who married Henry Ainley, and Edmund Gwenn in the cast. The play was a resounding flop, but the new recruit was in distinguished company from the start. Later the same year she moved to the St James's, then under the management of George Alexander, to play Cecily Cardew in a revival of *The Importance of Being Earnest*.

Gladys Cooper was not a rebel. She respected authority and those who knew more about the theatre than she did, but she considered the members of the St James's company carried their veneration for Alexander to absurd lengths, as they tiptoed about the theatre and conversed in hushed voices. They treated their chief as a demi-god and though she was only twenty-three she felt convinced he did not demand this treatment and would have been happier to have been on easier terms with his actors. He would like to have been regarded as a more approachable boss. She caused something of a sensation within those hallowed walls by refusing to wear the ugly dress supplied by the theatre wardrobe for Cecily. She not only refused to wear it, she even cut it up and announced her intention of wearing one she bought herself. Hers made her look far more attractive and there was fortunately no question of the colour clashing with the costumes worn by the other ladies in the cast. She said there was a frightful row. No other artist at the St James's had ever had the courage to defy authority so flagrantly. Looking back on the incident years later Gladys Cooper was inclined to think Alexander was really on her side. Though he did not express his own opinion, he did not fire her.

After *The Importance* she stayed on at the St James's to play in *The Ogre*, the Henry Arthur Jones comedy, and went on to the

Criterion to appear as Violet Robinson in a revival of *Man and Superman*, with Robert Loraine as John Tanner and Pauline Chase as Ann Whitefield. She was back at the Royalty in 1912 to play Ann in *The Pigeon*, the John Galsworthy phantasy, and then came *Milestones*, the play by Arnold Bennett and Edward Knoblock, in which she appeared as the Hon Muriel Pym.

After Isabel Jay, the popular musical comedy star married to the impresario Frank Curzon, had seen Gladys Cooper in *The Ogre*, she hastened home to her husband with the news that she had seen a young actress of quite dazzling beauty. Once Frank Curzon saw her he signed her up to play Dora in his 1913 revival of *Diplomacy* at Wyndham's Theatre. She earned £40 a week – her first big money – in this Sardou adaptation in which she took the part made famous by Mrs Kendal in 1878 when the play was first seen in London. Gladys Cooper was twenty-five, as was Owen Nares who was cast as Julian Beauclerc and some thought the management had lost its head to entrust two unusually young players with such important parts, but the youngsters more than justified the faith their elders had in them. Gerald du Maurier played Henry Beauclerc. Gladys Cooper was to play Dora once again in 1924, when the play ran for ten months at the Adelphi. Back at the Royalty in 1914, Gladys Cooper played Anne, Nina, Annette, Antje, Annie, Anna and Anita in *My Lady's Dress* by Edward Knoblock. Edith Evans, who played Moeder Kaatje and Miss Sylvia in the same production, was quite spellbound by Gladys Cooper's remarkable beauty and used to stand and stare at her quite gormlessly. Never had she beheld so ravishing a creature.

Like Maxine Elliott and Mary Pickford, Gladys Cooper was an actress possessing both brains and beauty. She was a remarkable business woman and at the age of twenty-nine joined Frank Curzon in the management of the Playhouse in Northumberland Avenue, now a BBC theatre from which radio shows are broadcast. During their association, which lasted some ten years, Gladys Cooper appeared at the Playhouse in *Wanted a Husband*, *The Yellow Ticket*, *The Naughty Wife*, *Home and Beauty*, *My Lady's Dress*, *Wedding Bells*, *The Sign on The Door*, *The Second Mrs Tanqueray*, *Magda* and *Enter Kiki*. In 1927 she became sole lessee of the Playhouse which she ran for six years, her most memorable productions being *The Letter*, *The Sacred Flame*, *Cynara*, *The Pelican*, *The Painted Veil*, *Flies in the Sun* and *The Rats of Norway*. During this period she also appeared with Gerald du Maurier in *The Last of Mrs Cheyney*, which they presented jointly at the St James's in 1925, and she played Peter Pan in 1923 and 1924 at the Adelphi.

Gladys Cooper once said she chose a play as she would choose a house to live in – by instinct. When she read a script she knew whether or not she could do it. Something within her told her whether it was right or not. The fact she was acclaimed as one of the most beautiful actresses of all time never went to Gladys Cooper's head; she was far too realistic and never lost sight of the importance of the play. She knew the public would not flock to the theatre to see a bad play just because one of their favourite stars happened to be in the cast. She even went so far as to maintain that there is no such thing as an actor who is a box-office attraction. Stars are capable of filling a theatre only when they have a good play to offer the public.

Even when Gladys Cooper read plays she never chose a script simply because it contained a big part for her. During the action of *Cynara*, the last successful production she shared with Gerald du Maurier, she remained in her dressing room for an hour. The part of the wife who slowly became aware of her husband's infidelities was a comparatively small one, but she liked the play by H. M. Harwood and R. Gore Browne, which ran for 248 performances at the Playhouse in 1930, with Celia Johnson enjoying her first real success in London. One cannot imagine any other star of Gladys Cooper's standing agreeing to play such a small part in her own theatre. She was never guilty of hogging the stage and when she put on *The Sacred Flame* by Somerset Maugham at the Playhouse she deliberately chose to play Stella Tabret, the faithless wife, and gave the more rewarding parts to Clare Eames and Mary Jerrold. She never type-cast herself and always enjoyed playing a wide variety of parts. She liked Leslie Crosbie, the hard-boiled murderess in *The Letter* by Somerset Maugham, which was the first presentation under her own management at the Playhouse; but she was equally at home as Paula Tanqueray and Peter Pan. There was no such thing as a Gladys Cooper part.

Not long before her death, as she looked back over more than sixty years on the stage, she told me the happiest time of her professional life was those six years when she controlled the destiny of the Playhouse. After the show she would often stay at the theatre until the early hours discussing possible new plays and planning the future with authors, producers and scene designers. She appeared in three Maugham plays. Out of *The Letter*, her opening production in which she later toured, she made £40,000 which was an astronomical figure in 1927. The other two Maugham plays, *Home and Beauty* and *The Sacred Flame*, which are still being revived, were also financial successes. The author denied writing these plays for Gladys Cooper. He wote them for themselves, as he admitted in the Sewell Stokes biography, but he bore in mind the probability that she might care to act in them and this coloured his invention of the characters.

Being on the Embankment, the Playhouse was affectionately known as the Seagulls' Rest at that time because birds flying up from the Thames estuary used to perch on the cornice which runs round the theatre. Edward Knoblock gave Gladys Cooper a large scroll as a moving-in present and she hung it behind her dressing room door. She used to ask distinguished visitors to sign it when they went round to see her after the show. Barrie was the first and among the many celebrities who followed during her six-year tenancy were the Duke of Windsor when he was Prince of Wales, Sacha Guitry and the enchanting Yvonne Printemps, at that time his wife, Rudolph Valentino, Georges Carpentier, C. B. Fry and the politicians, Asquith, Lloyd George and Baldwin.

Many admirers considered Paula Tanqueray was Gladys Cooper's greatest achievement at the Playhouse. At the time she revived the Pinero play, Mrs Patrick Campbell, the original 1893 Paula, was still playing the part spasmodically on tour at the age of fifty-seven. To use Gladys Cooper's own words, she was 'in a complete blue funk' when she started to study Paula and grew so frightened of the part she seriously considered giving it up. She decided she ought to look quite different from the Gladys Cooper people knew and she could not get started on the play until she was able to visualise how she ought to look.

She abandoned the script and rushed over to Paris to consult her favourite dress designer, Molyneux, about altering her appearance. He called in one of his mannequins whose hair was parted in the middle. The style appealed to Gladys Cooper and after much discussion they thought Paula's dresses should be trailing and clinging. Feeling a little happier about her visual conception of Pinero's character, Gladys Cooper went to the Casino de Paris that same evening and saw a most attractive, dark-haired woman wearing long earrings. She could have been Paula Tanqueray. The problem was solved. Gladys Cooper was convinced she had to be dark, with hair parted in the middle, wearing Molyneux clinging creations and long, glittering earrings. She raced back to London quite elated and started rehearsing in real earnest the next day.

She was always ready to experiment and open to new points of view when creating a character. She refused to be swayed by stick-in-the-muds who raised objections by maintaining certain things could not be considered because they had never been done before. She had cut up Cecily Cardew's dress at the St James's and she was responsible for some startling innovations when she played Peter Pan. Instead of the traditional high boots worn by Pauline Chase and other distinguished predecessors, she had sandals made from the skins of animals and used a sabre instead of a wooden sword for her fight with Captain Hook and, finally, she wore a pair of old cotton shorts belonging to Gerald du Maurier. She naturally sought Barrie's permission before the dress rehearsal and secured it. But how many other actresses would have dared to ask him? Most would have blindly followed tradition and done what all the other Peters had done since 1904 when Nina Boucicault first played the part at the Duke of York's.

'I am literally terrified of first nights,' admitted Gladys Cooper. 'When the time comes for me to go out of my dressing room for the first entrance I am seized with the most unbearable pains and the walk along the corridor to the stage is a veritable nightmare.' She always had word trouble. Learning lines never came easy to her. Until she settled down, which took at least a week, there were times when the words she actually spoke on the stage only approximated to what the author had written. She put his meaning across, but not entirely in his own words. When she played Rosalind in *As You Like It* at the Open Air Theatre in Regent's Park, Stephen Williams, one of the leading critics of the day, said there was more Cooper than Shakespeare in her part. Once again she conveyed the meaning, but the words she substituted for Shakespeare's played havoc with the music of the verse. As Rosalind and Olivia, which she also played, she looked magnificent, an inspiration to any painter. Like Edith Evans, she had similar trouble with Noël Coward, who expected her to be word-perfect when she presented herself at the first rehearsal of *Relative Values* at the Savoy in 1951. Relations were strained for some time but after she settled down as Felicity, Countess of Marshwood, the play ran for 477 performances which must have earned the author quite a considerable sum in royalties.

In 1937 Gladys Cooper came back to London after a period in America to appear in *Goodbye to Yesterday* by James Parish, directed by Basil Dean at the Phoenix Theatre. By this time she had married the English actor Philip Merivale and they appeared together again the following year at the Palace Theatre in Dodsworth, before going to the Open Air Theatre in Regent's Park to play Rosalind and Jaques in *As You Like It*, Oberon and Theseus in *A Midsummer Night's Dream*, Olivia and Malvolio in *Twelfth Night* and Lysistrata and Kinesias in the Aristophanes comedy. He also appeared as Prospero in *The Tempest*.

Philip Merivale was the actress's third husband. Her previous marriages to Herbert Buckmaster and Sir Neville Pearson had ended in divorce, but the Merivale union was a success and lasted until his death nine years later. He had four children by his first wife who had died and she had two by her first husband and one by her second and they all combined to make one large, happy family. Valentine Merivale, the actor's daughter, said her father and Gladys Cooper had the same sort of vitality and refused to accept defeat or bad luck without tremendous resistance. 'They both loved bright people, gay people and everyone was the brighter for their company.'

Professionally, their relationship in this country was not so easy. He was a fine actor, two years her senior, with a distinguished career behind him, but he had been in America for so long he was regarded in London as Mr Gladys Cooper, which was unfortunate and led to some unpleasant incidents. He had learned his job in the Benson company before joining Fred Terry and Julia Neilson. From 1911 to 1914 he was with Beerbohm Tree at His Majesty's, where he created Colonel Pickering in Shaw's *Pygmalion* when Mrs Patrick Campbell electrified London with Eliza Doolittle's 'Not bloody likely!' line. After the London run he went to America with Mrs Pat to play Henry Higgins in the New York production. He liked America so much he stayed there for twenty-three years, coming to London only to create the name-part in Clemence Dane's *Will Shakespeare* in 1921 and to play Hannibal in *The Road to Rome* in 1928. He was not much more than a name to the playgoing public of this country in the 1930s.

I assisted with the publicity at the Open Air Theatre and there were one or two tricky moments when press photographers went out to Regent's Park, eager to cover the productions. It was the first time Gladys Cooper had played Shakespeare in London so they were eager to get pictures of her as Rosalind; her figure was good and her legs shapely. Philip Merivale was ignored. On one occasion I managed to persuade a couple of Fleet Street cameramen to go over and take a picture of Philip Merivale, who was lounging neglected in a deck-chair while scores of pictures were being taken of Gladys Cooper. After securing his permission, one of the photographers asked, 'Could we have Miss Cooper in the picture as well?' That was the match to the dynamite. 'Why do I always have to be photographed with my wife?' he roared. She came over to pour oil on the troubled waters. Similar incidents which he deeply resented occurred continually during the season, but she dealt with them tactfully. He was a magnificent Shakespeare player, but she was sadly miscast. Before they played in the Park they had presented *Macbeth* and *Othello* at the Ethel Barrymore Theatre in New York. The Broadway critics liked her Desdemona because she gave the character a sense of humour, which it seemed to need in that production and made the part more convincing. Like Edith Evans, she felt Lady Macbeth did not flow as continuously as she would have liked because parts of the text seemed to be missing. After the London season she admitted Shakespeare was not her forte and never appeared in any of his plays during the remaining thirty years of her career.

The outstanding performance of her last years was the eccentric Mrs St Maugham in *The Chalk Garden* by Enid Bagnold, which she created in New York in 1955, a year before Edith Evans played the same part in the London production. Gladys Cooper appeared in a revival of the play at the Haymarket in 1971, the year of her death. Many consider Mrs St Maugham the finest part she ever played. It meant she was last seen on the London stage in a major star part, which showed her off to perfection at that most royal of West End theatres. It was a glorious finale.

Her success was due to the fact that as the years progressed and the beauty began to fade, Gladys Cooper became a more reliable actress. She also had a matey personality. There was no question of contriving a sort of act to be put on when she arrived at the stage door or when she left after the show. She would often turn up laden with parcels, which she had collected from various shops on her way to work. She was glad to greet anyone sufficiently interested to wait to see her. She always had time to stop and exchange a cheery word. There was no question of the grand beauty sweeping past the queue without so much as a glance in their direction. Her loveliness never produced a swollen head. Her energy and determination to enjoy life to the full never left her. I called on her just before her eightieth birthday. 'I've bought a boat today,' she told me, 'to use on the river at Henley. I suppose some people think I ought to have bought a bath-chair, but I just don't feel I need one. The boat will be far more useful.' With such a philosophy of life she never became an old lady. She spent her last years living at Henley-on-Thames, devoted to her family, who lived close at hand. For Robert Morley, who married her daughter Joan Buckmaster, she had tremendous admiration, both as a man and an actor. 'I think I'd have married him myself if Joan had not done so!'

We had a quiet chat one day about the great figures she had admired in the theatre. Just as Edith Evans used to be held spellbound by Gladys Cooper's beauty, she would gaze at Marie Tempest. When Gladys was beginning to make headway on the London stage she often went alone to lunch in the Carlton Grill, which was next door to Her Majesty's Theatre, so that she could sit and watch Marie Tempest a few tables away. She went alone so that she could give her undivided attention to Miss Tempest, fascinated by her elegance of dress, her manners and her exquisite poise.

Gladys Cooper's partnership with Gerald du Maurier played a significant part in her career. She was at her happiest and most relaxed when she worked with him. He would get the best possible performances from her when directing the plays in which she appeared. Unlike Noël Coward, he allowed her to do things her own way and in her own time. It was his policy to leave actors to play parts in the way which came most naturally to them and he never interfered during the difficult uncertain days of rehearsal, when they were groping to shape the characters they were playing. He let them try to solve their problems their own way and only came in to be helpful. There was never any question of imposing his will upon them and forcing them to play a part in a manner alien to their point of view. Their most successful show together was *The Last of Mrs Cheyney* by Frederick Lonsdale, seen at the St James's in 1925. He directed and also played Lord Dilling and she was the lady crook with a heart of gold.

She had great admiration for the versatility of today's run-of-the-mill actors. She was astonished to watch the boys and girls in *West Side Story*, each one an accomplished singer, actor and dancer. All so different from the days at the Gaiety when any good-looking girl could get a job on the stage. Today only highly trained and efficient youngsters need present themselves at auditions. The old Gaiety Girls, even up-dated, would never stand a chance in the demanding modern American musicals. Gladys Cooper doubted whether Edna May or Gertie Millar, idols of her youth, would electrify audiences of today. Gertie Millar had a very small voice and a few comparatively simple dance steps. Gladys Cooper was convinced no star of the Edwardian musical comedy stage could touch Cicely Courtneidge for versatility and vitality.

Sybil Thorndike is the only actress Dame Gladys ever envied. 'What I would have given to have played Saint Joan!' She was deeply moved by Eleonora Duse when the Italian tragedienne paid her last fleeting visit to London the year before her death to give one or two performances of Ibsen's *Ghosts* and *The Lady From The Sea*, which Cochran presented at the New Oxford Theatre, but she said, 'I was not impressed as I might have been because of Duse's greasy face. Why did she not use make-up?' Unlike her deadly rival Sarah Bernhardt, Duse scorned make-up in an attempt to make her performances as realistic as possible. Although Gladys Cooper said Sybil Thorndike was the only actress she envied, I think she could also have included Edith Evans because 'she is as good a first-nighter as I am a bad one.'

Films played quite a considerable part in Gladys Cooper's career. She had no intention of becoming a film star, but dabbled in some early British silent pictures, such as *The Bohemian Girl*, made in 1922 with Constance Collier, Ivor Novello, C. Aubrey Smith and Ellen Terry in the cast. Years later in America she was asked if she would like to go out to Hollywood for three weeks to play a small part. She had never seen the Pacific Coast. She felt she would like the climate and was told life out there was like a perpetual weekend. She accepted the invitation and even made her home in Hollywood for a time.

She did not find filming very rewarding, but it certainly helped the bank balance. 'You are just a puppet in films, which have no beneficial effect on your stage work. Film directors like stage players who know what to do and can be left to get on with it, leaving the directors more time to cope with the dumb blondes who are the box-office draws.'

No one ever doubted Gladys Cooper's utter professionalism, which is best illustrated by an incident related by Ronald Hayman in his biography of John Gielgud. In 1956 when Edith Evans was playing in the original London run of *The Chalk Garden* at the Haymarket, she was taken ill some three months after the opening and had to be rushed to hospital. Gladys Cooper, who had created the part of Mrs St Maugham in New York the previous year, was in Hollywood. Hugh Beaumont, managing director of H. M. Tennent Ltd, who were presenting the production, telephoned Gladys and she agreed to dash over and play Mrs St Maugham until Dame Edith was well enough to resume the part.

After flying for twelve hours she arrived at London Airport at eleven-thirty in the morning and met Binkie Beaumont and John Gielgud, who had directed the London production of *The Chalk Garden*, an hour and a half later at the Haymarket. After discussing the production in general, Gielgud ventured to ask when she would be able to take over. 'Tonight, of course!' she snapped, as if he had asked an utterly stupid question. She rehearsed with the company there and then, called a hairdresser during the afternoon, and played the long and exacting part that very night. Not bad going for a trouper of sixty-eight!

Anna Neagle 1904–

That Anna Neagle made any significant headway in the world of entertainment is nothing short of a miracle. Her girlhood ambition was to become not an actress but a teacher of dancing and gymnastics. Eventually she changed her ideas and decided she would prefer being a dancer. Being entirely devoid of self-confidence, it is surprising that she managed to get into the chorus of so many top West End shows in the 1920s. Even more astonishing is the fact that she managed to get out of the chorus to be in a position to reach the bottom rung of the ladder which eventually took her to the pinnacle of London's musicals and made her one of the most famous names in British films. Even now, in her seventieth year, she seems far too polite, gentle and considerate a human being to have fought her way through the savage show business jungle.

Had she not had the inconceivable good fortune to meet Jack Buchanan in the theatre and Herbert Wilcox in films at the right moment in her career, she might easily have fizzled out after a decade in the chorus line. Fortunately these two champions were not deterred by her numb fear of auditions and a crippling nervous tension that prevented her doing justice to her hidden talent. They both had powerful enough vision to disregard the young girl's handicap and realise that if treated with patience and given gentle encouragement, she could well respond and reveal the star quality they were convinced she possessed. They both took risks in their respective spheres and the result is Dame Anna Neagle, with a unique and unbroken career of close to sixty years behind her.

Born Majorie Robertson at Forest Gate in London, Dame Anna was the daughter of a sea captain, Herbert William Robertson, and his wife whose maiden name was Florence Neagle. Their son, Stuart Robertson, became a well-known concert singer, a protégé of Melba. As a child, sister Marjorie took dancing lessons from Judith Espinosa, with the daughter of an Australian lady her father had met aboard ship. There was no question of preparing for a career in the theatre, but the exercise was good for the child, who also acquired grace of movement. She was spotted with other children in class and at the age of thirteen was invited to dance with some of her fellow pupils in *The Wonder Tales*, J. B. Fagan's 1917 Christmas show at the Ambassadors Theatre. Marjorie's mother was quite enthusiastic about the idea and encouraged it, but her father disapproved. Their friendly family doctor considered Marjorie's disappointment, if forbidden to accept the engagement, would do her more harm than good. So she was allowed to make her début as a dancer. It gave her a taste for the theatre and no harm was done.

Then she went to boarding school at St Albans, where she acquired the unusual idea of wanting to teach dancing and gymnastics. During her four years at St Albans she took part in a good deal of ensemble dancing which figured rather prominently in the girls' lives. Marjorie learned a little of everything and could even execute a Highland Fling. The more she danced at school the more she liked it and became convinced she lacked the right temperament for teaching. She knew she would have very little patience with slow learners or clumsy beginners and decided it would be wiser to concentrate upon becoming a dancer herself. Her father would have to be told and she knew he would not willingly agree to his daughter going on the stage, but before the ordeal had to be faced he was taken seriously ill and had to give up the sea. By the time Marjorie left school money was getting short at home. Something had to be done to earn more, so she decided to try her luck as a chorus girl.

After a third audition she was taken on by André Charlot and appeared in a 1925 revival of *Bubbly*, which had been a First World War success. The revival was a decided flop, but it gave Marjorie Robertson the comforting feeling of being accepted as a professional. For the next five years she danced in the chorus of a number of top-flight West End shows which starred the greatest names of the day. For Charlot she also sang and danced in his 1925 *Revue* at the Prince of Wales Theatre, with Beatrice Lillie and Gertrude Lawrence at the top of the bill and she was in Charlot's 1926 *Revue*, which had Jessie Matthews as leading lady. She joined the Drury Lane chorus towards the end of the run of *Rose Marie*, with Edith Day, Derek Oldham and Clarice Hardwicke in the cast and was also in Edith Day's next Drury Lane triumph, *The Desert Song*, with Harry Welchman as the dashing hero and Gene Gerrard as the debonair comedian.

For Charles B. Cochran at the London Pavilion Marjorie danced in *Wake Up and Dream*, a glittering revue which starred Jessie Matthews and Sonnie Hale in London and Jack Buchanan in New York. She appeared in both productions. The highlight of her chorus career had come in *This Year of Grace* at the London Pavilion the previous year in 1928. Noël Coward contributed some of his finest numbers to this show, including 'Dance, Little Lady', which was sung by Sonnie Hale with show-stopping regularity. Coward had created an exciting new rhythm and Marjorie Robertson was one of the chorus girls who took part in this number, dressed as a robot wearing a rather sinister mask. Jessie Matthews, Maisie Gay and the enchanting Viennese dancer, Tilly Losch, were among the principals who starred in this milestone of sophisticated light entertainment.

'When I was in the chorus,' recalled Dame Anna, 'I had no idea what it meant to an actor given the responsibility of playing a leading role, nor did I realise the price idolised players had to pay for their stardom. Even so, it was exciting to be in shows with such famous people as Bea Lillie, Gertie Lawrence, Jack Buchanan, Jessie Matthews and Edith Day and a great advantage to be chosen to work with them in their numbers.

'I was most impressed by Edith Day's pure voice, which she projected so expertly into the vast auditorium of Drury Lane in *Rose Marie* and *The Desert Song* in the days before microphones had been heard of. She had a mercurial charm of manner which I always admired as she passed through the Green Room every night on her way to the stage. We chorus girls were not allowed in the wings until just before the cue for our entrance. Until then we had to wait in the Green Room, wearing protective cotton cloaks to keep our costumes clean. At a given signal we hung these garments on pegs at the side of the stage and then we were all ready to go on. I was also impressed by Edith Day's acting skill, being able to hold that enormous house throughout three long successive runs, starting with *Rose Marie*, followed by *The Desert Song* and concluding with *Show Boat*, which totalled more than 1,600 performances – quite a record figure in those days before *The Mousetrap* had run for more than twenty years.

'At the London Pavilion I was full of admiration for the versatile and talented Jessie Matthews, whose romantic partnership with Sonnie Hale brought them well into the public eye. She had a wonderful sense of comedy and a unique stage appearance, with that pixie face, the fringe hair-do and those enormous eyes. Few comediennes have been more genuinely loved by the public than Maisie Gay who was at the Pavilion in *This Year of Grace*. Arthritis was beginning to take its deadly toll. She could no longer run up and down stairs to her dressing room, so on stage level a corner of the chorus's quick-change room was screened-off for her use. Eventually she had to retire from the stage because of her crippled condition and she shrivelled to the size of an infant before she died, after much suffering, at the age of sixty-seven, seventeen years after we had worked together at the London Pavilion under Charles B. Cochran's banner.'

Charles Cochran was a unique showman. He had exquisite taste and encouraged such people as Noël Coward, Oliver Messel and Jessie Matthews early in their careers and in his productions he featured such dazzling creatures as Delysia, Nikitina and Lifar, the Dolly Sisters, Florence Mills, Tilly Losch, Eleonora Duse, Sacha Guitry, Alexander Moïssi, the Pitoëffs, Yvonne Printemps, Elisabeth Bergner, Katina Paxinou and Georges Guètary.

Cochran's chorus girls were known as 'Mr Cochran's Young Ladies' and Anna Neagle is very proud to have been one of them. 'We were all individual in personality and appearance, which made our troupe a star of any revue in which we appeared. Incredible as it may seem, he took an individual and personal interest in all of us and seemed to have some knowledge of the background of our private lives. "Are you all right for money?" he asked me on one occasion when there was a gap between a show closing in London and opening elsewhere. I was surprised that a man with so much on his mind and so many responsibilities should have time to consider me – just one of twelve girls in his chorus line. On another occasion when I had my tonsils removed, he took the trouble to send me flowers. Later, fourteen years after his death, I played Lady Hadwell in *Charlie Girl*, a former Cochran Young Lady who had married into the aristocracy, but had to throw her stately home open to the public to meet death duties. We played at the Adelphi Theatre, where Cochran had presented such successes as *Ever Green*, *Words and Music*, *Nymph Errant*, *Follow the Sun*, *Home and Beauty*, *Big Ben* and *Bless The Bride*. The Lady Hadwell link with Cochran gave me considerable quiet pleasure. I only wish he had been alive to see the show.'

When Anna Neagle returned to London after the New York run of *Wake Up and Dream* in 1930 she felt she really ought to do something about getting out of the chorus. She had enjoyed five years going from show to show and getting immense pleasure out of her work. In New York she acquired slight stirrings of ambition, so she took singing lessons and spent hours practising tap dancing, which was all the rage at that time. She felt something must be done about her career or she might continue dancing in the chorus until managements considered she had reached retirement age for that kind of work on the stage.

Cochran sent for Anna Neagle – who was still Marjorie Robertson – to tell her about a new musical called *Ever Green*, which he was preparing for the Adelphi. The theatre had been reconstructed and he had installed a revolving stage, the first to be used in the West End, only a few months ahead of the sensational *White Horse Inn* at the Coliseum.

Gladys Cooper's last show, a few months before her death, with Donald Eccles in *The Chalk Garden* at the Yvonne Arnaud Theatre, Guildford, 1970. *Photo: Donald Cooper*
Previous page: Gladys Cooper – a camera study by Angus McBean.

Freddie Carpenter, who went to Australia to direct Anna Neagle in *Charlie Girl* in 1971, escorts her to one of the many social gatherings in her honour.

Above left: Gladys Cooper postcards sold in their thousands whenever a new picture was published.

Above right: Another study of Gladys Cooper as a picture postcard beauty.

nna Neagle and Peter Graves in *The Glorious Days*, the 1953 musical, in which she played Nell Gwynn, Queen Victoria, a musical comedy star and an ATS driver in the Blitz.

Anna Neagle, as she appeared in *Stand Up and Sing* – London Hippodrome, 1930.

Anna Neagle as one of Mr Cochran's Y[ ] Ladies in *Wake Up and Dream*, 1929

Cicely Courtneidge and Jack Hulbert in the years just before the First World War. *Phot[ ]* *Foulsham and Banfield*
Right: Cicely Courtneidge as a male impersonator – a favourite picture she sent to her far[ ] in the 1930s.
Overleaf: Bobby Howes and Cicely Courtneidge in *Hide and Seek* at the London Hippodrome 1937.

Jessie Matthews was the star of *Ever Green*, in which she sang 'Dancing on the Ceiling'. The play was by Benn W. Levy and the score by Richard Rodgers. Cochran offered Anna Neagle the second understudy to Jessie Matthews, in addition to her chorus job. With tremendous courage she told him she thought the time had come to make a break and he respected her point of view. He was sorry to lose her. She had been one of his most attractive Young Ladies and he wanted her to know there would always be a place for her in his chorus line if she ever felt she would like to return at some future date. She left his office and when she reached the street she felt she must be crazy to have turned down a Cochran show, without having any prospects in view.

She failed to make any headway at auditions she attended because her nerves paralysed her, leaving her incapable of giving any indication of how good she could be in a show under public performance conditions. One agent thought she was photogenic and might get work in films. This led to a small part in *The Chinese Bungalow* with Matheson Lang, who was repeating his stage success on the screen. During this engagement she changed her name from Marjorie Robertson to Anna Neagle at the suggestion of the producer of the film who did not consider Marjorie Robertson a good name for an actress. She took her mother's maiden name of Neagle, which was easy to say, looked good in print and was easily remembered. There was no other Neagle in the entertainment world so there was no fear of her being mistaken for any other actress, if she succeeded in attracting attention. No work came along after *The Chinese Bungalow*. Anna became very depressed and wondered whether she had done the right thing in refusing Cochran's offer. Then it was Jack Buchanan's turn to make his entrance into the story of her career.

Jack Buchanan was the most elegant light comedian on the revue and musical comedy stage in the 1920s. He was always immaculately well tailored and was not unlike Edward, Prince of Wales, who later became the Duke of Windsor. There were occasions when both these well-dressed men set the fashions of the sartorial world. Jack Buchanan had a most attractive throaty voice which was instantly recognisable and his two most popular numbers were 'Who?' and 'Her Mother Came, Too', a song inspired by Elsie Janis, the American star, whose mother never left her side because she was so busy carving out her daughter's career.

When Jack Buchanan returned from his highly successful run of *Wake Up and Dream* in New York, he decided to take the London Hippodrome – now the Talk of the Town – and appear in *Stand Up and Sing*, which he had written with Douglas Furber. The show had music by Vivian Ellis and Philip Charig and also in the cast were

Elsie Randolph, Vera Pearce, Roma Beaumont, Anton Dolin and Charles Lefeaux. All they wanted was an *ingénue*, a youngster emanating youth and beauty. Anna Neagle heard of his plans and decided to go along for an audition. They had both been in the New York cast of *Wake Up and Dream*, but he was the idolised star and she was simply one of Mr Cochran's Young Ladies. They spoke on only one occasion when he asked her name before signing a picture for her. 'Marjorie Robertson,' was her reply and the picture which he inscribed to her still stands in a silver frame in Anna Neagle's sitting room.

Her tap routines made quite an impression at the audition and Jack Buchanan engaged her. During rehearsals when he discussed details of the small part she was playing he said, 'You are quite the most nervous creature I have ever come across.' But in spite of this and her surprising lack of self-confidence, he had faith in her and thought she would be adequate for the character of Mary Clyde-Burkin. Just in case she did not come up to expectations, her contract was for the prior-to-London try-out tour only and her part was pruned down to give her every chance of getting away with it. He left in things which seemed right and within the scope of her capability. At the end of the short tour he felt she was good enough for London and she was allowed to stay with the cast for the London Hippodrome opening in March 1931.

She had a comedy scene with Jack Buchanan, which was the great test of the evening as far as she was concerned. As it proceeded on the opening night she said, 'The audience seemed to care what happened to us. There was a hush in the auditorium which proved we were gripping their attention. I knew I had succeeded and I had been right to leave the chorus.' She was well received by the press and her glamorous pictures were all over the newspapers and illustrated magazines. She had arrived in a small way and the future was full of promise. Cochran still had a proud eye on her and sent a first-night telegram to the effect that hard work and perseverance had rewarded her with much-deserved success. When Anna Neagle reminisces about that London Hippodrome show, it is obvious that she has great affection for Jack Buchanan. 'He gave me my first glimmer of self-confidence. He was the most sensitive and understanding person and went to endless trouble in *Stand Up and Sing* to ensure that the part would not be too difficult for me and that I would be capable of coping with its demands. I felt it was within my reach and he knew that if I succeeded at that early point in my career I would gain confidence and be encouraged to tackle bigger things. His patience and sheer professionalism steered me through that show and opened the door into the film world.'

During the run of *Stand Up and Sing* Jack Buchanan had agreed to make a film, *Goodnight, Vienna*, to be directed by Herbert Wilcox.

Having failed to get an English leading lady, they were considering the engagement of a film star from the Continent. Herbert Wilcox was a bit uneasy about the idea as it would entail all sorts of tricky negotiation, and time was terribly precious. The entire film had to be made in three weeks, after the West End run of *Stand Up and Sing* and before the production set out on a long tour. He was desperate to get the matter settled, so on a matinée day he looked in at the Hippodrome to discuss last-minute details with Jack Buchanan.

He arrived before the end of the show, so he slipped into an empty box to wait for the final curtain. Then, for the first time in his life he saw Anna Neagle and was quite captivated by her beauty which he imagined would be remarkably photogenic. Why not use her in *Goodnight, Vienna* and save themselves all the trouble of discussions with the Continental star? He put the idea to Jack Buchanan as soon as he reached his dressing room. Jack thought it was brilliant and that is how Anna Neagle broke into films. Eventually she married Herbert Wilcox and they became the greatest husband-and-wife partnership in the British film industry. As the years rolled on she went to Hollywood and became a film star of international calibre, appearing in such memorable pictures as *Bitter Sweet, Nell Gwyn, Victoria the Great, Sixty Glorious Years, Nurse Edith Cavell, Sunny, I Lived In Grosvenor Square, Spring In Park Lane, Odette* and *Lady With a Lamp*.

During that between-shows dressing room discussion, Anna Neagle accepted the invitation to play the leading part in *Goodnight, Vienna* for a flat £150. They impressed upon her the necessity of completing the picture in three weeks, which meant unlimited working hours and a seven-day week. Once they started work she discovered she enjoyed the new medium and looked very attractive on the screen when the first rushes were shown. Herbert Wilcox was delighted with his 'find' and was convinced he would be using her over and over again in forthcoming pictures. Like Jack Buchanan, he was sensitive and understanding of the anxieties and inhibitions of artists. Once they had more time at their disposal and did not have to make a complete picture in three weeks, he was gratified to discover Anna was a perfectionist and as she gained more experience and authority in the studio she insisted upon working over and over again until she felt a scene was right before she faced the cameras. 'I go on until I cannot recognise Anna Neagle or her voice,' she explained. 'Then I know I'm lost in the character and it is time to shoot the scene.'

Anna Neagle's entry into films had a surprisingly beneficial effect upon her stage work. After making his pictures, Herbert Wilcox went to great lengths to see they were properly presented. He had a flair for showmanship, as Cochran had, and his films made an immediate and lasting impact upon the public, due partly to the manner in which he launched them. He gave Anna tremendous confidence in the film studio by encouraging her to do things which at first seemed beyond her capability. In this way she acquired faith in herself and made her name in the cinema. When his films were released he often arranged for Anna to make stage appearances in the cinemas showing her pictures. Together they would go round the big cities of Britain. The exhibitors would be lunched in style, with both Herbert and Anna making speeches, and then at the opening showing of the film Anna would also be seen on stage.

Some of these appearances were quite elaborate affairs. In *The Little Damozel* she attempted to get away from the English Rose image and appeared on stage dancing the waltz from *The Merry Widow* and also executing a lively Cakewalk. When she toured the Paramount Circuit she was accompanied by eight Tiller Girls. Herbert liked to get her back into the theatre in a show from time to time, using contact with a living audience to refresh her. The public could give her an immediate reaction which was missing in the studio and there were problems of timing which could be solved only in live performance. No one was more aware than Herbert of the fact that a film player is totally cut off from living people in the ivory tower of the film studio and he was determined Anna should not always be separated from the public he was trying to captivate with her films.

Her return to the stage – this time as leading lady – came in 1934, two years after the run of *Stand Up and Sing* and after her first experience of stardom in films. Phyllis Neilson-Terry, who had been engaged to play Rosalind in *As You Like It* and Olivia in *Twelfth Night* at the Open Air Theatre in Regent's Park, had been taken ill and Robert Atkins, the artistic director, was at his wits' end to get a suitable replacement at short notice. Anna Neagle was free and he considered the idea of presenting her in Shakespeare would be quite a feather in his cap. Anna's immediate reaction was to refuse the offer. The thought of playing two of Shakespeare's greatest parts terrified her. She was convinced she would never be able to learn the lines, after best part of two years in films when she only had to memorise a small section of the script at a time – just enough to cover the next day's shooting.

Robert Atkins was determined to go through with the idea. He worked with her on Rosalind's lines throughout one weekend and on the Monday she was joined by Jack Hawkins, her Orlando, and they started rehearsals with the company which included Robert Eddison as Jaques, Hubert Gregg as Silvius and the poet John Drinkwater as the Duke. She looked simply exquisite in that sylvan setting which Robert Atkins always lit so imaginatively. *As You Like It* was followed by

Twelfth Night in which Anna's Olivia was partnered by the Orsino of Jack Hawkins, the Viola of Margaretta Scott and the Malvolio of John Drinkwater. Her worst moment was the night she heard that Elisabeth Bergner – a legendary Rosalind of the time – was sitting in the front row.

Anna Neagle still looks back with gratitude on the kindness and co-operation of her fellow players in the Park. Taking an even wider view, she maintains she has never met with opposition from actors. They have always been most helpful and never, during the 1930s, resented her being a greater name on the screen than on the stage. Robert Atkins realised the learning of lines was quite an ordeal for her, so he had Rosalind's Epilogue written on an ornamental scroll, so that she could read it instead of having to commit it to memory. It was thoughtful gestures such as this which warmed her heart.

Peter Pan was another classic part she played, at the Palladium in 1937. She still recalls the rustle of sweet-bags and the aroma of oranges, when the curtain rose on a special performance given to a house packed with children, all guests of the Lord Mayor of London. George Curzon played Captain Hook and other names in the cast which were later to become famous were Max Adrian as Starkey, Jimmy Hanley as Slightly and Leslie Phillips as one of the Lost Boys. Nina Boucicault, who had created the part of Peter in 1904 and still took an interest in the annual revival, lent Anna her dagger. There were lots of famous names on the London stage that Christmas. Glynis Johns was playing Barrie's Cinderella at the Phoenix, Elsie Randolph was Aladdin to Arthur Riscoe's Widow Twankey at the Adelphi, Pat Kirkwood was Dandini and Madge Elliott Prince Charming in *Cinderella* at the Princes', Clarkson Rose was Mignonette in *Beauty and the Beast* at the Lyceum, Robert Helpmann was the Oberon to Vivien Leigh's Titania in *A Midsummer Night's Dream* at the Old Vic and Malcolm Keen was Long John Silver to Kenneth Connor's Jim Hawkins in *Treasure Island* at the Savoy.

Both on stage and screen Anna Neagle has played quite a number of famous people who actually lived, such as Queen Victoria, Florence Nightingale, Edith Cavell, Peg Woffington and Nell Gwynn. The private research she carried out in order to impersonate these historical figures proved most rewarding, mainly because the actress was not interested in knocking them off their pedestals. Her intention in every instance has been to pay tribute to their greatness and indicate the significance of their achievement. Her research concerning Peg Woffington and Nell Gwynn was confined to books, to looking up what had been written about them. But when it came to people who had lived more recently – Queen Victoria, Florence Nightingale and

Nurse Cavell, she was able to visit museums and art galleries which possessed vital personal material relating to them and to visit houses which had once been their homes. Even more exciting was her personal contact with elderly people who had actually known them.

When George VI heard of Herbert Wilcox's intention to make *Sixty Glorious Years*, a film on the life of his great-grandmother, Queen Victoria, he gave permission for the royal palaces to be used for location shots and arranged for Anna Neagle to meet two particular ladies who had known the ageing Queen intimately, so that she could gain valuable and accurate information concerning the Queen's mannerisms and personal appearance. One was Princess Helena Victoria, a grand-daughter who lived with Queen Victoria for some time and the other was the Dowager Countess of Antrim, one of the last ladies-in-waiting to the Queen. It so happened that Lady Antrim's father had been private secretary to Victoria, which made her an especially valuable link with the past. People at Court were so impressed by Anna Neagle's devoted and dedicated purpose in her search for historical accuracy, they went out of their way to help her and in some cases even presented her with priceless souvenirs relating to the Queen. In her sitting room Anna Neagle has an elegant glass-fronted cabinet in which some of these treasures are housed. The most remarkable item is Victoria's first notebook, consisting of a number of sheets of thin notepaper fitted into an ornate metal container designed in the form of a crucifix. Each sheet of paper is cut into the shape of the Cross. It had been a present to Princess Victoria on her fifth birthday from her mother, the Duchess of Kent. On the top sheet of this curiously fashioned pad, the little girl had written MAMA GAVE ME TIS (sic). Her pencilled words have been lovingly preserved since she inscribed them one hundred and fifty years ago. Anna Neagle also possesses an impressive photograph of the Queen in old age; it must have been one of the last portraits she signed and her expression gives a vivid indication of the impact the ageing monarch must have created upon all who met her even at the very end of her reign. This picture was also an inspiration to the costume designer searching for evidence of the Queen's taste in jewellery and style of dress.

Some of the episodes in *Sixty Glorious Years* were shot on location at Balmoral. Anna Neagle dressed at a near-by hotel, which during the Queen's last years had sometimes been used to accommodate the overflow of royal guests when the castle itself was full. One of the hotel's elderly employees, who had often taken orders from the Queen concerning the requirements of her guests, suddenly came face to face with Anna Neagle made up as the ageing monarch in one of the corridors. Rooted to the spot by shock, the old lady cried out, 'Our

Queen is risen!' Anna Neagle was deeply moved by what she considered one of the most remarkable and sincere compliments ever paid to her.

Anna Neagle visited Florence Nightingale's old home, Lea Hurst, in a tiny village near Bakewell in Derbyshire and she was even permitted to sleep in what had been the Lady with a Lamp's bedroom while the film company were working there on location. She met Florence Nightingale's god-daughter, but what was even more exciting was paying a visit to a woman who claimed to be the first Army Matron. At the time Anna Neagle met her she was in her one hundredth year. She was one of the first nurses specially trained to work with the Army Medical Corps and she gave Dame Anna a vivid account of being taken to see Florence Nightingale at her house in South Street, Park Lane, before being sent out to China.

While Anna Neagle was preparing to play Nurse Cavell she had the good fortune to meet Miss Wilkins who had been her personal assistant from 1912 and was with her in Belgium, taking part in the events which led to Edith Cavell being shot by the Germans in 1915 for harbouring refugees and facilitating their escape into Holland. Miss Wilkins knew what was happening and at one point while the Germans were actually in the process of interrogating Edith Cavell she collected some incriminating papers, tore them up, and flushed them down the lavatory pan, in the hope of saving the life of her dedicated chief. But it was too late; the Germans already had sufficient evidence of their own to condemn her. Apart from the gratification Anna Neagle obtained from playing these famous women, she gained immense satisfaction from the painstaking research which almost convinced her she had actually met the great figures she later impersonated.

Anna Neagle's first love in the theatre has always been musicals, ever since her days in the chorus. She had had long spells away from the stage to make films for Herbert – usually cast-iron box-office successes – and then she had swept back to gather fresh laurels as a West End leading lady. After her screen successes as Nell Gwynn and Victoria, both these characters were incorporated into *The Glorious Days*, a musical play by Robert Nesbitt, with a score by Harry Parr Davies, who wrote some of the best songs Gracie Fields ever sang. It was staged at the Palace Theatre in 1953 and ran for 256 performances.

As far as the stage was concerned, Anna Neagle imagined she had thrown her dancing shoes over her shoulder after *The Glorious Days*, which was followed by three different straight plays – *The More the Merrier* by Ronald Millar, *Nothing is for Free* and a thriller called *Person Unknown*. As far as the straight stage is concerned Anna Neagle's favourite part is Emma Woodhouse in Gordon Glennon's adaptation of Jane Austen's *Emma*. In the cast were Wynne Clark, Graveley Edwards, H. R. Hignett, Frank Allenby, Terry Randal, George Thirlwell, Gillian Lind, Grey Blake, Margaret Vines, Ambrosine Phillpotts and Cecil Ramage. She was extremely happy in that production which had the misfortune to open at the St James's Theatre in 1945 during the week the Germans sent their first doodlebugs to London. One of these flying bombs dropped in the neighbourhood of the theatre and that meant a very short run for *Emma*. It also meant London was no longer comparatively free from air-raids during daylight, so the old ladies who had ventured out to matinées made up their minds to stay at home and the theatres suffered a severe setback.

But the days of Anna Neagle's musicals were by no means over. One of the most spectacular of all her successes lay ahead. That was *Charlie Girl*, which Harold Fielding presented at the Adelphi Theatre twenty years after *Emma*, in 1965. It ran for more than 2,000 performances and then had another lease of life in Australia and New Zealand. David Heneker and John Taylor wrote the music and lyrics; Hugh and Margaret Williams, together with Ray Cooney, wrote the book on a story by Ross Taylor. Apart from Dame Anna, the original cast included Hy Hazell, Christine Holmes, Derek Nimmo, Joe Brown, David Toguri and Stuart Damon. There were various changes during the long run when contracts expired and artists had to leave the cast to fulfil prior commitments.

The production had no encouragement from the critics, but Anna Neagle and her devoted team of troupers kept the theatre packed for five years. 'I think it was the sort of family show audiences had been waiting for,' was Anna Neagle's opinion. 'There were good tunes; I think Derek Nimmo was very funny and it was the sort of show anyone could see without fear or embarrassment. You could take Grandma or any of the grandchildren and be sure they would all enjoy it. I think *The Sound of Music* was a success for the same reason and that had quite a slamming from the critics, but ran even longer than *Charlie Girl*. *Oliver!* was another ideal family show which ran even longer than *The Sound of Music*, but it had the good fortune to get rave reviews right from the start.

Anna Neagle has an undying affection for what is now called the old-fashioned musical. She cites the Drury Lane production of *Rose Marie*, when she was in the chorus. She would like to hear more leading ladies with a voice to equal Edith Day's and more staggering scenes with vast stages filled with singers and dancers. She fully realises no management could possibly afford to stage such productions these days unless they charged astronomical prices for the seats. Her ideal musical comedy leading lady would be one of the Phyllis Dare vintage, a fair English rose, in pastel chiffon, moving gracefully round the stage to the romantic lilt of violins in waltz time. Anna Neagle goes to see modern musicals, just to keep abreast with the times. Frequently she finds the score too noisy for her taste, which craves for melody, but she was most enthusiastic about *Sweet Charity*, the American musical which starred Juliet Prowse at the Prince of Wales Theatre in 1967. It had an amusing book by Neil Simon and music by Cy Coleman and lyrics by Dorothy Fields. The London presentation was based on the original production staged and directed by Bob Fosse.

When Australia decided to stage *Charlie Girl* in 1971 after the London run they invited Anna Neagle to play her original part and Freddie Carpenter was chosen to direct an entirely new production, with Derek Nimmo also in his original part. Discussing the Neagle magnetism, which is the envy of so many of her rival star colleagues, Freddie Carpenter said, 'The public adore her – especially the women – because she has all the appeal of a terribly nice person. She is the sort of good neighbour everyone would like to have. No star has ever been less theatrical than Anna Neagle. She gives the impression of being a genuine person, who looks most elegant through choosing simplicity as her guiding motif.

'Back-stage with her colleagues she is just as congenial. She never demands star treatment and because of that always gets it. After the run of *Charlie Girl* in Australia she went back to Her Majesty's Theatre in Melbourne a year later to attend a performance of *No, No, Nanette*. The stage hands treated her like royalty, lining up to welcome her like a Queen. They were delighted to see her back again, just because they liked her as a person and not because she had bought her popularity by giving them parties and presents.

'She is always prepared to meet her colleagues half way and makes no special demands. When we were arranging rehearsal schedules for *Charlie Girl* she made one suggestion to me. "I try to rest after the lunch-break and would be glad to have the afternoon free, if that is possible. I'll work as long as you like in the morning and again in the evening. If this idea would throw your rehearsal plans out of gear, please forget it and I'll fall in with your plans. On the other hand, if you can arrange the work so that I am not required in the afternoon I would be grateful." Who could resist so gentle and reasonable a request?

'She never threw her weight about. Her film legend was never mentioned and she was more than considerate with the rest of the cast. On the New Zealand tour of *Charlie Girl*, the production played one theatre which had not been used for live shows for a long time. The underground dressing rooms were in bad condition and a musty odour pervaded the whole of the back-stage area. She never complained. She just took it in her stride and roughed it with the rest of the company, who found her more endearing than ever.

'Herbert Wilcox came out with Anna and they were much together. He used to escort her to rehearsal and call for her afterwards, but never interfered with the production or with her performance. He would never dream of staying to watch unless expressly invited to do so. I have never seen a more natural actress than Anna Neagle. She uses less make-up than any other star; her stage make-up is so light she could wear it in the street without attracting attention. She is a professional down to her fingertips. She was never late for rehearsal and never created any fuss about doing her job. She just got on with it to the best of her remarkable ability and worked at her exercises quietly at home. Once the show has opened her performance never deteriorates, either in acting, singing or dancing. She is one of the most reliable artists I have ever worked with. She never has an off night. Her off-stage modesty is quite genuine. It was rumoured that when she was on holiday during the London run of *Charlie Girl* the box-office figures dropped by £1,000 a week, but she was never tempted to boast about it. Unlike so many actresses, she has no time for gossip. Because it is of no interest to her, she turns a deaf ear to it, but with great charm. Her manners are never less than beautiful at all times.'

As Peter Saunders once said, 'Anna lives in a dream world which Herbert Wilcox created for her.' He has isolated her from reality, but also made it possible for her to earn the money with which to build that private world and maintain it. Whenever she is in a stage production, Herbert is always about. As Freddie Carpenter observed, he never interferes, but does everything possible to interest the right people in whatever Anna is doing. Anna, known to him as 'the Girl', plays her part and never lets the side down, on stage or off. Peter Saunders is full of admiration for the gracious manner in which Anna always behaves. 'She always dresses up to face the fans at the stage door. She would never dream of just pulling on jeans and an old sweater to drive home.' She is a past-mistress when it comes to creating the illusion of glamour on the stage and is not stupid enough to shatter it the moment the curtain falls.

The fascinating Neagle-Wilcox relationship has long intrigued Herbert de Leon, an old and trusted friend of theirs, who also happens to be Anna's agent. Anna and Herbert have a wonderfully close and understanding relationship. The entire theatrical profession, together with a legion of fans, admired her great courage when Herbert Wilcox was bankrupt. She sold her jewels and worked like a Trojan until their debts were paid. During the run of *Charlie Girl*, Herbert was the victim of a serious illness which took him to the very threshold of death's door. Anna never missed a performance. She kept faith with the public who had paid to go and see her, even though there were many nights when she felt convinced he might die during the performance and the news would be kept from her until the end of the show.

While she is in a production he is constantly at her side or at the other end of the telephone line. When she went to Australia to play in *Charlie Girl*, Herbert flew out to see her on three different occasions and he also saw her in New Zealand. He is a great showman and in de Leon's estimation might have rivalled Cochran had he concentrated his interest entirely upon the theatre. He knows what is right for Anna. She has blind faith in him and he has never failed her. He attended all the ten or so previews which preceded the opening of *No, No, Nanette* at Drury Lane in 1973. He sat in front, choosing different parts of the house each time, and concentrated upon the audience's reaction. After the show he went back to report to Anna, so that she could benefit from any lesson he felt he may have learned. He invited influential people and took them round to see her afterwards as a means of boosting her morale.

'She has great and gracious qualities as a woman,' maintained Herbert de Leon. 'She is high-minded and I always feel she would have made a wonderful nurse. Herbert Wilcox knew what he was doing when he cast her as Florence Nightingale for one of the most moving films he ever made.'

As a child Anna had been taken to the theatre to see the two greatest ballerinas of the day, Adeline Genée and Anna Pavlova, and that may have had some influence upon her decision to devote her life to dancing when she first thought seriously about a stage career. When she had to dance in the *Nell Gwynn* and *Peg Woffington* films she studied with Serafina Astafieva, the famous dancer who came to London from the Imperial Ballet in St Petersburg and taught Markova, Anton Dolin and Margot Fonteyn. Anna Neagle was also coached by Stanislas Idzikovsky, the famous Polish dancer considered by many to have been the equal of Nijinsky. For modern dance she worked with Betty and Philip Buchel and with Alfred Rodrigues for *Charlie Girl* and with the American Donald Saddler for *No, No, Nanette* at Drury Lane. She always took her dancing very seriously and sought the best available teachers to correct her faults and give her the right point of view.

Peter Graves was one of her four leading men in *The Glorious Days*, the other three being James Carney, Olaf Olsen and Patrick Holt. As a result of being associated with her in films and of sharing a good deal of her leisure during the prior-to-London tour of *The Glorious Days*, Peter Graves had the opportunity of getting to know Anna as a close friend and the words he has generously jotted down speak for themselves, giving a vivid impression of a unique and admirable woman:

'It is difficult to talk about Anna Neagle without including Herbert Wilcox. To me they are almost one. I certainly never think of one without the other.

'I suppose Anna is the greatest example of a very pretty girl with brains and talent being "discovered" by a film director, Herbert Wilcox who, by his knowledge of film-making, showmanship and remarkable presentation of his protégée, made the very pretty girl with the brains and talent into a star. And having achieved that, saw to it with the right combination of part, script and presentation that she remained one for many years.

'The fact that she has survived through her film years and remained a star in the theatre speaks much for her amazing appeal to the public – the kind of appeal that if she's in difficulty or trouble as she was with Herbert's bankruptcy and subsequent illness, made them feel they wanted to help her and go and see her in the theatre in return for the tremendous pleasure she has given them and to salute her courage.

'I joined them in 1947 in *Spring in Park Lane* and stayed with them in their *Maytime in Mayfair, Derby Day, Lady with a Lamp* and *Lilacs In The Spring*, before being cast as one of Anna's leading men in the musical play *The Glorious Days*. Six years in all – the happiest of my working life, which I can only describe as a holiday with pay – with two very dear people.

'It was during the twenty-seven-week tour of the musical, before it came to London that I got to know Anna. She loved to go for long walks. So did I. So we used to meet around eleven in the morning on the non-matinée days and pace the streets, promenades and country lanes of the larger cities and talk. Not gossip. She's an exceedingly kind person and gossip isn't in her make-up. It's impossible not to be fond of her, to want everything to be all right for her, to be protective even.

'Her marriage to Herbert is even more remarkable than their relationship at work. Total absorption in each other, the one complementing the other – not just occasionally, but always. Their behaviour to each other is touching and exemplary. Her example of discipline in the studio and in the theatre is derived from Herbert's enthusiasm and direction, so that the confidence they give to the other actors is relaxing and enjoyable.

'Anna is, then, a Dame by reason of the example she sets in her private life, her service to her job and the charities she looks after and her appeal to the public.'

If you ask Anna Neagle what she would like to do in the future, as far as her career is concerned, she will tell you she never plans far ahead.

'I don't set my sights,' she says, 'and things seem to come to me.' In other words, she leaves it to chance. She feels people who write about the theatre these days are obsessed by the question of age in her case, constantly referring to the fact that she is on the brink of seventy, instead of concentrating upon her artistic achievement. 'They never harped upon Ellen Terry's age or Bernhardt's age, even when at fifty-six she played the ill-fated son of Napoleon in *L'Aiglon* and received thirty curtain calls on the opening night in Paris. The Divine Sarah was playing the part of a sick boy who never reached the age of twenty-one and she scored the supreme triumph of her later career. She moved her audiences to tears in this part every time she played it. That was enough in itself. Quoting her age would have made no difference to her amazing achievement.'

Anna Neagle is no fool and knows she can look half her real age on the stage, without the aid of fantastic make-up, but she is never allowed to play a new part without her age cropping up somewhere in almost every written comment on her performance. She would still like to play Beatrice in *Much Ado About Nothing*, to add to the Rosalind and the Olivia she played in Regent's Park all those years ago, and she would indeed look ravishing in the part. Mary Queen of Scots is a temptation, but far too many plays have been written about her. Anna Neagle regrets there was no romance in the life of Flora Macdonald. She would have made a new heroine for the stage, but her life was once closely examined with the idea of writing a film scenario for Anna. It transpired that Flora was only with Bonnie Prince Charlie for three days and was far too busy engineering his escape to get any romantic ideas about him.

So there is no heroine Dame Anna is desperately eager to play, but after the pleasure she derived from appearing as Jane Austen's Emma she would obviously like to go back to the straight stage. If she is still pursuing her policy of leaving her future to chance, perhaps something will turn up and surprise everyone as much as the long run of *Charlie Girl*.

Cicely Courtneidge 1893–

Cicely Courtneidge admits she owes more than half her success to the inspiration and imagination of her husband Jack Hulbert who has been her stage partner, as leading man and producer, since 1913 when they first appeared together at the old Shaftesbury Theatre which faced the Shaftesbury Avenue side of the Palace Theatre, in a musical comedy called *The Pearl Girl*. Like Sybil Thorndike and Anna Neagle, she had the good fortune to marry a man who has given her a lifetime of congenial companionship and has also been her vital Other Self throughout all the ups and downs of their professional life. Their partnership caught and retained the public fancy so securely they were able, when already in their early eighties, to revive *The Hollow*, one of the lesser successful Agatha Christie thrillers, and nightly pack provincial theatres on the touring circuit with loyal and affectionate followers for months on end.

Cicely was born in Australia where her Glasgow-born father, Robert Courtneidge, was in Sydney playing Gringoire in a comic opera called *Esmeralda*. On his return to this country he was to direct the Prince's Theatre in Manchester for seven years, where little Cicely played her only Shakespearean role, Peasblossom in *A Midsummer Night's Dream*, at the age of eight. He settled inLondon at the turn of the century to produce *The Duchess of Dantzic* for George Edwardes and such popular musical comedy successes as *The Blue Moon*, *The Dairymaids* and *Tom Jones* and in 1908 he became the lessee of the Shaftesbury Theatre where he produced *The Arcadians*, a smash-hit which ran for two years, quite a record-breaking achievement for those days. Such was the world in which Cicely Courtneidge grew up, daughter of one of London's most successful showmen, running a West End theatre of his own.

Having decided to go on the stage, she naturally appeared in her father's productions and at the age of fourteen played Rosie Lucas in *Tom Jones* in Manchester and then moved to the Lyric Theatre to make her London début later the same year in the same part. In 1909 she took over the part of Chrysea in her father's production of *The Arcadians* at the Shaftesbury from an actress who left the cast to get married, leaving behind an unsuitable understudy. The following year she was promoted to the part of Eileen Cavanagh in the same show. Another milestone under her father's management was *The Pearl Girl*, when she appeared for the first time with Jack Hulbert, making his début on the professional stage, after having shown great promise as an actor during his undergraduate days at Cambridge. Three years later they were to marry.

Robert Courtneidge did not spoil his daughter. She received a salary of £5 a week, but was allowed to handle only £2, out of which she had to buy her own clothes, pay her travelling expenses in London and get any meals she did not have at home. Her father retained £3 to pay her Academy fees, to cover insurances and to put a little away in a savings bank account. All seemed set fair for success until her father's good luck changed alarmingly. He had a succession of flops, the most spectacular being *The Cinema Star* and *The Light Blues*. He lost his money and, what was worse, he was heavily in debt. So in 1915 for the first time in her life Cicely had to look for a job outside her father's management. The future looked decidedly bleak. Not having known the gruelling business of calling on the Charing Cross Road theatrical agents to look for work, she was inclined to sit at home and wait for the phone to ring, with the offer of an attractive part for Robert Courtneidge's daughter. But the phone never rang.

At that point in her career Cicely Courtneidge had no idea of becoming a comedienne. She fancied herself as a young charmer, a magical Gertie Millar in the making. She was really not all that good as the Edwardian chocolate-box girl. She was apt to giggle too much and overdo the arch fluttering of the eyelids. Her father had a sneaking idea Cis would make a good male impersonator and sent her to watch Vesta Tilly over and over again. Vesta Tilly's work was highly polished, her technique faultless, and there was always a touch of feminine charm about the young males she chose to impersonate – yet they were not effeminate. The same applied to Ella Shields of Burlington Bertie fame; but when Hetty King came along she preferred the tougher butch characters exemplified by her famous Jack Tar. Cicely Courtneidge at that time did not see herself in trousers, she saw herself in floating chiffons. She could not get away from the chic, magnetic Gertie Millar, with those graceful wrist movements.

Losing patience with the silent telephone in the family home, Cicely Courtneidge went out and about to explore the work situation, but the only gleam of hope she discovered was the possibility of a music-hall engagement. It was no good hankering after the theatre of

Marie Tempest or Charles Hawtrey, which had no place for her, with experience limited to her father's musical comedies. So it was a question of going on the halls or doing nothing at all. But going on the halls meant working up an act capable of fitting into a variety bill and that in turn meant an outlay of £100, which she did not possess and there was no question of turning to her father for a penny. She accepted the challenge and managed to raise the money. Her father helped her to prepare the act, insisting upon a male impersonation number. The First World War was still on and that sort of song went down very well.

She got a date at Colchester, where Gladys Cooper had first appeared on the stage ten years earlier as Bluebell in a touring production of *Bluebell in Fairyland*. For Cicely Courtneidge it was far enough away from London not to matter, if the experiment turned out to be a disaster. 'There was a lot at stake. In the first place I never wanted to be a comedienne; I had no faith in trying male impersonation; I was gambling with borrowed money and I had never faced a music-hall audience in my life. But I was twenty-four and it was time I made a positive impression on the stage. Appearing in my father's productions was not enough and for all I knew he had gone out of business for good.

'Surprisingly enough, Colchester turned out to be an unqualified success and for the first time in my life I really felt I was making an impression on the stage – and it was as a male impersonator the audience liked me best of all. My final cameo, sung in an airman's uniform, was called "The Knut in the RAF". I swaggered, I sang my heart out and burlesqued the character. The audience loved it. I knew they did and I had the glow of feeling they were with me. They stamped their feet, they clapped their hands, they whistled and they laughed. That was the most wonderful thing of all – to hear their laughter. I knew I had found a place in the theatre – playing to make people laugh.'

Before the end of the week at Colchester Cis knew she had been accepted on the halls, but it took many long months of experimenting before she felt at home in that particular medium of light entertainment. 'If you want experience of your fellow men at their kindest and cruellest, go and stand alone on a music-hall stage on a Saturday night in some provincial town and try to amuse them.' Jack was in the Army by this time, but he used to telephone every night after the show to hear how she had fared. He used to dictate gags over the line and tell her to try them out and he would give her some idea how to put them across. Next night he would ring back to discover how they had been received. If the result had been disappointing he would make adjustments or scrap the idea and dictate new material. Even today the

Hulberts adopt the same method when trying out a new show and Cis is a fiend for hard work as she searches for the best possible script and the best possible way of putting it over. There is no question of her saying 'That'll do,' if she feels there is still any chance of improving it. 'I was brought up by my father to believe that minute attention to detail, coupled with self-discipline, was the only way to achieve success in the theatre. But success doesn't just mean having your name in lights and earning a high salary. The ultimate aim of all artists is to give the best possible performance of which they are capable.'

The boys impersonated by Cicely Courtneidge possessed a decided dash. There was something unique about her smart young men. She went to a military tailor for her uniform and later she appeared in faultless Savile Row tails. She knew she had reached the peak of success when she received a fan letter from Vesta Tilly and she continued giving male impersonations in shows for more than thirty years. She even impersonated Noël Coward in the Coronation revue, *Over the Moon* at the Piccadilly, but perhaps her most popular number of all was the Guardsman singing 'There's Something About a Soldier'. This type of entertainment has rather gone out of fashion. Perhaps it has not survived because there are no longer actresses capable of appearing as a convincing boy, with a fascination which appeals to both sexes in the audience.

After her first variety theatre tour Cis discovered, 'No two audiences are alike, their mood is affected by the weather, good news and bad news and a number of other conditioning factors, such as what they have eaten for dinner. So every time the curtain goes up the audience present a challenge and when you have won them over you have a feeling of triumph which never palls.' On the halls, as she enhanced her reputation, her act was considered good enough to appear on bills with such big names as Charles Hawtrey in comedy sketches, Nellie Wallace, Harry Weldon and Harry Tate. She gained confidence through facing tough audiences who did not hesitate to throw pennies on the stage when artists did not meet with their approval and there were times when Cis herself suffered this humiliation. She never ceased to be feminine in manner and taste, which had a strong audience appeal and helped to make her the darling of the public which she still is.

Cicely Courtneidge had not started to be funny when she first met Jack. He improved her acting technique and impressed upon her the all-important factor of timing until she became a comedienne without an equal in revue and variety. Robert Courtneidge was first to cast Jack and Cis together and afterwards they cast themselves together. 'Jack always had a high opinion of my work,' maintained Cis. 'He believed in me when I was still playing romantic parts in musical comedy. He believed in me when nobody else did, including myself. His faith in my ability kept me going when I was out of work and for those two years following the collapse of my father's shows. Only Jack firmly believed I could switch from romantic parts to the hurly-burly of the music halls.'

There was no question of Jack blindly hero-worshipping his young wife. He was always critical. 'But Jack has the sort of critical faculty,' continued Cis, 'which leaves a sweet taste in the mouth. When I'd do something wrong, Jack used to tell me I was doing it well, but he was certain I could do it far better and then proceed to show me how. It is because he understands me so well that I have always done my best work for him.' They worked extremely well together, but they did not become household names in a night. 'One success does not do the trick,' she explained. 'We had to make several attempts before we could truthfully say in 1929 that the managements and the public accepted us without question as a husband-and-wife team and by then we had been married thirteen years. We then had four major successes to our credit in the space of six years, beginning with *By-the-Way* at the Apollo Theatre, continuing with *Lido Lady* at the Gaiety, *Clowns in Clover* and *The House That Jack Built*, both at the Adelphi. These shows gave us an uninterrupted run to enable us to get firmly established in the public eye and Jack's contribution was tremendous. He wrote, organised and produced them all. They not only made us a lot of money and consolidated our position for all time in the West End but they gave us the chance to be together on the stage and at home. I consider *Clowns in Clover*, with the exquisite June in the cast, was our greatest success.'

There were ups and downs in their career, but they remained devotedly together through thick and thin. Their friend, Paul Murray, took charge of the administrative and financial side of their joint career. In all good faith he engaged the Hulberts in a series of theatrical commitments beyond their resources. He gambled and lost, and at the height of their success in the 1920s they found themselves without a penny and faced with debts that amounted to thousands of pounds. Undaunted, they accepted the challenge and also the grim truth that they could no longer afford to appear together as a husband-and-wife team because they could earn more money apart. Jack could fill one theatre while Cis was filling another, so he went to the Winter Garden in *Follow a Star* with Sophie Tucker and she went to the Piccadilly with Nelson Keys in *Folly to be Wise*. Then they became successful film stars. There was no financial risk for them in films and one picture, which took eight weeks to make, earned them more money than a year's run in the theatre. So after a comparatively short time of very,

very hard and exhausting work they managed to recoup their lost fortune. They were both blessed with good health and able to stand the enormous physical strain. About that time, a doctor told Cicely Courtneidge she burnt up more nervous energy in one performance at the theatre than an office worker would in eight weeks.

Edith Evans once said, 'Don't go on the stage unless you want your heart broken.' Cis admits she has had her heart broken on the stage – shattered, bitterly and abysmally – on several occasions, but when such disaster strikes the Hulberts they just pick up the pieces and carry on. 'Failure anywhere for any reason,' observed Cis, 'resounds everywhere in the theatre. People are very ready to applaud you when you are at the top, but they are equally ready to join in the hue and cry if you stumble. I forget who said *There is something not displeasing in the misfortune of our friends*, but I think it is more applicable to my profession than any other. I think an actor or actress who reaches the top is in a similar position to a champion boxer. With every new show, like every new fight, his title is at stake.'

Their mutual devotion has helped the Hulberts to weather the storms which broke over their happiness. Jack was taken seriously ill when they were touring in *Oh Clarence* in 1970. He was rushed into the intensive care unit of a Newcastle hospital and Cis and the company had to proceed on the tour without him. At one moment his heart actually stopped beating. Cis travelled hundreds of miles to visit Jack as often as possible, when the towns where she was playing were not a fantastic distance from Newcastle. On days when there was no matinée she would take an early morning train and return in time for the evening performance. She never once missed a show and never gave a mediocre performance. There were times when Jack was so ill Cis was not allowed to see him, but she had the satisfaction of knowing she had been under the same roof and she had been there to see him, had it been humanly possible. Such devotion played no small part in Jack's recovery and helped to bring him back into circulation long before the doctors imagined they would be sending him home.

And no one knows better than Cis how to make a home. As her old friend Herbert de Leon observed, 'Cis has no real hobby apart from the theatre, her home and her family. All her dynamic energy is divided between those three interests. She loves giving dinner parties under her own roof and those who have the good fortune to be invited regularly have the pleasure of meeting time and time again the same old and tried friends of the Hulberts' circle. Cis looks after the house, does the shopping and the chores and as a result is the perfect hostess. Nothing is left to chance in the home or at the theatre. Cis knows what she wants and makes sure she gets it and she relieves Jack of all the business side of their lives by looking after the contracts, the cheques and the conditions of their engagements.'

Vivian Ellis wrote tuneful music for several shows which Jack Hulbert directed, with Cis in the star part. There was *Folly to be Wise* at the Piccadilly with Nelson Keys; *Hide and Seek* at the Hippodrome with Bobby Howes and Patricia Burke; and *Under Your Hat* at the Palace, with Cis and Jack, as well as Leonora Corbett and Peter Haddon. He also contributed numbers to *Clowns in Clover* and *The House That Jack Built*. After this long succession of musical successes Cicely Courtneidge toyed with the idea of 'going straight' and appearing in a play. The radio had whetted her appetite and given her confidence. For several years Cis had a radio programme every week and each one contained a miniature play written for a guest-star from the straight stage, who appeared opposite Cis. In this way she had worked with Gladys Cooper, Flora Robson, Diana Wynyard, Eric Portman, Dirk Bogarde, Jack Hawkins, John Mills and a host of others. Having thus established herself as a straight actress on the air, she felt she might be accepted by playgoers whose interest lay in the legitimate theatre.

Cis did not rush things and in 1946 chose a sort of half-way-house vehicle at the Phoenix Theatre. Called *Under the Counter* it was a comedy burlesquing post-war Black Marketeering, with music by Manning Sherwin. Directed by Jack, it had Irene Handl, Thorley Walters and Hartley Power in the cast to support Cis. Arthur Macrae submitted this light comedy to Jack; it had an actress as the leading character and Jack, always a pioneer, realised musical numbers could be added quite naturally in the course of the action and even lend a touch of realism to the plot. And so a new form of entertainment was conceived, a comedy with music, a play with songs, which was half way to being a straight play. Apart from *Lido Lady*, in which Cis appeared as Jo Fox, a glamorous musical comedy star, *Under the Counter* was the first show which gave her an opportunity to get away from all those heavy revue disguises as stern schoolmarms and Colonels' wives from India. She skilfully blended beauty with buffoonery and had a real story instead of a series of disconnected sketches. She was rather bewildered to be playing in a set with real furniture, as cosy as her own Mayfair drawing room, and suddenly realised she had never sat down to play a scene in any of her previous musical shows. It was an immediate success making fun of the lengths to which people would go to overcome wartime shortages and regulations and Cis enjoyed this challenge and it was the first show in which she had starred alone. She gained new confidence and felt sure she could cope with a conventional straight play when one eventually presented itself. She had to wait another ten years before she went into *The Bride and the Bachelor*, but Ivor Novello's *Gay's the Word* came in between.

Ivor Novello always said Cicely Courtneidge made him laugh more than any other comedienne and he wanted to express his appreciation by writing a musical show for her. It was agreed that Arthur Macrae should write the book and Ivor would be responsible for the score. Cis was ready for a success, having had three rather difficult years in the theatre. *Under the Counter* had run for only three weeks in New York because it dealt with wartime Black Market conditions in this country which Americans could not be expected to understand; so the humour fell rather flat. An Australian tour followed and on her return to London Cis had a rather short run in *Her Excellency* at the Hippodrome and when she went back on the halls she knew she had been away from the variety stage far too long and her material was not broad enough for the changed taste of the public. While the Novello-Macrae show was being written Cis went abroad for a holiday. On her return she was met at the airport by Jack with the shattering news that Arthur Macrae could not meet the deadline with the book for the new musical and had withdrawn from the agreement.

That same night the Hulberts went to see Ivor Novello in his flat above the Strand Theatre to break the disastrous news and to express the hope that he would still consider writing the music, in collaboration with a new librettist. Ivor thought it over for a few moments and said, 'I'll be very pleased to work with myself!' The Hulberts were somewhat baffled by this pronouncement, until Cis suddenly saw the light and cried, 'Do you mean you are going to write the book yourself, Ivor?' 'Precisely,' was his quick reply. The Hulberts were on top of the world again. Ivor's musical, called *Gay's the Word*, told the story of Gay Daventry, a not-so-young actress who tries to make both ends meet by opening a drama school and Cis had the chance of a lifetime to sing 'Vitality,' which has since become her theme song. Ivor wrote this glowing testimonial to the staggering vitality of the comedienne he had admired so often and she put it over with a verve that stunned the audience. The number went like a bomb and the show was a success from start to finish, though Ivor's sudden death three weeks after the opening night at the Saville Theatre was a blow from which the Hulberts never quite recovered. The show went on for Ivor's sake and for the sake of all the artists whose teamwork contributed so much to the enjoyment of those who flocked to see it.

Alan Melville wrote the breezy lyric for 'Vitality', which paid tribute to that magic quality which puts top-liners on top and gives them the power to knock us for six without having to rely upon microphone tricks. Very cunningly he worked in the idolised names of Gertie Millar, Marie Lloyd, Lily Elsie, José Collins, Phyllis and Zena Dare, Gracie Fields, Dorothy Ward and Shaun Glenville, George Robey, Billy Merson and G. H. Elliott, all exciting names which left the audience in a glow of nostalgia. As Cis has a flair for pathos, like all great clowns, there was another number concerning an actress trying out a show which at heart she knows to be a flop. 'It's bound to be right on the night,' she cries, but she really knows it isn't all right, it's all wrong. It doesn't go on, it comes off. The house was on the verge of enjoyable tears when Cis put that number over. Looking back on it all twenty-odd years later Cis declared quite definitely, '*Gay's the Word* was the most important first night of my career.' Jack directed the show when Cis was approaching sixty and other names in the cast included Lizbeth Webb, Thorley Walters, Maidie Andrews, John Wynyard, Dunstan Hart and Molly Lumley.

On the musical stage Cicely Courtneidge's unique gift was her ability to sing speech, which is not the same thing as speaking to music and she could also express any mood or sentiment under the sun. One moment she would be assuring us that Home is the place where the Heart is and Things are getting better every day. In a more frivolous frame of mind she considers what would happen if she wore Napoleon's 'at, all expressed in a homely French accent. Romance is in the air when she confesses:

> The moment I saw you
> I said to myself
> You're too nice a baby
> To leave on the shelf.

As far as sketches are concerned in musical shows, she never surpassed *Laughing Gas*, introduced into *The Little Revue Of 1932*. At the reading of a will in which a husband leaves his wife no more than his income tax demands, a child turns on a cylinder of laughing gas and in consequence all the gathering whose hopes have been dashed, unite in a state of wild hysteria. The recording Cis made is just as potent today as her first stage performance of this sketch forty years ago.

Cicely Courtneidge is very proud of her career on the musical comedy stage. 'Playing in musicals is the hardest job in the world – you have to sing, dance and act, which all calls for highly specialised training and proves a great asset when an artist decides to leave musical shows for the legitimate stage; in plays there is also the question of having to use a lower pitch and I had to do this in *Dear Octopus*. Both Marie Tempest and Gladys Cooper gained their early experience in musicals, but not so many people flit from the legitimate stage into musicals. There are more, of course, since Rex Harrison made a success as Henry Higgins in *My Fair Lady*, when he showed how it is possible to more or less speak numbers to music. 'It is almost impossible for young people to learn their job in musicals today. In my youth when a show finished at Daly's or at the Gaiety there would be as many as three different companies on the road at the same time. Any promising beginner could get a start in the chorus of the Number Three tour and if she made a good impression she could get promoted to small parts in the Number Two tour the following season. The next step would be a chance to get tried out as a lead in the Number One tour and then London would be within reach. Lily Elsie toured for years before she captivated London as the Merry Widow and Gertie Millar spent ten years in the provinces before she was engaged to play Cora in *The Toreador* at the Gaiety. When her chance came she was ready to take it and to remain the Gaiety's leading lady for the next seven years. Young people with similar ambitions these days would find it very difficult to gain enough practical experience to equip themselves for the heavy responsibilities the leading lady of a musical is called upon to shoulder.'

The time was at hand for Cicely Courtneidge to think about shouldering the responsibility of taking the leading part in a play without a note of music and without her husband to direct it. The play was *The Bride and the Bachelor* by Ronald Millar, with Charles Hickman to direct and Naunton Wayne and Robertson Hare in the cast. In the first instance Ronald Millar sent the script to Edith Evans, who returned it saying, 'You need to farce it up a bit and in that case it would not be for me.' He saw her point and decided to take her advice. After the play had been 'farced up' a whole year was spent in trying to get it placed. Then someone suggested Cis. Jack was touring in *The Reluctant Peer* by William Douglas Home, and Cis, who hated being at home doing nothing, was eager to appear in a straight play.

She was interested enough in the idea of *The Bride and the Bachelor* to invite Ronald Millar to tea at the Hulbert home in South Audley Street. 'Are the lines complicated?' was her first question. She feared the play might be an intellectual exercise, such as one might expect from Christopher Fry or Robert Bolt. She was afraid there might be some symbolistic significance in the lines which would need a good deal of explaining to her. All she wanted was to play a straightforward woman who spoke like people she met every day of her life and she also hoped the lines would provide her with an opportunity to make the audience laugh. She had no songs to fall back on, neither had she Jack beside her to give his opinion concerning how key lines should be put over. She had been used to gags all her life, playing characters which did not necessitate sticking too closely to the script, as long as she got the meaning across. A glance at the new play whetted her interest and she asked Ronnie Millar to leave it for her to read.

Two days later his telephone rang and Cis said she was prepared to play the part and take the risk of really going straight. She had a nodding acquaintance with Naunton Wayne and Robertson Hare, but she felt lost at the prospect of being surrounded by so many new faces. She missed the environment of the musical comedy world; she had thrived in large casts, with singers and dancers rushing about at rehearsals. 'I was very lost and nervous and on the opening night I missed the sound of the overture, which always gave me a lift in my previous shows.'

Ronnie Millar went out with *The Bride and the Bachelor* on its prior-to-London tour, while it was being licked into shape and he was astounded by Cicely Courtneidge's ruthless professionalism. Everyone realised the show presented a tremendous challenge because there was a good deal of rewriting to be done, which meant considerable adjustments to the shape of the production originally mapped out by Charles Hickman. 'Nothing mattered to Cis except the job in hand,' said Ronnie Millar. 'She was prepared to work night and day and try any suggestions which looked promising. That is what I mean by her ruthless professionalism. Having accepted a part she was one hundred per cent loyal to it and had no time for defeatism.

'The opening night reviews on the try-out tour were bad, but that did not daunt or deter her. She had taken the job and was determined to make a success of it. Every night – for quite a long time – we would go back to the hotel and hold a *post-mortem* – Cis, Charles Hickman and myself, as well as other people connected with the production and the management. We would talk into the small hours and various suggestions were analysed and either accepted or rejected. Finally Cis would ask if I could produce some new material by the morning. Fortunately, having worked in revue, I am a quick writer, especially when engaged on the surgical job of trying to get a script into the right shape. So during what was left of the night I would write new lines at points in the play where the old ones had not proved as effective as we had hoped. A new treatment would be ready for Cis by breakfast time. She was not a particularly quick 'study', but in every instance she devoted the best part of the day to committing the new lines to memory and adjusting her performance accordingly. She always insisted upon trying out the new material the very next night. There was no time to lose. The new lines did not always go down as well as we had anticipated and then we would be faced with the prospect of trying all over again at supper after the show the following night. If

Cis was a bit uncertain on some lines, having had insufficient time to memorise them, she would have them written on slips of paper and hidden on the set. It was trial and error with a vengeance, but in this way we knew exactly what the audience thought about our combined efforts. As part of her dedication to her job, Cis was always first at rehearsal and she expected everyone else in the cast to be punctual. She had no time whatsoever for people not prepared to bother.'

Cis never takes No for an answer at rehearsal. She refuses to discard a promising suggestion until it has been tried out. She constantly says, 'You can do anything if it is organised.' She had carried out amazing quick changes in her revue days with such speed the audience could hardly believe their eyes when she was back on the stage she had only just left, looking totally different. She might have three people waiting to pounce on her in the wings to transform her appearance – one to deal with her shoes, another with her wig and a third with her costume – and Cis had her own part to carry out in the exercise, all timed to a split second. Such drill was worth 'bothering' about. The audience loved the result and both Cis and her collaborators were amply rewarded by the pleasure they gave the house. During the rehearsals of *Move Over, Mrs Markham* Cis kept on complaining, 'I'm not happy!' The management and the authors were dismayed, fearing she was about to quit the show, until her agent, Herbert de Leon, explained she merely wanted the part revised and rewritten in certain places to provide her with better material to make a more powerful impact. She has an uncanny instinct for what is right and wrong and is prepared to move heaven and earth to get things right. Peter Saunders recalls an incident when Cis was telephoned by her then agent during the try-out of a play which was giving every indication of being doomed to disaster. By way of cheering and comforting her, he said, 'Don't worry, I'll find you something else!' Cis exploded with indignation at the other end of the line. Just as if she would give up the ghost! Peter Saunders indicated that Cis sacked the gentleman before she rang off.

The Bride and the Bachelor had a poor press in the provinces and a ghastly first night at the Duchess Theatre. It was in the days when the BBC used to televise excerpts from West End shows – and that saved the day. The box-office sold out the house for six months within a week of the television and the show ran for 590 performances at the Duchess, which proved to Cis that she could carry a straight play, even without Jack's magic touch of direction.

Twelve years later, this time at the Haymarket, the most aristocratic of all West End playhouses, Cis had her greatest triumph of all on the legitimate stage when she played Marie Tempest's part of Dora

Randolph in Dodie Smith's *Dear Octopus*. She had Jack in the cast to play her husband, but yet another director, Frith Banbury. 'He really made a straight actress of me!' Cis had never been quite so nervous as she was on the first night of *Dear Octopus*. Perhaps Marie Tempest's ghost was drifting about the dressing room. Cis had seen her in the part she was about to play, but did not recall any details, apart from remembering her at the head of the long table laid for the family reunion dinner and also sitting by the fire in a reflective mood. This was no time to delve into the past, so Cis paced the dressing room, going over one or two vitally important lines. There was a knock at the door. Hurriedly a well-wisher slipped a first night gift into her hand and was gone. Cis looked down and found herself holding an illustrated souvenir of the original production of *Dear Octopus*, with Marie Tempest gazing out at her from the cover. 'It nearly killed me!'

Frith Banbury was the most understanding and considerate of directors. Cis had complete faith in him and obeyed him unquestioningly. 'I shall never forget his consideration over an incident at rehearsal. I said a line in a way which made the cast laugh. "Shall we keep that in?" I asked. After a slight hesitation he replied, "I'll think it over." Instinctively I knew it was not right, but had he said "No" instantly it might have crushed me. I was always grateful to him for the gentle manner in which he treated me on that occasion.' Cis naturally had to change her way of playing when she went into straight plays, but she firmly maintains she never altered her technique of putting over comedy.

The morning after the provincial première of *The Bride and the Bachelor*, Peter Saunders saw Cis breakfasting at the hotel as he was about to go out and buy the morning papers to see what the critics had said. 'Which paper shall I get for you, Cis?' he asked. 'I never see the papers the day after one of my first nights,' she replied, 'in case I might be tempted to read the review of the play.'

Generally speaking I am apt to distrust actors who boast about never reading reviews. The temptation is so very great. But I have no doubt about Cicely Courtneidge's claim, after asking her point blank, 'Is it true that you never read what the critics say?' 'Yes,' she replied, 'and now you are going to ask why. It is because I am very easily hurt that I never read reviews at the beginning of a run, before the play has settled down. I am much too nervous to rush out for the papers the morning after a première because I would go down like a pricked balloon if I had been ignored entirely or if I felt I had been hit below the belt. If a play is not an instant success, it is more important than ever that I keep up my spirits. As leader of the company, the cast look to me to inspire confidence; as I cannot do my best after being hurt, I feel it is better not to know what the critics say . . . just to be on the safe side. The actor is quite helpless and has no come-back. After working weeks and weeks on a part he can be torn to shreds in a night. I always know the next morning whether or not the show is a success, without looking at the papers. The phone buzzes with exciting calls if it has gone well and looks like settling down to a run. If it is silent I know my friends have their doubts about it. They don't quite know what to say, so they don't ring at all. They are afraid and the silence at my end of the line has the most depressing effect.'

A failure is not always the fault of the artists. Long after the short run of *Under the Counter* in New York, Cicely Courtneidge heard there had been a move to take the show off the next night, not just because the Americans failed to appreciate the effect of wartime shortages in Britain but because of political troubles which were responsible for adverse comments in the press. *High Spirits*, the musical version of Noël Coward's *Blithe Spirit*, failed to run in London, where Cicely Courtneidge played Madame Arcati, the eccentric spiritualistic medium created by Margaret Rutherford in the original Coward comedy. There was a certain amount of confusion as far as the public was concerned; they did not all realise Noël Coward was not responsible for the music. His play had inspired this musical but the music, book and lyrics were by Hugh Martin and Timothy Gray. To make matters even more confusing Noël Coward himself supervised the production at the Savoy Theatre in London where it was directed by Timothy Gray and Noël Coward's friend Graham Payn. It had previously been staged on Broadway with Beatrice Lillie as Madame Arcati. She, rather than the show, had been the success, so by the time it reached London Cicely Courtneidge was presented with a part which had been turned into a vehicle for Beatrice Lillie, which did not happen to work for anyone else. Cis was devastated at rehearsal, but it was too late to turn back. She had expected a part not unlike Margaret Rutherford's creation, but who could be further from Dame Margaret than Bea Lillie?

One thing the Hulberts try to avoid at all costs is sitting in their Mayfair home without a play to keep them occupied in the evening. If they cannot find a show likely to run in London, they are quite content to go on the road for months at a stretch in a revival such as *The Hollow* by Agatha Christie, which they played after they had passed the age of eighty.

Malcolm Farquhar, artistic director of Cheltenham Everyman Theatre, had hero-worshipped Cicely Courtneidge since his schooldays, but they never met professionally until he was invited to direct *The Hollow* in a 1973 production geared for a provincial tour. After an opening season at Cheltenham, the show went on to Norwich, Southsea, Guildford, St Annes-on-Sea, Brighton, Bath and Bournemouth. Christmas was kept free because that is a season very dear to Cis, with her love of entertaining family and friends.

Before rehearsals started Malcolm Farquhar began to worry. Although Cicely Courtneidge had made her entrance into the straight theatre quite late in life and won her laurels in *Dear Octopus*, he could still not forget she had been the undisputed queen of musical comedy, the doyenne of revue and a loner on the music halls. In other words, she was a lady who had been used to standing alone on a stage uncluttered with furniture, a stage which left her free to make exits through wing spaces rather than through more specifically marked practical doors.

'I was rather disturbed by these reflections,' admitted Malcolm Farquhar, 'when we called the first rehearsal. I was soon to discover it was she who did all the worrying. She is a prize worrier about getting the character right and she is in constant need of being assured that the mood of the scene is correct and her performance moving in the right direction.

'I had admired Cis's work for years and felt I was on a sympathetic wavelength with her particular brand of humour. Happily, this proved correct. I decided to strengthen the comedy in the script and provide her with the sort of material audiences expect from her. With the author's permission I wrote new lines, imagining how Cis would utter them. How incredibly rewarding to hear them come to life when the Courtneidge voice took hold of them! It is difficult to define what makes her comedy unique and such a joy to the audience. Certainly some physical attributes are in evidence. Her neat, jaunty walk, a quick sit on the sofa with her feet splayed out at a quarter to three, and a shrewd yet baffled expression on her face have a lot to do with it. Yet, most of all, she is blessed with cadences in her voice that can gurgle a comic line to full effect. Such a gift can easily fool you into believing really weak lines are very funny.'

What sort of parts would she like to play in her eighties? She would have enjoyed playing Queen Mary, the greatest success of Wendy Hiller's career in *Crown Matrimonial*, which told the Abdication story, because she knew Queen Mary well and had great admiration for her. People have suggested Shakespeare to Cis, whose only Shakespeare part still remains Peasblossom in *A Midsummer Night's Dream*, in which she made her stage début seventy-odd years ago. The Nurse in *Romeo and Juliet* has been suggested, but she points out that it has been so well played within living memory by Edith Evans, Ellen Terry, Peggy Mount, Marie Ney, Martita Hunt, Athene Seyler and others, why should she try? Her age has to be considered. But within reason, she does not think age matters as long as the actress can look the part. 'If a management sees you in a part, if the producer has faith in you, and they take the risk, you would be a fool not to play the part, if you happen to like it, even though you would never have thought of playing it yourself. I would never have considered myself for the eccentric lesbian I played in the film of *The L-Shaped Room*, but someone had the imagination to see me in the part and I took it.' The shows by which she would most like to be remembered are *Something in the Air*, *Under the Counter* and *Dear Octopus*.

The Hulberts have always exploited their personal popularity by giving curtain speeches after the show, in London and on tour. At the height of their success in those musicals at the Palace, shows such as *Something in the Air* and *Under Your Hat*, Jack's epilogues were known to last twenty minutes, with the entire cast standing behind him, itching to get out of their make-up and on their way home. After the leading players had taken their individual calls, the company would get into position to make a background for Jack who would be discovered, as the curtain rose once again, walking from one side of the stage to the other. Suddenly looking across the footlights at the audience, he would exclaim, 'You're still there!' and proceed to have a cosy chat with them. Then he would indicate that his wife would like a word. So the audience went home feeling they had met the Hulberts, quite apart from having been entertained by them. On their octogenarian tours Jack thanks them: 'How very kind of you to clap. You've no idea the difference it makes to us because we live on it. It rather suggests you've enjoyed the show and that makes us feel jolly good. I'm talking too much, but I know my wife would like a word with you.' As Jack turns to Cis, her face lights up and she looks quite beautiful as she tells the audience what a joyous evening she has had and how she can always be sure of getting a warm welcome when she returns to their town.

Peter Saunders enjoys employing Cis, who worked for him in *The Bride and the Bachelor* and *Move Over, Mrs Markham*, because she is such an inspiration to her fellow artists. She missed only two performances in the three and a half years covered by those two productions. The theatre is her only interest, and especially the show in which she happens to be playing, which means she arrives at the stage door an hour and a half before the rise of the curtain because she hates to rush and wants to make her entrance feeling completely calm and collected, knowing full well she is about to give the very best performance of which she is capable.

Cis was once caught out by the public, not looking her best off-stage. She was in New York playing in the revue *By-the-Way* and she went to see a matinée performance of Al Jolson's show. He spotted her in her seat and invited her on to the stage so that he could introduce her to the audience. Cis was not prepared. It was a wet afternoon. She was wearing an old mac, carrying an old umbrella and wearing splashed stockings.

'From that day forward I have never gone out in public without being properly groomed and polished. There is no such thing as being off-stage if you want to be a star, except in the seclusion of your own home. In my opinion it is not fair to the public who are, after all, our employers. In the theatre we create an illusion and to break that down outside is not only unfair to yourself but to them. I suggest that the young women who think it proper to wear slacks, an old jumper and wind-swept hair off-stage or off the film set should think again. Don't let your public down or you will soon wind up with an audience of one, and a non-paying audience at that.'

There is a suggestion that Cis never goes to bed. Her favourite pastime is entertaining her friends to supper after the show at her Mayfair home and to sit at table till the early hours. She and Jack have lived all their married life in Mayfair – in Curzon Street, South Audley Street, Shepherd Market and Charles Street. 'Such fun,' is how she describes her first drink after the show. 'People mean more to me than anything and I enjoy letting my hair down in my own home as we all sit round the table talking shop – as actors always do – and recalling wonderful players who have thrilled us in the theatre – Robert Donat, the Lunts, Gladys Cooper as Paula Tanqueray and my favourite of all – the matchless Yvonne Arnaud.' No wonder the dawn breaks over the Mayfair streets before the Hulberts say good morning to their last guest.

Bibliography

Who's Who in the Theatre (Pitman)
The Oxford Companion to the Theatre (OUP)
Dictionary of National Biography (OUP)
The Stage newspaper
Ivor Novello – Man of the Theatre, by Peter Noble (Falcon Press)
A Talent to Amuse, by Sheridan Morley (Heinemann)
Flora Robson, by Janet Dunbar (Harrap)
Noël, by Charles Castle (W. H. Allen)
Ellen Terry, by Roger Manvell (Heinemann)
Ellen Terry and Bernard Shaw – A Correspondence,
    edited by Christopher St John (Max Reinhardt)
Early Stages, by John Gielgud (Falcon Press)
Dame Madge Kendal by Herself (John Murray)
Marie Tempest, by Hector Bolitho (Coben-Sanderson)
John Gielgud, by Ronald Hayman (Heinemann)
Peggy Ashcroft, by Eric Keown (Rockcliff)
Sybil Thorndike Casson, by Elizabeth Sprigge (Victor Gollancz)
Lewis and Sybil, by John Casson (Collins)
Cicely, by Cicely Courtneidge (Hutchinson)
Margaret Rutherford – an autobiography as told to Gwen Robyns (W. H. Allen)
Without Veils, by Sewell Stokes (Peter Davies)
Gladys Cooper by Herself (Hutchinson)
Twenty-five Thousand Sunsets, by Herbert Wilcox (Bodley Head)
Sybil Thorndike's recording of a talk she gave on Ellen Terry at the National
    Portrait Gallery
Bryan Forbes' television documentary on Edith Evans, screened by Yorkshire
    Television on March 6, 1973